A MEMOIR

Undercover DEBUTANTE

The Search for my Birth Parents and a Bald Husband

CHARLOTTE LAWS

Copyrighted Material

Undercover Debutante

Copyright © 2019 Charlotte Anne Laws. All Rights Reserved.

No part of this publication may be reproduced, stored in a retrieval system or transmitted, in any form or by any means—electronic, mechanical, photocopying, recording, or otherwise—without prior written permission from the publisher or author, except for the inclusion of brief quotations in a review. Some names in this book have been changed to protect privacy.

For information about this title or to order books and/or electronic media, contact the publisher:

Stroud House Publishing

Offices in New York and Anaheim, California

StroudHousePublishing.com

Contact@StroudHousePublishing.com

ISBNs:

978-0-9961335-6-2 (Print)

978-0-9961335-7-9 (eBooks)

Printed in the United States of America

Photo in "Bonus Stories I" by Robyn Feeley of Bungalow Art Studio (BungalowArtStudio.com)

Contents

Preface v
Introduction ix
Chapter One - Private Eyes and Private Parts 1
Chapter Two - The Glitz Blitz 21
Chapter Three - Strip Clubs and the President 35
Chapter Four - The Secret 53
Chapter Five - Westwood Bound 65
Chapter Six - The Search for My Biological Family 81
Chapter Seven - The New York Baby Daddy 97
Chapter Eight - Kayla: My Precious Twig 109
Chapter Nine - The Gunman and Sheena's Scheme 131
Chapter Ten - Desperately Seeking Sharon 143
Chapter Eleven - The Wife Résumé 167
Chapter Twelve - The Dud and the Dead Guy 187
Chapter Thirteen - My Date with an Unindicted
    Co-Conspirator 203
Chapter Fourteen - Whips, Chains, and the UCLA Professor . 219
Chapter Fifteen -Return of the Menacing Particle? 237
Chapter Sixteen - Surprise! Married by a Witch 247
Chapter Seventeen - The Trip to Nowhere 261
Bonus Stories 1: Additional Autobiographical Experiences ... 281

    How to Fake Your Way into a Celebrity Party: Frank Sinatra and George Clooney • My Adventure Presenting Animal Rights Philosophy to the FBI • The Nun with the Ruler • Party Crashing for Political Access: Arnold Schwarzenegger and My Pantsuit • Pigeon Man • Bill Cosby and Drugging: My 34-Year-Old Secret • Playing Pranks on the Governor • Fundraiser Mania • Seat Filling for the Stars: Sitting Pretty or Slave Labor?

Bonus Story 11 - The Devil Made Me Do It: My Grandpa's Life and Murder 321
Author Biography 335
Endnotes 337

Preface

"Charlotte Laws is a tsunami."

Snatch Magazine

"She is such an amazing and inspiring woman."

Buzzfeed

"Undercover Debutante is witty, illuminating, engaging, unguarded, and gorgeously written. In a word: triumphant."

Every Way Woman Show

"Charlotte Laws is a champion of the underdog."

New York Post

Undercover Debutante reveals the often-outlandish exploits that transpired in Charlotte Laws' life from age twenty-two to thirty-nine when her primary goal involved finding and securing love. Specifically, she hoped to track down the family that relinquished her at birth and pinpoint the "perfect" man to marry. From the start, she knew success was not a guarantee, and she was braced for perilous turns and off-road mishaps. It's her hope that through the pain, joy, humor, and bizarre antics in this book, you will gain insights that aid in your own life's voyage.

> "Undercover Debutante is a fascinating trip through Charlotte Laws' unorthodox, yet fascinating, life. Dr. Laws has the mind of a CIA operative. She can make a missile out of sticks."
>
> Dr. Bruce Goldberg,
> bestselling author of Exploring
> the Fifth Dimension

> "My Goodness, she does a lot!"
>
> L.A. Talk Radio

> "A beautifully crafted memoir full of family struggles, self-reflection, and celebrity party-crashing hijinks. You will laugh out loud. Thank Charlotte Laws for sharing her extraordinary life."
>
> Ralph Cissne,
> bestselling author of Angel City Singles

> "Charlotte Laws is the kind of woman you'd always want on your side."
>
> Vox

> "Undercover Debutante is a funny, probing, masterful memoir that gives a big shout out to fearlessness and what's important in life: helping animals and humans

in need. The book is more than a dose of honesty and emotional resonance. It includes the author's outlandish escapades. No adventure is off-limits from schmoozing with President Reagan to visiting a sadomasochistic dungeon and working at a dingy strip club. Don't miss the roller coaster ride of Undercover Debutante."

> Pamelyn Ferdin,
> actress and animal activist.

"This book is an incredible testament to the power of persistence. Charlotte Laws blasts through naysayers and self-doubt and is an inspiration to us all."

> Mandy Stadtmiller,
> Daily Beast columnist and bestselling
> author of Unwifeable

"Charlotte Laws reveals her success is all down to her fearless attitude and gusto."

> Daily Mail

"The conversation we need to hear from an honest, brave voice. Writing at its best."

> Paulette Mahurin,
> author of the best-selling novel
> The Seven Year Dress

"I love this book. Charlotte Laws is a delightful disturber of norms."

> Sue Jones, Hollywood Report TV

"Unbelievable! That's what most people thought when Charlotte revealed the exploits and escape plans she hatched underneath the serene surface of buttoned-up Atlanta in the 70's and 80's. We shared our teen years inside 'the body bag' of Atlanta society, as she describes it in her new book, living across the street from one another on a quiet, manicured and muggy Atlanta street. Back then I knew that all this had to end up in a book one day. I'm so glad it finally did. Readers will be, too."

Chris McGinnis, columnist for
SF Chronicle / SF Gate

"In Undercover Debutante, Charlotte Laws rebounds from abandonment and family put-downs to earn the respect of presidents and A-list celebrities. This beautifully written story teaches you how to see around the obstacles in your own life. It will have you laughing out loud while at the same time dabbing a tear from your eye. Enjoy this rollicking ride with a most daring woman at the helm."

Ken Lawrence, novelist and former Publisher
of the Association of Corporate Counsel,
Government Institutes, and Bernan Press.

Introduction

I am a recovering debutante.

Although I attended private school and was raised by an affluent adoptive family, I was never drawn to "old guard" values, preppy styling, or the "old money" mindset, which encased upper-class Atlanta like a body bag. Pretentiousness was too tart for my Everyman taste, and my daily battles against prejudice made me feel like the outsider that I was. I lived as a clashing sword. My values were at odds with almost everyone I knew.

The conformity in my community was both dizzying and claustrophobic. As a child, it felt like I was trapped in a rolling barrel. I was tumbling downhill and could never catch my breath, find my balance, or escape from the dread of it all. Most days felt bleak, caged-in, and airless. I dreamt of escape. Suicide was that fire extinguisher in the glass case. It was there in case of an emergency. It was an ever-present option.

My only hope lay in the television. The Sony provided a glimpse at the rest of the world—a world that did not seem one-note, a world of diverse ideas and interesting lifestyles, a world where there could be a sunny tomorrow. Those on TV seemed to lack the racist attitudes that I originally thought were standard practice throughout the globe. Those on TV donned glamorous sequined gowns. Those on TV did not seem bent on getting dead presidents (money) from dead relatives in order to lead a dead existence. Those on TV did not seem superficial.

This was ironic. Show business is often perceived as a platform for pretend, a microcosm of superficiality, a mosh pit for pretty people. It is arguably a haven for stretched faces, forced smiles, glitzy jackets, and happy endings. Yet this make-believe world seemed more authentic to me than the highbrow society in which I was raised. I wanted to touch the bright lights, to be a part of them and find out if my hypothesis was true.

In my late teens, my perception morphed into reality. I taught myself how to party crash any event, anytime, anywhere. I routinely got past security, including the Secret Service. I hobnobbed with entertainers and VIPs at parties and events. I finagled my way into an audition to land my first movie role, and I asked actor Burt Reynolds to my prom. (He could not attend, but it was cool chatting with him.) Famous folks struck me, on the whole, as more real and down-to-earth than the supercilious upper crusts who had waltzed through my formative years. Go figure.

One celebrity was a standout: pop star Tom Jones, who had been the target of my affection for some time, even though he was forbidden fruit for a debutante like me. He was a "new money" entertainer who had been dubbed "morally inferior" by Atlanta society gatekeepers. Luckily, rebels do not listen to Atlanta society gatekeepers, so I launched a number of outlandish schemes with hopes of stirring the embers of his heart. My Cinderella dream came true just before my nineteenth birthday, and I ended up dating Tom for three years, traveling to various cities while he was on tour.[1]

Show business became the family I never had.

On paper, I had adoptive parents and an adopted brother, Buddy. But in reality, my family was a rattletrap, a broken-down shanty, a fraud. To the neighbors, all looked primed and painted, but I was well aware of the termites beneath the surface.

My adoptive mom was aware as well. She led a dead existence without a job, hobbies, friends, or interests. Opening cans was her idea of a meal, and watching cartoons was her daily diversion. Her grandest achievement was winning the "most ladylike" contest in high school. A tasteful three-inch trophy rested demurely on a closet shelf adjacent to a stack of hats. The statue was a reflection of reserved elegance. It was most ladylike, too.

Mom and I were opposites. We clashed like discordant piano notes. But we had one thing in common. On some level, we shared a desire to escape. Mom was a ball of clay, directionless, waiting to be molded into the expectations of others. Her aim was to please Dad and Atlanta society, but in so doing, she lost herself. She ended up a distortion, a blur, a maze of confusion, a purposeless form without identity. I was a ball of clay as well, but I was stubborn. I refused to let others leave their imprint without permission. I was determined to forge ahead. Alone, if necessary. My identity would belong to me, while Mom's identity belonged to everyone else.

I grasped the fullness of her pain one muggy morning in July. She pulled me aside and offered the only advice she would ever give: "Don't buy a fur coat until you are old or you won't have anything to look forward to in life." It is ironic that I became an animal rights advocate. Two years after the fur coat remark, Mom locked herself in the bathroom, popped pills, and slashed her wrists and neck with a razor blade. She became a quasi-vegetable, hooked up to life-support machines.

Dad immediately filed for divorce and commanded Buddy and me to never mention our mother's name again or visit her in the hospital. Dad admired strength, and Mom had proved herself weak and unworthy. She had blown our ruse as the perfect family. Folks could no longer be bluffed. She was an informant, a stool pigeon, a snitch. Her existence was a reminder of the irreparable crack in the foundation.

I was initially scared of Mom, but as time passed, I softened, perceiving her as a victim. She was not a weakling as Dad intimated but merely a product of cause and effect, prey to forces stronger than her. They swallowed her. It was not her fault, and I suddenly felt compassion. I decided that if she snapped out of her semiconscious state, I would invite her to live with me. I would take care of her because she had no one else. Mom never retained her faculties and never came home. She perished a decade later.

Mom had two fur coats when she died.

Dad was nothing like Mom. He was all about running a construction company, chatting with his buddies via his extensive HAM radio setup, pitting Buddy and me against each other in daily competitions, and watching his favorite station: The Weather Channel. When I left for college, he hired a detective to keep tabs on me.

Dad was competitive and goal-oriented. Folks who failed were ousted from his life. His brother, Tween, was a case in point. When Tween attempted suicide ten years before Mom cut her wrists, my father cut off all ties. Dad considered himself a leader. Tween was a follower. Dad lived in the fast lane, while Tween was the guy hitchhiking on the shoulder of the road. Dad was tough and unemotional. Tween was sensitive. Tween was a lot like mom.

Buddy died in a car accident two years after Mom slashed her wrists.

It was a rainy day. He was sixteen. He was hit by an oncoming vehicle, and his body crumpled like a piece of cardboard. I was attending college in Florida and flew back to Atlanta. Dad was in the kitchen. His words are seared into my flesh: "You were always the bad one. Buddy was the good one. You're the one who should have died, not him."

Dad's words were a cannon, propelling me west.

I moved to Las Vegas, where I took oddball jobs with hopes of puffing up my spindly bank account. I worked as a bodyguard for a prostitute, a backup singer for an Elvis imitator, a bandit cab driver, and a chip chatter—a bizarre job I invented that brought me a mind-boggling $278,000 per year.[2] In my off-hours, I schmoozed with entertainers, politicians, and royalty backstage and at events. I was twenty years old, and Las Vegas was my puppet. I had it on the end of my string, and I could bring it to life on a whim.

Dad remained the captain of cruelty, the master of the barbed tongue. When he visited or spoke with me on the phone, he treated me like a flop, an outcast, a disappointment. Did he hate me for rejecting the role of proper Southern belle? Was I a pesky reminder of a tainted family life? Did he dislike my innate ability to get around rules and think outside the box? This quality, which I called "smart talent," was why I could party crash and hobnob with entertainers and heads of state. It was why I could visit Mom at the hospital behind my father's back. It was why I could investigate off-limits areas of casinos without getting caught and why I could raid hotel kitchens in the middle of the night. It was why I excelled at philosophy, and it was why I would eventually make a good private eye. I had an inferiority complex about intelligence but never about smart talent.

No matter how far from Georgia I got, it seemed like Dad was in pursuit, trying to mold me into his specifications. He was the architect, and I was the raw building material. I was the blank slate he had adopted. He was becoming increasingly agitated, as if the building material was becoming weathered and unusable. I knew that on a whim he could deem me a loser.

I could wind up in his basement "discards closet," where he tossed his rejects, such as the dragon china that I'd given him for Christmas and the unworn department store clothes that he couldn't be bothered to return. I could end up like Mom and Tween, tossed out of Dad's life like scrap paper. Part of me didn't care.

But for some odd reason, part of me did.

Chapter One

PRIVATE EYES AND PRIVATE PARTS

"I'm curious about my birth parents." I donned a second sweater because my adoptive father kept the house so cold. "What do you know about them?"

I was twenty-one and staying for a week at Dad's place on Orcas Island. Although his main residence was in Atlanta, he had vacation properties in Colorado, Florida, North Carolina, and Vermont, in addition to this one in the state of Washington. Orcas Island is picturesque, only twenty-four miles from Canada, and shaped like a half donut or a horseshoe. It curls around a bay called Eastsound.

"The adoption records were destroyed." Dad did not lift his eyes from the weather forecast on television. "You can't find *those people*."

This had always been his answer. Dad was

nonchalant and convincing. He was a record player, a well-oiled machine, an equity actor delivering his lines like a pro. I always nodded as if I was swayed, as if I was an easy mark, as if I was a model child. But part of me knew he was lying. Otherwise, why ask him the very same question every two or three years? Why revisit the issue again and again? Why be repeatedly bombarded with the phrase "those people"? Insanity is doing the same thing over and over and expecting a different result, but I was not crazy, and I was not gullible. I was wary. I suspected he was fibbing. I aimed to catch him off guard by posing the question at the right moment, on the right day, when he was looking to the left and not the right. I hoped to catch him in the midst of a mental nap and force him to blurt out the truth in frustration. But Dad was not an "off guard" sort of fellow, and he rarely became frustrated. He was too controlled, too rehearsed, and just too darn composed.

I shrugged, knowing "those people" would remain a mystery for a while longer—maybe even forever—and ventured into the kitchen to make some lunch. There were two choices: frozen or canned. These were what Dad called "the primary food groups." Packaged products or so-called convenience food had sustained me since babyhood with four exceptions: iceberg lettuce, carrots, Red Delicious apples, and tomatoes. I had been taught that broccoli, spinach, green beans, and orange juice came from the freezer. Pears, asparagus, mushrooms, and peaches lived in tin cans. Whole grains were kooky, and only wackos on the West Coast ate them. In fact, as I grew up, the only bread in the house had been white and pre-sliced. Tofu, quinoa, sushi, chia seeds, bean sprouts, and other "hippie foods" were simply never discussed. My childhood was all about Twinkies, tater tots, sugary cereals, pretzels, frozen pizza, and Oreos. Bad habits are hard to break, so my diet changed little after I left for college. In fact, on this very day, the fridge back in my Las Vegas apartment was stocked with my parents' Kool-Aid.

"Why didn't you at least get a midsize, Missy?" (Family and friends called me by the nickname "Missy" back then.)

"What?" I popped my head into the living room to find Dad peering out the window at my economy rental car. I braced myself for another sideswipe.

"You should have gotten a midsize. You're supposed to be a debutante."

"This car's fine," I mumbled. "I'm a little short on cash." It was a blunder. I knew it as soon as I said it. I had given Dad a reason to gloat, a reason to climb I-told-you-so hill and reign down on me like a tyrant.

"Of course, you're short." The wood-chipping machine that was my father roared with laughter. He always cushioned his cruelty with chuckles, a tactic meant to soften the blow. Dad had ground down my family tree, and now he was crushing my confidence. My head dropped, and I stared at the white shag carpet.

My father had always thought I would fail. It was his refrain. I would fail at paying my bills without his golden wallet. I would fail at finding a husband because, as he put it, why would any man want to marry me? I would fail at life. Maybe his words were an attempt to spur me on, to motivate me, to shove me toward success. Maybe he thought he was doing me a favor. Or maybe not. It's possible he wanted to feel needed as the adoptive father of a renegade debutante who had trampled on his rules for years.

"So, what happened? Why are you short?" His expression was a soup of righteousness and glee.

I stood there in silence. I was ashamed. I was disappointed in myself. I had spent my entire chip-chatting fortune on antiques, designer clothes, and travel in an effort to keep up with my entertainer friends. I had been jet-setting like a Rockefeller, but reality had caught up with me. I was not rich or famous. I was poor and obscure with a measly $500 in the bank.

"Did you gamble it all away?"

"No," I shot back. "I bought some really nice things."

Dad shook his head as if to say that overspending was immature, classless, and thoroughly unbecoming of a high-born. "Well, I guess you'll be moving back to Atlanta." He returned his gaze to the set.

All air left the building, and I felt queasy. Moving back was not an option. Moving back would extinguish my dreams. Moving back would douse my fiery spirit. I gathered my courage and spoke. "I'm sick of Vegas, Dad. I'm moving to Los Angeles."

"That's where the fruits and nuts live." He loved delivering his standard line about California. Then he swallowed his laughter, and his face became solemn. He made me an offer that he thought I couldn't refuse.

"If you move to Atlanta, I'll give you $500,000. I'll buy you a townhouse, give you a Mercedes, and support you. If you move to L.A., you get a Volkswagen to drive and that's it. You get nothing."

"You want to give me half a million dollars, a place to live, and a new car?" I was dumbfounded.

"Or you can fail in Los Angeles." He gazed back at the meteorologist on TV.

My initial shock shifted into reflectiveness, and then the truth hit me. Dad's offer was not about generosity. It was about power. It was about controlling me with his money. Dad wanted to turn me into the obedient socialite that he'd always dreamt I'd be. He hoped to prop me up in that "old money" world, a place I saw as flawed, as wooden, as stifling, but that he perceived as the only respectable place for his daughter.

Dad aimed to make me dependent on him and to convert me into a fan of cotillions, curtseys, and pointed pinky fingers. He wanted me to be another Mom, only emotionally stronger.

But Atlanta had been my coffin for eighteen years, and I had finally escaped from the darkness of its belly. Nothing could tempt me back, not even excessive riches. So I thought about Dad's offer for as long as it takes me to get bored watching the weather report: namely, ten seconds.

And I moved to California with only $500 to my name.

Half of my designer clothes were piled into the Volkswagen Rabbit that Dad was letting me use, while the rest were stashed in a Las Vegas storage unit with my antiques. I was on the road to self-discovery and once again thinking about "the secret." I had kept it from Dad and from everyone I knew. It had occurred many months prior in what was the most disastrous and frightening day of my life. I was lucky to be alive, but I felt dead—emotionally dead. I was a wounded wallaby, devoid of my usual feisty spirit, no longer able to jump to great heights or kick with great strength. My spirit was shredded, in a tailspin, on a harum-scarum highway toward collision. I could not tell Dad. I could never tell Dad. If he knew, he'd take me hostage, placing a noose around my neck and dragging me back to that scaffold called Atlanta. He'd blame me, calling me unclassy or disgusting or both. To his mind it would be proof of tainted genes, that I was infested with a disease picked up from *those people*—the birth family whom I had never met. I would no longer be a renegade debutante. It would be worse. I would be hideous, irredeemable, a fetid corpse of a daughter. I would be disowned. I knew my father well.

I willed my thoughts away from "the secret" and back to

my journey. Los Angeles was sprawling and overwhelming. It was the goddess of the metropolis, the master of all trades, expertly coordinating her disparate parts: beaches to the west; deserts to the east; mountains to the north; and tourist attractions, such as Knott's Berry Farm and Disneyland, to the south.

I was a pebble in her presence. I felt helpless. I was confused by the hodgepodge of her freeways and by the unfamiliar faces. She was nothing like Las Vegas, which I had easily brought under control. Los Angeles was much too diverse, much too complicated, much too self-reliant to be lassoed or tamed.

I thought about the awkward week with Dad and how his offer to support me had not been tempting. A vault full of cash, by itself, would be airless and alienating. I had dreams to fulfill, and Atlanta had been a nightmare. Rebels don't play it safe. Rebels don't give up their goals to please their dad. Rebels don't arrange their lives around a fur coat and the title "Most Ladylike." I knew I could fail without my father's safety net, but I was willing to gamble, to venture outside the gray area. My to-do list was exhaustive. I hoped to obtain a university degree, establish a career, save money, buy a house, and find a man to love and marry, in spite of the fact that only a fool would search for a husband in L.A., where commitment-phobes are more common than suntans. I planned to track down my birth parents, in part because I was curious about my roots, and in part because I needed to find family in order to make sense of myself and the world.

I knew the journey would be challenging. I had no college diploma. I had two useless skills: chip chatting and bandit cab driving. I had bills to pay: for food, for gasoline, for car insurance, and for doctors because my chronic migraines had not improved. In some respects, my unpleasant childhood was a blessing. It meant going back was not an option. There was nothing to distract me from the future, no lures to suck me into the past. Atlanta was an empty, dark shell. It felt like another planet.

I exited the freeway and veered down Melrose Avenue with its trendy boutiques and punk rock influence. It was the pinnacle of pink hair and West Coast cool. Then I drove to Beverly Hills, where I scoped out the grand mansions with their rolls of green grass, fancy fountains, and bevy of gardeners. From there, I headed forty miles south to upscale Villa Park, where I planned to live. Villa Park is the smallest and most politically conservative city in Orange County. The population was 5,900 in 2014, and probably lower when I was there.

I parked in front of a home with Frank Lloyd Wright flair. This was my new beginning, and I felt like the phoenix, a mythological creature being reborn. I was rising from the ashes of my former self and sawing at the shackles of "the secret." I had rose-colored plans to prosper—materially, emotionally, and spiritually—wrapped in the loving embrace of the California sun. My first gig would not be glamorous or brag-worthy, because I would be hobnobbing with dirt rather than superstars. I would be doing windows rather than the waltz. I would be wearing an apron rather than a ball gown. Yes, I was taking a job as a maid. I was going from debutante to dust buster, a fact I planned to hide from Dad.

Thank goodness my housekeeping duties were light, because cleaning was not my strong suit. Feather dusters and I were not on friendly terms. My recurring nightmare as a child had involved an odious vacuum cleaner situated in the front yard that kept me prisoner. It was the gray devil with its menacing cylinders, humming motor, and chord that whipped around in the wind. Terrorized, I'd run from window to window, feeling like a bug in a box. Then I'd wake to both good news and bad news: I was relieved that there was no hell-sent Hoover but sad that I was still trapped in Georgia.

In addition to my shortcomings in the housekeeping department, my cooking skills were subpar. When I was twelve, Dad and my brother, Buddy, had laughed at my quiches and soufflés, calling them "sissy foods." They refused to eat anything I made during my stint as an amateur chef, so I never cooked for the family again. Plus, the butler sheltered Buddy and me from what most kids consider normal contributions to the household. All I had to do was feed the dogs and make my bed. My brother did zilch, probably because he was male and not expected to need domiciliary skills.

Although I was now a maid, I received no pay per my deal with Bernie and his fifteen-year-old son, vacationers whom I had met six months earlier at the pool of a Vegas resort. They needed a housekeeper and offered me free accommodations if I would move to California and do some scrubbing and tidying each day. I slept on a twin bed in an otherwise empty room, using an electric blanket each night because they kept the house so cold. At the time, I did not know that electric blankets create a magnetic field that penetrates the skin by six or seven inches. Some studies link them with cancer.

I hated being a domestic servant but figured physical labor was good for my soul. It was a way to remain cognizant of the back-breaking tasks some people do regularly to survive. Cleaning helped me maintain a balanced outlook on life. At least, that's what I told myself.

The worst part of the job was Madge, Bernie's jealous girlfriend, who had frightened off the former live-in. She was sixty-two, hated having a younger woman in the home, and regularly berated me. "Don't you think you should go on a diet?" "It must be horrible being so short." "Do you think you'll *ever* get married?" One day, she made a confession about snooping and my predecessor. "When that slut wasn't home,

I went through her room and found a douchebag." Then she stared at me in horror. "*You* don't have one of those, do you?"

I shook my head feverishly, appearing guilty, even though I barely knew what a douchebag was, apart from the living, breathing kind.

Madge looked me up and down. "I suppose sex is the only way some girls can get male attention."

I never fought Madge. She was technically my employer, too. But I immediately started searching for a less hostile living situation. I call this the "hear no evil" phase of my California residency. I had to pretend to be deaf.

The "see no evil" phase began when I rented a room in an 800-square-foot Huntington Beach house occupied by a young couple. The rent was cheap at $150 per month. The wife was obsessed with penises, and one particular "man part" was shoved in my face every day. It belonged to her husband. She had an oversized naked photo of him on the wall. She was proud of his large corvette, so to speak. This woman had nothing else going on in her life: no job, hobby, or friends. She reminded me of Mom, minus the penis envy.

While in Huntington Beach, I spent most of each day sewing. I sat cross-legged on the floor in my tiny room hand-beading custom blouses, sweaters, and gowns. I hoped to make my party crashing profitable, selling entertainers and VIPs my one-of-a-kind creations. In addition to peddling the designs to celebrities, I planned to put some on consignment at Rodeo Drive shops. I figured each item could bring five hundred dollars or more. It could take two or three weeks to finish one garment

"I don't think you like my husband's picture." The Huntington Beach wife confronted me one day, waving the framed phallic masterpiece in the air. She seemed to want me to move out of the house, so I did.

The "speak no evil" period began when I took a job as a nurse. I was not an RN. This was a live-in job for minimal pay, taking care of a paraplegic named Tad on South Garfield Avenue in Paramount, California. I slept at one end of his modest mobile home, while Tad stayed at the other end. Paramount, which is largely industrial, is not upscale. According to the 2010 census, the median income for a household is $44,934, and 22 percent of the population lives below the poverty line.

Tad was not your average paraplegic. He worked at Cypress College, providing services to students with disabilities, and he was one of the delegates from California to attend the 1976 White House Conference on the Handicapped. He had become injured in a motorcycle accident at sixteen, but this did not stop him from being an advocate for the disabled. There were always important-looking papers on the tray attached to his wheelchair. I had to cook and clean and bathe Tad. Again, it was not a job that suited me, but it was a new experience that probably helped that "balanced outlook on life" thing, plus I knew it was only for a short time.

"My last nurse would fondle my penis sometimes," Tad told me one day when I was dressing him after a bath. "I can't feel anything anyway."

"I'm not going to do that," I said.

"Well, you could talk about sex."

"Nope. Sorry." I lectured Tad about how dirty talk was not part of the job description. Thus, the "speak no evil" link was born.

There seemed to be only one way to escape douchebags, penises, and sordid live-in jobs: I needed to get my own place. This required finding a job, but not just any job would do. I wanted to blossom into a star. Like so many newcomers to Hollywood, I was a wannabe actress with naivety, optimism, and dreams of castles in the clouds. I was convinced that the head hogs and producer types were all but waiting for my grand entrance and my signature on the purple, sequined line. So I donned my best "say cheese" dress and drove to the Screen Actors Guild on Sunset Boulevard to be "discovered." This seemed like a logical place.

Folks in the lobby were absorbed in paperwork and seemed unaware that I was dripping with talent. I approached a woman behind a counter. "I'm looking for the leading lady department."

"We don't have a leading lady department."

"Really? Where would I go for an acting role?"

"The Guild doesn't give out roles. You have to do that on your own."

"I do?"

"Yes. But you may want to check for auditions over there." She pointed to index cards thumbtacked to a bulletin board. "Sometimes there are postings."

"Private Investigation Company seeks Actress. Undercover Mission. $500."

These were the enticing words on an index card. The gig seemed adventuresome, profitable, and even doable. After all, I had a natural-born predisposition for getting around rules. I had sneaked Buddy to the convalescent home to visit Mom behind my father's back. I knew how to crash VIP events, tiptoe into hotel kitchens at night, and investigate off-limits areas of casinos all without getting caught. I figured maybe I would make a good private eye.

Rudy and Patrick were my bosses for this undercover operation. I had to pretend to be a newcomer in town. This was easy because I was. I had to pretend to be an aspiring actress. This was easy because I was. And I had to pretend to be promiscuous. This was not so easy because I had, thus far, agreed to have sex with only one man: Tom Jones.

"Dolly" was the fake name I was told to use because it would make me seem voluptuous and loose. My assignment was to wear a come-hither dress, call a certain film producer named John, and arrange to meet him at a bar for a drink. Rudy and Patrick would sit at a nearby table for protection. I was supposed to say that I'd gotten John's name and number from a friend of a friend. A movie studio had hired my bosses to find out if their employee was making porn flicks on the side. I was wired, so any confession could be used against John by studio heads.

Although I was excited to go undercover and make money, I was not excited about being thrust into another sex-related situation. To my mind, posing as a porn star was not all that different from rooming with a framed penis or being the unwitting heartthrob of a paraplegic playboy. If the world was a stage, I was being repeatedly cast as a sex object. It felt misogynistic and frankly uncomfortable.

"I have a stomach ache. I'm on an all-nut diet," John said after we introduced ourselves at the bar.

"Like a squirrel?" I asked. "No fruits or vegetables?"

"Yep. Nothing but nuts. I'm trying to lose a few pounds."

My sob story seemed pretty darned believable. I could hear the teeny violins in my head. I told Squirrelly John how I'd been robbed in Beverly Hills just after arriving in town. This had actually happened, but the thief, who drove away in a Mercedes, got only seventeen bucks. I told him how I could not find a job, and my landlord was threatening to evict me. My actual living situation was indeed tenuous, so this was an easy line to deliver.

Like a baseball pro, I tried every kind of pitch. There were curveballs, straight balls, grease balls, underhanded throws, and foul balls. But he would not hit. Being a private eye required more chatting than I'd had to do as a chip chatter. No matter what I said, nothing made Squirrelly John want to cast me as the new Linda Lovelace. *Deep Throat* did not seem to be in my future.

"If you hear of any job openings, let me know." I gave him my number and left.

Afterward, my bosses congratulated me for being believable, but I felt like I had failed. "I would have hired you," Rudy said. "Maybe he's on the up-and-up."

A week later, I got a call from Squirrelly John, who said he had a part for me in a movie. I was not sure whether he wanted me to be something respectable like a prison inmate or a dead body, or whether he was hinting at a sleazy role in an adult film. I was hesitant but figured I should not turn down his offer, because it was either good news for me personally or good news for my former bosses.

"Be here in two hours," he said.

I hung up the phone and immediately telephoned Rudy and Patrick, but they did not answer. I left five messages. I had to make a decision: either nix the whole idea or meet a strange squirrel in an unfamiliar location. I dumped my tape recorder into my once prime chip-chatting purse and rushed out the door. I figured I could at least eyeball the meeting place to see if it looked scary.

It didn't. In fact, according to the lobby directory, he worked in a building with other entertainment professionals. I flipped on my tape recorder and knocked on his office door. I considered it odd that he had no waiting room or secretary.

Squirrelly John had been hibernating alone in a cramped and downscale room with piles of papers, movie posters on the walls, and cheesy plaques on a bookshelf. I was worried that I was walking into a trap, so I kept a clear path to the door. John settled at his desk. I sat across from him, placing my purse, which concealed the tape recorder, between the two of us. I was not sure if recording someone without his knowledge was legal in California, but I figured if he killed me, the authorities would have audio evidence.

"Dolly, you said you need work and have acting experience. So I thought you might be right for a new project."

"That sounds good." I smiled.

"You will need to take off your top, Doll." The slimy words came out of his mouth as if he had said them to a thousand girls before me.

"Sorry. I don't do nudity." I rose from my chair.

"Hey. Sit down. All the famous actresses do it. It's no big deal."

"Sorry." I backed toward the door with my purse.

"Doll, you can make a couple grand. Maybe more."

"I gotta go." I bolted from his office. I gave the tape to my bosses, who presented me with a hundred-dollar bonus. I never found out whether the studio heads fired Squirrelly John.

❧

I went from (James) bonding with a squirrel to (James) bonding with a hamster, a rabbit, and two potbellied pigs. In other words, I was landing detective work (sometimes through Rudy and Patrick, and sometimes on my own), and I was envisioning the "persons of interest" or "targets" as tiny animals. It was a way to maintain perspective and a sense of humor during these nerve-racking undercover missions.

Gretchen was a hamster because she was on the relationship wheel to nowhere. Her boyfriend hired me to root out her infidelity, and Halloween made this task easy. On October 31, I knocked on her door wearing a mask and sporting an orange-and-black candy bag.

"Trick or treat," I said, while spying a male specimen in the next room—shirtless and seductively positioned on her bed. Case closed, plus some Hershey's Kisses and Mr. Goodbars to boot.

Andy and Cliff—the potbellied pigs—were twin brothers with jet-black hair and a penchant for hoarding. After an alleged accident, they filed for workers' compensation, claiming they were unable to lift heavy objects, thus not fit for employment. They had been working at a warehouse, loading boxes. I was paid by their employer to stake out their house and record unusual activity. On the fifth day, I claimed victory when the brothers lugged a large television from their car to the front door. I was able to memorialize the heavy lift with a photo.

Madeline's husband, Roger, was also the target of my private eyes. He was a rabbit. But unlike Roger Rabbit, he was in no way framed. Instead, he incriminated himself. Like the gentle, furry creatures, Roger was fond of trying to procreate. He had slipped into more sexual encounters than a truckload of Trojan condoms.

"I just know he's cheating." Madeline sobbed into the phone. "He keeps saying he isn't and telling me I'm crazy. I've seen so many psychiatrists. Please help me find out the truth."

I had never met Madeline, who was calling from Boston. She wanted to hire me as a sleuth because she'd heard of my success with Squirrelly John. I needed to act quickly. Roger was on a business trip in Beverly Hills and dining at a restaurant. Soon he would return to his hotel room at the Four Seasons.

"I think the other woman is on the business trip with him," Madeline said. "You have to hurry over to the hotel and catch them."

The Four Seasons was extravagance and elegance like a Renaissance painting. In the lobby, there were iron chairs with silk seat cushions. Lush greenery arched out of oriental vases, and the chandeliers were shaped like bursts of tentacles. The lights resembled white sea anemone. It was in this picture-perfect setting that I sat waiting for a scruffy, short blond man wearing baggy pants and a brown motorcycle jacket.

Madeline had said he would be easy to pinpoint, and she was right. When he walked through the door, the Renaissance painting suddenly seemed marred. Roger seemed much too plebeian to be a guest in the hotel. He was not alone. He had a plebeian accomplice: a cute, thin, blonde gal in jeans.

I followed them while pretending I wasn't. They turned the corner. I turned the corner. They went up steps. I went up steps. They stopped at their suite, and I walked past them as if I was searching for another room. After they were out of sight, I circled back to listen at their door. I thought about how there were probably cameras in the hallway and figured hotel security would be along any moment to nab me as a Peeping Tom. I also thought about how the socially acceptable occupation of private investigator was actually much shadier than being a chip chatter. Go figure.

Five minutes later, I heard sex sounds and pillow talk. Roger Rabbit was living up to his name. As I eavesdropped, I jotted down every "ooh," "aah," and "do it again" in my trusty notebook. I felt like a pervert with my ear against the door, but I needed every detail so I could give a full report to my client back in Boston. When I had enough evidence to convict, I telephoned Madeline and communicated the heartbreaking truth.

"Go to his room," she said, "and tell him to call his wife."

I figured Roger and his cutie would ignore my knock, since they were clearly preoccupied, but I was wrong. Roger opened the door wrapped in a white towel.

"Your wife wants you to call her," I said, and walked away.

He stammered, "Uh, okay."

Roger Rabbit spent an hour on the phone trying to convince Madeline that he and his cutie were only watching a porn movie. Eventually, he broke down and confessed the truth, including the fact that he had been unfaithful for years. They divorced soon thereafter. Cutie was probably pleased. Madeline certainly was. Madeline got to keep half of the estate and all of her sanity.

∾

Although I was 2,200 miles away, Dad was still trying to wrangle me into submission. This was nothing new. His attempt to place a tether around my neck had begun decades earlier, after adopting me from "The Agency." As a child, his put-downs and manipulations felt like an ever-tightening rope, hoisted upon me as part of a package deal. I would get a roof over my head, an education, three meals a day, and—ding, ding, ding—the grand prize: a lifetime of verbal abuse. To Dad's mind, the needling, the hostility, the denunciations were necessary in order to drag me toward high-society Atlanta and the proper role of Southern belle.

But dragging had never worked with me. I was like an ornery old oak, unwilling to budge. Dad retaliated by calling me "hardheaded." Then he'd issue a footnote: "Remember, young lady, you'll never be as stubborn as me." And just like that, I was thrust into bullheaded badminton, pigheaded polo, the hundred-yard dash for the obstinates. Everything was a contest in Dad's world, and money was king. Whoever died with the most stuff won. Maybe my father would have been all compliments if I'd waived a little white flag. Maybe he would have changed his tune if I had not been a rebel. Then again, maybe not.

Our tug-of-war was most obvious when we spoke on the phone. Seconds into the conversation, I'd want to explode. Yet I'd remain polite, composed, and meek. I hated conflict. It was my nature. Plus, getting rattled could bring blood to my head and trigger a migraine. I was a master of disguise, a sea dragon when it came to anger—blending into the flora, fading into the background. I was skilled when it came to calmness and stoic resolve.

On this particular occasion, my father was being more than mean and controlling. He was making a bizarre accusation. I fiddled with the phone cord, knowing I had two options: hang up—an aggressive move and wholly out of character—or stick it out. I opted for the latter.

"Your brother would *never* have done something like this." Although Buddy had been dead for three years, Dad saw him as a diamond while I was a tray of smashed glass destined for the rubbish bin.

"What are you talking about?" I asked.

"You stole my gun."

"What gun?"

"Don't lie to me, Missy."

"I don't know what you're talking about."

"It was in the top drawer of the old chest. You took it."

I knew Dad had a six-foot-tall cabinet full of shotguns, but did he also have a revolver? I had never seen it. Was he inventing it? Was he losing his mind? And if there had been a gun, who could have stolen it? No one was ever inside the Atlanta house except the two of us and the housekeeper (who was not capable of theft, in my view). In addition, this was an alarming situation. Wasn't there a law that made a registered gun owner responsible for crimes committed with his weapon? Would there be a shooting? Would someone die? Would Dad go to jail?

"I didn't know you had a gun in the chest. I only know about the rifles in the cabinet. Who could have taken it?"

"*You* took it. There are lots of lowlifes out west. I know you're mixed up with them."

"No, I'm not."

"Face it. You're a loser and you're mixed up with losers!"

"Why are you yelling at me?"

"You need to move back to Atlanta. And bring my gun with you."

"I like it here." I began to wonder if Dad was inventing the missing revolver as a ploy to force me back to Georgia.

"And I need my Volkswagen."

"You have three Mercedes, Dad. You don't need the Volkswagen. Plus, I don't have money for a new car."

"That's not my problem."

"I have to go." I hung up, figuring I'd have to dodge Dad's calls for weeks, maybe months. If he made good on his threat, I'd be carless in Los Angeles, and this was as bad as being coatless in Antarctica or boatless in the middle of the Pacific.

I paced the room, wondering what Dad's next move might be. I envisioned him on the phone with the cops. "Officer, my daughter is in that liberal cesspit called Los Angeles with other lowlifes. She stole my car! Arrest her! And be careful. She's got a gun!"

I settled on the bed, feeling anxious and alone. I examined an array of beaded blouses that I had tediously and lovingly sewn while brainstorming on how to acquire used-car funds. And that is when the idea hit me. I would launch a scheme called the Glitz Blitz. It would lift my spirits. It would give me access to high-end clothing customers. It could bring me hundreds of dollars. On the other hand, it could land me in jail.

Chapter Two

THE GLITZ BLITZ

The Glitz Blitz is a party-crashing maneuver I invented. It required transforming into a human Christmas tree, a five-foot-tall diamond, or a shiny space alien. In other words, I needed to look outrageous, temporarily blinding security guards with my garish glitter as I waltzed past them into an event. When embarking upon this strategy, I had to pretend to be famous—often part of the evening's entertainment—while manifesting confidence, charisma, and that indescribable attitude of "step aside, darling, and let me through the door." If I'd been flush with cash, I might have commissioned actors to pose as fans, screaming for my autograph and snapping paparazzi shots.

It was Glitz Blitz day, and my target was the Grammy Awards. The event was held at Los Angeles' Shrine Auditorium, and I wore my "Cher special," a sexy fishnet body stocking with a sequined one-shoulder dress and fake feathers. I had two beaded blouses tucked inside my oversized purse and hoped to show them off—possibly even sell them—to well-heeled attendees. After leaving my Volkswagen in a motel parking lot, I stepped around broken glass and empty soda cans as I made my way through the streets of south Los Angeles and toward the affair. The area was humming with traffic, short on parking spots and long on security officers.

Since arriving in L.A., I'd heard about periodic headliners at the Greek Theatre, Universal Amphitheatre, and other local venues. It differed from Vegas, where I could pop backstage any time at a wide array of showrooms to hang with entertainers and to meet VIPs. I wanted to invent new and exciting challenges in the realm of "crashing" and hoped that award shows, such as the Grammys, Emmys, Oscars, Golden Globes, Saturn Awards, and the People's Choice Awards, would be my new playground. In addition to the adventure, I could add friends to my show business family. Plus, there could be employment-related benefits: I might get acting role offers and gain customers for my one-of-a-kind beaded creations. There seemed to be no downside to party crashing.

This was my first awards show, and I had no idea *if* I could sneak into the affair, much less how. I was a rebel in high heels but without a plan. As I neared the Grammy venue in my stilettos, I came upon a long line of shiny limousines filled with celebrities and VIPs. The vehicles were inching toward their destination: a lavish red carpet, where the rich and famous would disembark, wave to screaming fans, and strut up to a security guard who would confirm their ticket and superstar status. Then they would sashay into the festivities.

I needed fancy wheels. A real celebrity does not hobble up to the theater loading dock, rap on the metal door, and mumble, "Do you think I could… maybe… come inside?" Hitchhiking was my plan. So I ventured from limo to limo, smiling at the reflective glass and wondering if Michael Jackson or Madonna was inside sipping champagne and laughing at my dopey grin. Eventually, a man rolled down his window.

"Are you going to the door?" I asked. "I'm so tired of walking." I feigned exhaustion. "Do you think I could have a lift?" He graciously invited me to join him.

This man (who was traveling solo, apart from his driver) confessed that he would not be exiting the vehicle. He didn't say why, and I did not recognize him. I assumed he was a commoner like me and lacked a ticket or wanted to get more use out of his rented car. His decision to stay put was disappointing because I had hoped to glide into the event on the weight of his credentials. On the other hand, disembarking alone would seem downright impressive. I'd look like a bona fide star.

When the anticipated moment came, I stepped onto the red carpet by myself. I floated toward the entrance, waving at the crowd, sending air kisses, signing autographs, and posing for paparazzi. However, the entire time I was acutely aware of the security guard in the distance, watching my every move. My Glitz Blitz performance was solely for him.

When I reached the door, this guard asked me for my invitation, and I feigned surprise. "Oh no. My agent has it. I'm supposed to meet him at the door. What should I do?"

The guard sighed. My transportation was gone, and he did not have the heart to send me back down the red carpet in my ostentatious outfit, past the huge throng and into the dark and possibly dangerous street.

"Okay. I guess you can wait here on the outside of the building until he arrives."

I spent the next ten minutes befriending this guard, hoping that he would eventually let me pass. As we chatted, I inched from the outside of the entry to the inside, and then I made my big move. "I need to go to the restroom. Is there one nearby?"

With a knowing smile and what seemed to be a half wink, he said, "If I let you go, you're going to come back, aren't you? Because if you don't, there's nothing I could do about it." He seemed to be hinting that I should let him off the hook, save him from the painstaking dilemma of "should she stay or should she go." If I was to disappear into the labyrinth of party dresses and black tuxedos, it would make his job easier. So I thanked him, gave him a quick hug, and headed backstage to hobnob with the rich and famous.

The backstage area was packed with entertainers, including Tina Turner, Rick Springfield, Marie Osmond, and Mickey Gilley. I was thrilled when former *Hello, Dolly!* actress Carol Channing approached me, struck up a conversation, and eventually asked to see the beaded blouses in my purse. She fawned over my designs and agreed to buy one for a whopping $500! After lots of schmoozing, I left the backstage and ventured into the audience section, where I was approached by a woman with a clipboard. She seemed frazzled and desperate for help.

"Please, would you like to be a seat filler?"

"Okay," I stuttered, unsure what I was agreeing to do.

I learned that seat fillers are generally placed in vacant seats in the first few rows of the auditorium for television purposes so that when cameras pan the audience, there are no gaps. This woman placed me in the third row between singer Glen Campbell and football player Lynn Swann. I sat there for the remainder of the show. I imagined someone back in Georgia pointing at my gate-crashing mug on TV and saying, "What in heaven's name is that little Missy Laws doing at the Grammy Awards?"

After the show, I sneaked into the after-party by slithering under a curtain. The event was held in a ballroom adjacent to the stage. But I immediately caught sight of a man outside the ropes who was not a cheerful chipmunk. Security refused to let him enter. This man was singer James Brown, and he had been a presenter at the show. I motioned James over to the ropes. "Do you need help getting in?"

"Yes, I do. I lost my ticket."

"Don't worry. Wait here." I trotted off to track down the head of security.

Five minutes later, James was allowed to join the party. It was ironic that little ole me was able to gain entrance easily while the King of Soul had difficulty. The City of Angels was deliciously devilish. It was a paradise of paradox. Thus, it was the perfect place for me.

~

A night of Grammy glitz led to a hunger for more glitz, and what better place to find it than in Las Vegas? I loaded up the Volkswagen and headed to Sin City for a three-day vacation. I planned to hit showroom dressing rooms, introducing myself to entertainers and other VIPs as I had done routinely while living there. I knew fun could turn into profit, meaning I might be able to sell more of my beaded creations, get acting gigs, and collect interviews for a book I planned to write about party crashing.

On this trip, I had a date with teen idol Andy Gibb. Unfortunately, it was as enjoyable as walking on broken glass. Andy's dreams were shattered all over his suite at the Riviera Hotel, and I didn't want to get pricked, so I fled. Although it saddened me that he was in so much pain, I could not be the tourniquet in his life. He didn't need a superficial fix. His wound was clearly too deep.

It all started when Louis Cabaza, the keyboard player for singer Natalie Cole, arranged for me to see the show. (I had befriended dozens of musicians and other show business folks while living in Las Vegas, and sometimes they comped me to performances.) Natalie was the warm-up singer in the Riviera showroom that night, and Andy was the main act. This was after Andy's much-publicized breakup with actress Victoria Principal and before his six-week drug rehab stint at the Betty Ford Center.

Louis arranged for me to sit in Natalie's private booth and later to join the band for bowling at the El Rancho Hotel. "Everyone's going there to play," he said when I went backstage at the conclusion of Natalie's act. "You can join us if you want."

"No, I'm going back to the booth to watch Andy's show," I replied. "I'll head over after."

While backstage, I asked a Riviera employee for the name of Andy's manager. He told me that it was "Dan." I figured this information might come in handy when attempting to "crash" Andy's dressing room. The question of crashing never hinged on "if." It was all about "when."

Back in the showroom, I questioned the maître d', "Where is Mr. Gibb's private booth?" I was aware that each Vegas headliner was allotted a table for family and friends. He pointed, and I stored the all-important information for future use.

When the show ended, I eyed Andy's private booth guests and followed them into the backstage area and up the carpeted steps toward the headliner dressing room. I planned to fool security into thinking I was part of their group. But a silver-haired man in the group was wise to my scheme. He wheeled around with a scowl on his face.

"Where exactly are you going?" Mr. Silver Hair shot daggers.

"I'm supposed to go to the dressing room to see Andy Gibb."

"I'm sorry, but no one is allowed back here."

It was time to whip out my secret weapon: the manager's name. "Dan asked me to come backstage." I worried that my lie would be exposed, and I prayed this man was *not* Dan.

Mr. Silver Hair didn't seem to know whether to believe me. He put away his daggers and proceeded down the hallway with the other guests. I tagged along. As they entered Andy's dressing room, I ducked inside just before the door was shut. This prompted Mr. Silver Hair to come unglued. He threw up his hands as if to shove me back into the hall.

"All right, you can say hello to Andy." He sighed. "Then you *must* leave."

The room was silent. Everyone had heard his stern words, including Andy. I felt like an idiot and a nuisance, but figured I could not turn back now.

"The girl would like to say hi," Mr. Silver Hair said to the singer.

I moved toward Andy with my hand extended while Mr. Silver Hair reopened the door, prepping it for my speedy exit.

"Nice to meet you, Mr. Gibb," I said in a formal tone.

The guests stared at me, anticipating humiliation and rapid ejection. But that's not what happened.

"Come on in. Sit down." Andy welcomed me. "What would you like to drink?"

In one broad stroke, he erased my embarrassment. The other guests went back to their conversations, and Mr. Silver Hair closed the door with me on the inside. Andy fetched me a glass of orange juice, invited me to sit with him on the couch, and flirted. He told me he had a fondness for blondes and that he would like to have dinner with me on the following evening.

"I'd ask you out tonight, but I'm going to see some tame orangutans." He explained that Bobby Berosini, a Czech-born American performer, had an animal comedy act at the Stardust Hotel across the street. Although I was an animal advocate who disapproved of using animals in entertainment,[3] I listened quietly. I did not want to say anything that could put a damper on a promising friendship.

Andy veered the conversation into less controversial terrain. "I'm English by birth. I've lived in Australia, Spain, and England." He told me about his tour and his affection for his brothers, the Bee Gees. He also revealed that he was only two years older than me. I was proud of myself for treating him like an equal. I had a tendency to treat males my age as if they were kid brothers. "Why don't you come by tomorrow night after the second show? We can have dinner in my suite."

"I don't usually go to guys' suites," I said.

"Okay, we can eat here in the dressing room."

I accepted the dinner invitation. He gave me a peck on the lips, and I left for the bowling alley.

On the following evening, I arrived backstage for my date with Andy, but he was not there. A crew member was reviewing some papers.

"Are you Missy?"

"Yes."

"Andy's waiting for you in the suite."

"We aren't having dinner in the suite. He's supposed to meet me here."

The crew member seemed confused. He called the singer from the dressing room and handed me the phone.

"I have some other guests up here," Andy said to me. "Give me ten minutes, then come on up."

"I thought we were eating in the dressing room."

"No, just come on up. We won't be eating alone anyway."

I was reluctant, but agreed since he had said others would be present. The crew member escorted me to Andy's room.

There was a degree of comfort in going out with a famous guy. If he were to do something inappropriate, he risked bad publicity, a costly lawsuit, and a possible end to a fruitful career. It gave me a degree of control over an otherwise risky situation with a stranger. Only a stupid star would gamble it all on a girl he barely knew.

As I entered Andy's suite, I looked down to see something utterly disgusting: a used pair of women's underwear balled up on the carpet. I pivoted back toward the door, but the crew member had departed. Clearly no one was joining us for dinner. I felt duped. I was alone with Andy.

Although I was naïve about behavior with respect to drugs and alcohol, it was obvious that Andy was not himself. He'd seemed normal on the previous night. Now he seemed to be an entirely different person. His charm had turned to callousness. His previous good manners were bordering on crudeness and disrespect. There was an insecurity and sadness in his eyes. He seemed to be in emotional pain. I think he perceived me as temporary relief, as a faceless person who might help him get through an agonizing evening. I got the sense that every evening was agonizing. I had expected a date of lightheartedness and comedy, but Andy was all tragedy.

"Where's the dinner?" I noticed there was no food in the room.

He stood at the window. "Isn't that beautiful?"

"The lights on the Las Vegas strip?" I asked.

"No. My name on the marquis."

I wondered if hotel management intentionally gave some showroom entertainers suites with a view of the sign. At the time, I thought Andy was trying to impress me, but looking back, I think he was trying to impress himself. He did not seem convinced of his own worth. He did not have an ego problem. He had an inferiority complex.

"Where's the dinner?" I repeated.

"I'm not really hungry." He sat on the couch. "Come sit next to me."

I reluctantly obeyed, but I was starting to get angry. Andy

made small talk for no more than five minutes before grabbing me and kissing my lips while moving his hands all over my body. I jumped up furious and in disbelief, wondering what had happened to the courteous guy I had met the previous night.

"I think you have the wrong idea."

He opened the double doors that led into the bedroom of his suite and started shedding his clothes. The bed was in disarray. I figured the girl who'd lost her panties had been there. I stood in the living room, incredulous. Seconds later, Andy was fully nude on the bed, begging me to join him.

"I think you're a total jerk," I roared, and marched out of the suite. The door slammed with a loud thud.

I was still fuming when the elevator doors opened on the casino level of the Riviera, where, to my surprise, Andy's band members were congregated.

"Andy Gibb is the biggest jerk I've ever met," I bellowed loud enough for the band members and half of the casino to hear. I could see shocked looks as I stomped out of the building.

I don't think the real Andy was a jerk. He had become overpowered by extraordinary success at a very young age. Fame had caught him off guard, and it had devoured him. It had sucked the soul out of him. Andy had lost himself. Like drugs and alcohol, he saw me—and probably other females—as a diversion, as a crutch, as temporary gauze. But we were not the answer. His injuries were just too serious.

Andy died a few years after our date. He was only thirty.

❧

I'd always been able to bring Las Vegas to life, to trigger memorable moments. Therefore, it was not surprising when on the following evening, I found myself on another unforgettable adventure. It happened at the Sands.

The Sands Hotel and Casino had come on the scene in 1952. It was the seventh resort to open on the strip. Las Vegas had been segregated in the 1950s, but this hotel was a pioneer when it came to hiring blacks and allowing them to gamble on the premises. The Rat Pack—Frank Sinatra, Dean Martin, Sammy Davis Jr., Peter Lawford, and Joey Bishop—had performed in the intimate 385-seat showroom in 1960.

I saw the place as cozy, inviting, and mellow; it seemed devoid of anxiety and pushiness. It did not give the impression that it was clamoring to reel in tourists like a pedestrian flagging down a bus. It was painted a deep pink, which I saw as the color of old money and class, probably because Dad's parents had spent time in Naples, Florida, at a similar-looking vacation spot.

I delighted in the Sands' naturally flowing floor plan and its delicious private patios off some of the suites. I'd had a conversation with *The Odd Couple*'s Jack Klugman in the Sands coffee shop, hung out with Robert Goulet backstage, and attended dozens of parties hosted by Wayne Newton on the premises. On the evening following my ordeal with Andy, I had my first date with Tony Bennett at this establishment, although I did not initially realize it was a date.

I had briefly met Tony at the Chastain Park Amphitheatre in Atlanta when I was in high school. I had "fat face complex" that night. My cheeks were puffed out because my wisdom teeth had just been removed. Despite my embarrassment, I sneaked backstage to meet Tony after his show. We had a ten-minute conversation—nothing that set me apart from the hundreds, even thousands, of folks he met each week.

Flash forward to the evening after my date with Andy. I ventured backstage to reintroduce myself to Tony and to mingle with his backstage guests. After an hour of small talk, I said my good-byes and headed for the door. Tony shouted at me, "Why don't you give me a call in a couple of hours? Just have the hotel ring my room."

"Oh… O… kay." I was confused. I didn't think Tony could possibly be asking me on a date, because I was so much younger. He was fifty-six at the time.

"Would you like to join me for dinner?" Tony asked when I phoned.

"Oh… O… kay." I was still bewildered, assuming this was a "friend thing."

Tony gave me his room number. Although I normally refused to dine in a guy's suite, regardless of stature, I had the impression Tony would be a gentleman. Plus, I didn't think he was romantically interested.

I navigated the winding hallways to Tony's suite, and the singer answered the door with his usual friendly smile. I stepped into an alcove, which opened into the living room, where there was a couch, a bowl of fruit, a guitar, and plates of food on a cart. Each dish had a silver cover, which Tony removed to reveal steaming hot entrées.

"Thanks for coming." He motioned to a chair. "Would you like to sit down?"

We enjoyed tasty food and good conversation, but I clearly noticed our generation gap. I had been comfortable with Tom, who was twenty years my senior, but Tony was thirty-four years older than me. He brought up people and experiences that were before my time. Of course, when he mentioned his participation in the civil rights march of 1965 in Alabama, I was impressed. At the time, he was one of the few Caucasian performers who was willing to take a stand on the issue.

"I've been learning how to play the guitar," Tony said as we retreated to the couch after dinner. "Could I sing you a couple of songs?"

"Wow, I would love that."

I felt honored. No one had ever given me a private serenade. Tom had belted out a few bars here and there in his suite and in the dressing room, but it had never been directed at me.

Tony played the guitar and sang. It was romantic and reminded me of one of my favorite movies, *Love in the Afternoon*, starring Audrey Hepburn and Gary Cooper. Ironically, I had always been drawn to that movie because of the huge age difference between the two leads (since I'd always preferred older men). I also liked the rare "woman pursues man" plot.

Tony was charming and knew how to make a woman feel special. He might have swept me off my feet that very night had I been a spontaneous soul. But "sweeping" had never worked with me. I was too deliberate, too cautious, and just too practical.

After four lovely tunes, we continued our conversation. Tony did not have a negative thing to say; it was not part of his nature. He demonstrated a rare ability to perceive the bright side of a situation. Although I had spent only a few hours with him, I considered him to be one of the nicest people I had ever met.

I noticed it was getting late. "I should probably be going."

"Let me walk you out." He held open the door and then reached over and kissed me passionately on the lips. I was shocked. I had no idea he was attracted to me. I did not pull away from the kiss as I would have with most guys. I was confused and unsure how I felt. I thought Tony was handsome but also felt the age difference was a problem due to the conversational disconnects. He was from the world of "I had to walk to school every day in the snow" while I was from the age of computers. We had grown up in different eras.

"Are you married?" I asked him after the kiss.

"I wouldn't have asked you out if I was married."

I smiled and left, giving careful consideration to whether I might want to see him again. A week later I decided the answer was yes, and he invited me to Illinois—where I got an earful from a high-profile heckler.

Tony was participating in an all-day neighborhood festival in Chicago, and he was the headliner, performing the final act at five p.m. There was a twenty-seven piece orchestra and a crowd of 100,000. Tony gave me a ticket to sit ringside next to Mayor Jane Byrne, but he only made it through two songs before the heckling began.

The mayor kept interrupting the performance and shouting out song titles with instructions, such as, "Do this one!" and "Not that one!" Plus, she was squirming around in her seat like a fidgety child. I was in disbelief, but Tony stayed calm and did as the mayor requested, changing the sequence of his songs as needed and adding tunes that had not been part of his repertoire. He was a seasoned performer, so the interruptions surely did not fluster him, but I felt bad for the orchestra members who had predesignated song sheets on their music stands. The mayor was making it difficult for them. I also figured that any other audience member who caused this sort of ruckus would have been booted. The mayor acted as if she was the only observer, but there were thousands of people seated behind us who were no doubt annoyed.

Afterward, I said to Tony, "I couldn't believe it. The mayor was heckling you."

"I just hope she liked the show."

"She should have." I laughed. "She directed it."

Tony and I had dinner that evening with television host Merv Griffin in Tony's antique-appointed suite, and the next day I returned to Los Angeles. Although I never fell in love with Tony and we never had sex, I enjoyed his company and met him periodically for dinner and conversation. As for Jane Byrne, she only served one term as the mayor of Chicago. She lost her reelection bid. It could have been due to heckling.

Chapter Three

STRIP CLUBS AND THE PRESIDENT

I was at a café in Los Angeles, studying a blob of ink on a piece of paper. I had intensity. I had concentration. Then I spoke with confidence. "It's an L."

"No way." My friend Laura snatched the paper from my hand. "It's a capital T. See?" She pointed to a different mark, poking out from under the blob. It did not look deliberate but appeared to be a smudge or a coffee stain.

"I don't think so." I furrowed my brow.

We were trying to decipher the redacted words on my adoption paperwork. Two weeks prior, I had called "The Agency" in Atlanta and requested the names of my birth parents. A woman on the phone had told me that it was illegal for me to have this information.

"We'll send what you're *allowed* to know."

Allowed to know? Who were they to tell me what I was *allowed* to know? I was being held prisoner. The adoption agency was like my father. It was keeping me emotionally captive, tethering me to my tragic childhood, forcing me to remain ignorant about my ancestors and my genes.

When the package that contained what I was "allowed to know" arrived, I tore it open to find that some annoying stickler for rules had used a black marker to scratch out my real name and the names of my birth parents, as well as their hometowns. The blobs of ink on the paper were stab wounds to a thirsty heart, lacerations on a soul that needed answers.

"Why am I wasting my time? I'm never going to find my birth parents," I said to Laura.

"You're probably right." She bit into her sandwich.

"You're supposed to say, 'You can do it,'" I replied.

She gave me a long, hard look. "I don't think you'll find them." Then she took another bite of her sandwich.

I liked Laura, but she was a naysayer, skillful at smashing my dreams with a nimble whoosh, the way a Globetrotter stuffs a basketball into a hoop. Laura's favorite phrases were "You can't do it," "Dream on," "Forget it," and "It's not possible."

I had met Laura at a gas station just after arriving in Los Angeles. We marveled over the fact that we both had red Volkswagen Rabbits owned by our parents, and we joked about paying for only one insurance policy that could secretly cover both cars. Laura had a fourteen-year-old daughter but no husband. We became fast friends, even though we differed in the looks department. Laura was tall and redheaded. I was short and blonde. Laura wore yoga pants. I was the queen of cinch-waist circle skirts. Laura was stylish and Twiggy thin, while I resembled a fire hydrant.

Suddenly, there was an unexpected stench in the air. Were

there rotten eggs in the café kitchen? Had a bag of dirty diapers dropped from the sky? Was there a corpse seated at the table next to ours? No. It was my friend Larry, who resided at a budget motel, weighed over three hundred pounds, and habitually wore the same purple velvet tuxedo. He was not a chameleon; he did not blend in with the crowd. He was a jigger of Tabasco sauce; his appearance was a wake-up call. Plus, Larry smelled like a landfill. This is not meant as an insult. Every nose knew it was true. Larry showered only once a month because he had a psychological malady called aquaphobia, or fear of water. Although you could smell Larry from twenty feet and see him from two hundred yards, he had no trouble hobnobbing with the rich and famous, and many—especially old-timers in Hollywood—knew him affectionately by name.

"It's a bird. It's a plane. It's sewer man," Larry announced as he sat at our table. His odor-related quips stemmed from a desire to be liked and to ease everyone's embarrassment. Larry preferred to shower people with jokes rather than shower himself with water.

I had first met Larry at the Saturn Awards. We had both sneaked inside the affair. Despite Larry's less-than-spiffy appearance, he could gate-crash with the best of them. He was confirmation that no special skill or look was required to experience a glimpse of glamour or a moment of celebrity. Because of him, I had started writing a step-by-step party-crashing guide for the masses called *Meet the Stars*. With the book, I hoped to assume the position of doorman, lifting people up to the prestigious penthouse as well as toward their dreams.

A "doorman" is a go-between or a person who tiptoes up to the exclusive high-rise for a glance at the VIP penthouse and then darts back to the sidewalk to tell ordinary folks how they, too, can taste the lifestyle of the rich and famous. Rather than stay at the party and play insider, I preferred to hold the door open for others. I wanted to inspire people to pursue their dreams—both fleeting (such as attending star-studded events) and long term (such as snagging employment by making connections with CEOs and bigwigs). I wanted to encourage folks to explore gray areas, to think outside the box, and to reach for success. One theme of my book was that anyone could relish adventure and glamour, not just tycoons and movie stars.

"Are you ready for your big night?" Larry took a seat at our table.

"Not really." I laughed, hiding the adoption paperwork in my bag.

"Don't worry, kid. You'll break a leg." Larry was referring to the Hollywood Appreciation Society award, which I would be receiving that night. He had arranged for me to be one of the recipients even though I was in no way deserving of a fancy certificate and a room full of applause. He had done this for only one reason as far as I could tell: out of selflessness. Larry was the opposite of the Hollywood casting couch. He was a giver and billed himself as "the platonic Casanova," furnishing young women with small-time publicity and encouragement to follow their dreams. He was perfume in the area of optimism and never asked for anything in return. Lots of young ladies owed him for their fifteen minutes of fame.

Larry had already gotten me bit parts in a couple of local commercials, selling carpets and car wax. They had come with "bit pay." Larry had said, "It's not much money, but it's exposure, honey. And that's what you need to make it in the biz."

Larry had also landed me two unpaid gigs: as a presenter at the American Guild of Variety Artists award show and as a hostess at a Golden West Magazine–sponsored celebration. I was not accomplished enough to be thrust into these illustrious roles, but Larry was a public relations guru who had started his career at the *Chicago Tribune*. Later, he worked as a publicist for the Rat Pack and Goldwyn Studios.

Six hours after the café lunch with Laura and Larry, I stood on a stage in front of a small crowd making a speech about the merits of Tinseltown, going on about how the Hollywood community supports deserving causes. I could not thank all of the little people because, of course, I had no little people. In fact, I had no "people" at all—other than perhaps Larry. So I publicly praised this quirky but warmhearted man. He beamed with pride from the back of the room.

And that is the moment I saw him. I couldn't believe it. It was my father's private investigator, Ike. He wore a light gray jacket over a blue plaid shirt. Ike had surveilled me when I lived in Las Vegas. I'd spied him outside of my Nevada apartment building in a shiny, white Dodge. I'd noticed him here and there at casinos, coffee shops, and the Las Vegas mall where I'd worked as a Saks Fifth Avenue clerk. Once, I'd sashayed up to him and informed him in a teasing way that his cover was blown, that the fish was out of the water, that the owl had to find a new tree, that his target was wise to his prying eyes. He'd acted ruffled and surprised but did not stop spying on me. I hadn't reported the "unmasking" to Dad because I liked Ike and did not want him to be without a job.

What was he doing in California? He wasn't in the state to pan for gold. Would he stalk me in perpetuity? Did he plan to nab my car, search for the mysterious gun, or strong-arm me back to Georgia? I was eager to confront him, to bombard him with questions, to verify that he would not be taking subversive action against me. So I headed off the stage in his direction. "Excuse me." "Pardon me." I slid past audience members. "Sorry, I need to get by."

Then, in a flash, Ike was gone. I scanned the room in a panic. Where was he? How could he have disappeared so fast?

Although I felt on edge about his motives, I suddenly felt less hated by Dad. Would my father place me under surveillance if he truly loathed me? Would he expend his precious dollars in that way? Would he really want "activity reports" on a daughter whom he'd written off as a "disappointment" and a "kook"? In addition to feeling slightly less shunned, Ike's existence made me feel less alone in the behemoth city of Los Angeles. I left the award show with my certificate and a bizarre sense of serenity.

୶

Several months after the Hollywood Appreciation Society event, I sat in the back of a police car outside of my new North Hollywood apartment. I was distressed and almost in tears.

"Excuse me, sir," I spoke to a police officer through the open car window. "What's happening? I'm really worried about them. They may be dead."

"Just stay put, ma'am," he replied.

"I think you need to go inside."

"We have everything under control."

I fidgeted with my brown corduroy purse. I was in agony over Fred and Buffy. Were they dead? Were they injured? They had been alone in my apartment with the gunman. I had deserted them, and my body was wrapped in a blanket of guilt. I'd learned how I would act under pressure. I'd saved myself and left others behind. This was not altruistic. This was not commendable. But it proved one thing: I was a survivor.

Coldwater Canyon Avenue—which was lined with 1950s and 1960s apartment buildings—was normally buzzing with cars, but that morning it had been evacuated by official orders. There were ten law enforcement vehicles in my line of sight and what seemed like one hundred police and SWAT officers scampering to and fro, hoping not to get nailed by the gunman who could have poked his rifle out of my apartment window. The incident had the distinction of being Los Angeles' number one news story for the day.

Despite my pleas, the officers did not care about Fred and Buffy. They were only animals. Fred was a German shepherd, and Buffy was a striped golden cat. Both belonged to my roommate, Lynn. I had met Lynn six months earlier at an audition for a game show, after which I'd appeared on-air as a contestant and become the lucky winner of a lamp. I had to pay taxes on that stupid lamp. Lynn had moved to Los Angeles from Florida. We had that "southeastern state" connection.

Lynn had wanted to offset the cost of rent, so she'd offered me the distinguished position of "roommate" in her one-bedroom flat. I'd been there for only a few weeks before the gunman incident. We had to share a bed unless I was willing to make the pint-sized couch or porcelain tub my sleeping quarters. I opted for the bed, sleeping fully clothed each night in shorts and a T-shirt. In an attempt to save me from myself, Lynn was forever seeking hiding spots for the Cheerios and Lucky Charms. Without her, I would consume an entire box of cereal in one sitting and turn into a human oat balloon.

At two that morning, I'd woken to find a gunman hovering over our bed with an assault rifle aimed at Lynn's head. I'd recognized him as Mack, a twenty-year-old guy who was obsessed with my roommate, although they were not romantically involved. He often took Fred to the dog park and Lynn to lunch. Mack had broken down the front door and the bedroom door, both of which had been locked. He'd thought she was with another man, but he had been wrong. It was just the dog, cat, and me—the cereal fanatic and soon-to-be ex-roommate.

I did not scream or panic like they do in the movies, nor did I jump into action like Indiana Jones. I knew I could not count on physical strength with my five-foot-tall build. My only hope was my brain. Could I outsmart this guy? That is when I left Lynn, the dog, and the cat behind.

I yawned as if Mack's presence was routine, even boring. I folded back the covers with an air of detachedness and calmly slid out of bed. I slipped on my flip-flops and casually collected my purse from the bedside table. Thank goodness I slept dressed.

"Well, I'm already up. I might as well go to the grocery store," I stated in an aloof and tranquil way.

To my surprise and relief, Mack said nothing. He allowed me to walk right past him out of the apartment, his gun still firmly fixed on Lynn's face. Maybe he thought I always hit the supermarket at two a.m.

As I descended a staircase toward the street, I heard Lynn pleading, "I need to go to the store with Missy. I need to go to the store with Missy." Moments later, she jetted onto the sidewalk beside me. I was relieved that she made it out, and we dashed to her car. As we took off for a nearby phone booth to call the cops, I looked back to see Mack standing at the top of the stairs in the semi-darkness with his gun aimed at the stars. He looked like a statue.

Several hours passed while I sat in the back seat of the police car, agonizing over the fate of Fred and Buffy. Lynn was out of sight, briefing officers on details about the assailant. The SWAT team strategized for what seemed like forever on how to get this young man to surrender. Their megaphone efforts to coax him out had failed. They were understandably cautious because they had searched Mack's pickup truck and found enough assault weaponry and ammunition to equip half of the stalkers in Hollywood.

A strategy was finally agreed upon at six a.m., and tear gas was tossed through our apartment window, shattering the glass. The SWAT team rushed inside to find Mack facedown and lifeless on the carpet in the living room. He had been dead for hours, apparently shooting himself when Lynn and I drove to seek help. I was relieved to find that before taking his own life, he had compassionately confined Fred and Buffy to the bathroom. I knew it was compassion because he had set out bowls of food and water for them. The animals had not been exposed to the tear gas, the gruesome suicide, or the armed SWAT team members bursting through the door and prepared to shoot anything that moved. They were safe.

Lynn and I stood over Mack's body. The scene was surreal. Wind—which I had never felt to that extent in North Hollywood—whipped through the broken window with tremendous force, whirling dozens of twenty- and hundred-dollar bills through the air. We were immersed in a tornado of green. It was like being inside one of those game-show glass booths where contestants attempt to catch flying cash. This was other people's money. In fact, it had belonged to Mack. Why he had brought thousands of dollars to our apartment, no one knew. The incident was a mystery to Mack's family and friends. "Out of character" was the phrase they used. Tests later revealed that Mack had no drugs or alcohol in his body. I was packed and moved out of the apartment by noon.

◈

I believe in a woman's right to shoes. In fact, I had more clothes and accessories than twenty celebrities combined, and half of them were jammed into my Volkswagen Rabbit. I could barely see out of the rearview mirror. To this day, I am uncertain as to whether there was a Sparkletts truck behind me, or whether I was looking at my raindrop-print halter top. The other half of my wardrobe was in a Las Vegas storage facility with my furniture.

My new, cramped one-room apartment was in Van Nuys and a mile west of Lynn's crime scene. It was not ideal, but for $275 per month and short notice it was the best I could do. I hauled beaded gowns and blue jeans into my new place while an elderly neighbor explained how graffiti had sprung up in the area like an out-of-control morning glory.

"Some gang scribbled all over that wall." He pointed at black lettering. "And when it's not gangs, it's the blasted homeless." He gestured at two shopping carts resting on the curb. I pretended they were street art.

My main complaint about the apartment was the lack of air-conditioning and heat. Temperatures could fluctuate up to ninety-six degrees and down to freezing. I learned that when I am physically uncomfortable temperature-wise, I sleep. Morning, noon, night, anytime, I sleep. Since "being unproductive" was one of my seven deadly sins, this was utterly unsatisfactory. I dreamt of completing tasks, such as finishing the book I was writing, and then woke to find that I had only accomplished getting my clothes sweaty. Studies show that those who sleep more than eight hours per day or less than six and a half hours don't live as long. My landlord would be held responsible for my early death.

The apartment was located in a commercial zone, adjacent to hole-in-the-wall shops that served the bus-riding community. I popped into these stores in search of a bed and a table to fill my cubbyhole of an apartment, assuming prices would be lower in this less affluent neighborhood. I assumed wrong. As I expanded my furniture search by car into well-to-do Studio City and Sherman Oaks, I found identical items at a lower cost than in Van Nuys. It was disappointing to learn that some businesses took advantage of low-income folks who lacked the means to comparison shop. Wasn't it Toni Tennille's mama who said, "You better shop around"?

My theory about "gouging the poor" was confirmed again and again. A Subway restaurant in a low-income South L.A. neighborhood charged me a full dollar more for my vegan sandwich than did the Subway I regularly patronized in upscale Encino. And a dental establishment in a low-rent district quoted Laura considerably more for her daughter's braces than did orthodontists in swanky office buildings in Santa Monica. Go figure.

I eventually felt obliged to phone Dad. "I want to give you my new number. I had to move because a guy killed himself in our apartment." I blurted it out like a nitwit, as if my brain were made of cornmeal, as if my tongue were on speed dial. Dad already believed that his disaster of a daughter was cavorting with hooligans in a state all too lenient on crime, and now I had reinforced this view and adorned it with a big red bow.

There were five long seconds of silence, and then my father spoke. To my surprise, he did not inquire about the particulars of the ordeal, feign concern, or even ask whether his (supposedly) stolen gun had been used in the suicide. Instead, he let out a chuckle. "You've got a screw loose, Missy. I bet you're broke, too."

"No," I lied. "I'm doing fine." I quickly gave him my new number and hung up.

My next call was to Laura because she was my confidant, my sounding board when I wanted to vent or seek advice.

"You should go cold turkey on that whole dad thing," she said.

"I think I feel a sense of duty… like it's my job to stay in touch."

"It's not your job. He's the dead weight around your neck.… But let's talk later. I have to leave for work. The streets are jammed. Reagan's in town."

"He is? I'd love to interview him for my book and get a photo."

"Are you crazy? You can't interview the president!"

Luckily, I'd never been swayed by the Debbie Downers in my life. I possessed an innate "I'll show you" attitude. Perhaps this rebelliousness stemmed from genetics, from my real ancestors who had fought starvation, war, disease, poverty, or headhunters. Or maybe not. Negative words had always been my fuel, propelling me into high gear for another challenging adventure. So I quickly shifted into gate-crashing mode and called the White House to request permission to interview Ronald Reagan.

"The president will have no part of something like that," a staffer chastised me. She made me feel small but did not dissuade me from my goal.

I waited fifteen minutes, phoned the White House again, and requested contact information for the press department personnel who were traveling with Reagan in California. I hoped to have better luck with them. I was told to call Mark Weinberg at the Beverly Hilton. It turned out he was a Debbie Downer, too.

"Everyone in the country can't get their picture taken with the president! And he is not doing interviews for six weeks! I'm sorry. It will not be possible."

Weinberg's words prompted me to do what any renegade debutante would do: hop in the car and drive to the Beverly Hilton for a face-to-face showdown. Upon arrival, I found two men setting up camera equipment on a grassy island in front of the hotel's entrance. I had a hunch they were with the president and initiated a conversation. One man was Dean Reynolds, a White House correspondent for CNN and the son of television journalist Frank Reynolds. The other was Reggie, the White House's chief photographer.

I chatted with them for a while before popping the all-important question. "So what are you doing for New Year's Eve?" I was aware that publisher and diplomat Walter Annenberg hosted a social gathering in Palm Springs on New Year's Eve each year, which the president attended.

"We're going to a party," Reggie replied.

"That sounds fun. Do either of you happen to need a date?"

"Sure. I could use a date." Reggie smiled. "But the party is in Palm Springs. Do you want to drive all the way down there?"

"No problem.... Will the president be there?"

"Of course he will," Reggie said. "But I'll need your social security number for a background check." I gave it to him.

The party turned out to be an exclusive reception prior to the Annenberg estate event. It was held in a well-guarded ballroom at a ritzy Palm Springs hotel. At the agreed-upon time, Reggie met me in the lobby, and we headed for the metal detectors—that is, until I was stopped by a Secret Service agent because my name was not on the approved list. Reggie pulled him aside and did some fast talking while I did some fast praying. Thankfully, I was given the green light.

Inside the party, the president wore a white turtleneck and a plaid jacket. He glided around the room, holding brief conversations with guests. When he came to me, I asked if I could interview him for my book, and he agreed. In addition to answering my questions, we discussed his political goals for the upcoming year, animal welfare issues, and his holiday plans. An event photographer snapped a picture of us.

"So you lucked out and met the president," Laura conceded on the following day. "But it's going to be impossible getting your book published."

"There you go again," I said with my best Ronald Reagan impersonation.

⁓

I wanted to evaluate my life, to size up whether I was conquering

Los Angeles or whether it was conquering me. Was I on the path to victory? Or was I backpedaling toward the abyss, toward lifelong penury, and toward a godforsaken road trip back to Georgia? I sat on the bed in my pint-sized apartment and made a list of accomplishments and setbacks, of crazy antics and scary predicaments, of that which I would someday tell Dad and that which I would forever hide from him. There were admittedly a lot of bizarre situations listed on that paper. I'd been held at gunpoint, spied on by my father's private eye, and robbed by a guy who drove away in a Mercedes. I'd crashed award shows, gone on celebrity dates, and received a prize for doing nothing. I'd worked as a housekeeper, had drinks with a chipmunk, and been told by "The Agency" that I'd never meet my parents. I'd been mocked by a jealous girlfriend, badgered by a lady with a penis photo, and propositioned by a hot-to-trot paraplegic. I'd stalked Roger Rabbit, lived in a mobile home, interviewed the president, and been asked to make a splash in the porn world.

Yes, a lot had happened, and in one sense I was barreling along, racking up unforgettable experiences. But in another sense, I was stagnant. I had done nothing to increase my bank balance and become financially stable, to find a husband, to track down my real family, or to land a career. I was in survival mode. I was running in place. It was not long before running in place morphed into dancing in place. I found myself shimmying on a podium at a sleazy bikini bar. This was admittedly not a typical career choice for a debutante.

I did a jazz turn and a forward kick on the tiny stage. Then I flung my arms into the air, thrusting my head upward. I was wearing my usual thick ballet tights and a one-piece leotard. I looked like a Danskin ad for kiddie ballet. I did not manifest sexiness, but it was not about sex appeal in my book. Unfortunately, my employer had a different book.

"You need to wear something more revealing," she reprimanded me, as usual, during my ten-minute break.

I nodded as if I agreed, but my fake smile was routine. Since landing this go-go dancing job several months prior, I'd always acted as if I would comply but then showed up on the next day in the same puritanical garb. I felt comfortable bucking the system and ignoring authority, but I did not feel comfortable with confrontation. It was easier to nod in agreement and then later disobey orders.

I felt the job was about talent, about dance as an art form, and not about seductiveness—probably because this was my only hope for tips. Men came to this bar called One for the Road, located near the corner of Beverly Boulevard and Normandie Avenue, to drink beer and to watch girls in skimpy swimsuits swinging their hips in a suggestive way. They handed out dollar bills and often quite a bit more. I never made as much as the bumping, grinding gals, but I did fine due to my technical training in dance. The customers who appreciated skill and effort were my loyal supporters.

The twelve-by-six-foot podiums were like little islands, and they were scattered around the room. I had to be careful when doing split leaps, axel jumps, and other large moves. The bumping, grinding gals rarely changed position, so it was easier for them. There were usually three or four of us dancing at one time. Customers would dock themselves in chairs near our feet and put dollar bills, or fives or tens, on the stage. The more creative spectators were origami experts. They would fold their money into shapes—such as planes, flowers, fish, or birds—and toss them onto the platform.

When I spotted Talia across the room, I was elated. She was another me. She wore a demure one-piece leotard, did real dance moves, and ignored the sex-crazed customers. She held her head high as if she were part of the Royal Ballet. I knew that, going forward, I wouldn't be the only dancer singled out and scolded by the club's owner.

"I live nearby," Talia said to me after introducing herself. "Could you drop me off after work?"

It was one a.m. when we climbed into my car. I noticed that a customer in a strange green hat had staggered out of the bar behind us; he was heading toward a Ford Galaxie. Because I had always been Miss Careful (arguably bordering on paranoid), I hurriedly started my engine; jetted onto Beverly Boulevard; and whizzed past a car wash, a liquor store, and a pizzeria. I kept tabs on the street behind us via the rearview mirror. Twenty seconds later, Green Hat was on our tail.

"Some guy's following us. What should I do?"

Talia did a swift look-see and then yelled, "Quick. Turn."

I veered onto New Hampshire Avenue. For a moment, it looked as if the street was coming to a dead end at the Rosewood Methodist Church, but then I realized I could make a left at a stop sign. Green Hat did not slow at the sign. He whipped around the corner behind us, almost hitting our rear bumper.

I made an immediate right onto Normandie Avenue, and so did our pursuer. That is when Talia spotted an unmarked police car. Apparently, they have municipal license plates, tinted windows, and a specific kind of radio antenna. I have no idea how she knew this.

"It's an undercover cop." She pointed. "Honk your horn."

When the officer heard my honking, he triggered a flashing light on his dashboard. I pulled over to the curb, and to my surprise, so did Green Hat. The police officer promptly arrested the man for drunk driving and instructed Talia and me to hurry home.

I had been inducted into the treacherous world of go-go dancing by a stripper friend, who claimed to make "tons of cash fending off creeps."

"I doubt they're all creeps," I joked. "Maybe some of them got lost on the way to the library."

This friend had put me in touch with her booking agent, Carmen. Carmen also got me a job at a North Hollywood club called Star Garden, which was a block from the Debbie Reynolds Dance Studio. The place had a long mirrored bar, soda shop tables, red velvet chairs, and a pool table in the corner. All dancers were required to go topless. Since this was out of the question for me, Carmen booked me as a barmaid. I got beer for customers and worked the cash register. My most memorable experience at this establishment involved finding two one-hundred-dollar bills on the floor one evening after everyone had left.

Although I hated working in these one-stop shops for vices and fending off raunchy men, there were aspects of the job I liked. It gave me flexibility to work on my book, sell beaded gowns, snag private eye gigs, get cast in bit-part acting roles, and take respectable dance jobs in commercials and trade shows. Also, I liked getting exercise and entertaining onstage. The job reminded me of my childhood hobbies—sneaking into vacant homes to sing and dance for my dog and slithering into hotel conference rooms when on vacation in order to perform onstage to the applause of empty seats.

However, after a year of go-go dancer work, I yearned to quit. I wanted to sprout in a new direction but knew it would not be easy. I didn't think I could cover my monthly bills without a steady dancer (and barmaid) paycheck. I had become dependent and vulnerable. I felt like an alcoholic who craves to get clean.

Then luck placed a dollar on the stage.

My father came to California. As he entered my Van Nuys apartment, he mumbled, "Low class," and shook his head in disapproval. He poked his nose into the microscopic bathroom, the wee closet, the efficiency kitchen, and the not-so-tidy trash can. His facial expression was one of horror and revulsion, and for the second time in my life, he made me an offer that he thought I couldn't refuse. This time the offer didn't require blossoming into a socialite or returning to Atlanta. It had nothing to do with a townhouse, a Mercedes, or caverns full of cash. It was a different kind of overture.

Dad stared at me as if he were negotiating a high-level business deal. "I will buy a condo in Westwood where you can live while you finish college." He added that I would still need to work part-time but said that he'd help support me in Los Angeles as long as I agreed to attend school.

I was in shock. It was almost as if Dad had declared defeat. His bribes had not worked. His threats and fear-mongering had failed. Ignoring me and cutting me off financially had been losing strategies. It seemed to finally dawn on Dad that his recalcitrant daughter was going to remain in California even if she had to live in a low-class hovel of an apartment with an unkempt rubbish bin.

My father waited patiently. He seemed to expect defiance and a rejection of the proposal. But that's not what happened.

I said yes faster than Green Hat could barrel around a corner. It *was* an offer I couldn't refuse. Dad's generosity may have saved my life. I never set foot in a dangerous strip club again.

Chapter Four

THE SECRET

An adopted child is always undercover. She lives a lie, a split personality of sorts, rarely speaking about the pain of being in the dark about her roots and the fraudulence of pretending she is not. She silently ponders the question "Who am I?" while mourning for the family she has never known. She is immersed in a battle—an internal revolt, a genetic rebellion, a fight to uncover identity.

Of course, many adoptees are skilled at fitting in. They are wizards at performing as if they are insiders and at drumming up applause. I was not that way. I was a rabble-rouser and a misfit, who by fourth grade gave up on appeasing debutante society and the golden-coated gods of conformity. I was more like a demolition derby, ramming into the morals and mores of my community and then accepting my lot as a scapegoat for backlash. I was criticized not only for my outsider ways but for what seemed to be hereditary differences between myself and those in "old money" Atlanta.

For all adoptees—even those who suppress or camouflage their feelings—there persist questions, ancestral ghosts, turbulence, curiosity, confusion, and inner dissonance, whether they admit it or not. The unsolved mystery lurks. It lingers, and it is aggravating—mildly for some adopted children but severely for others.

Compartmentalization can ease the pain—a method I embarked upon to escape internal conflict, to alleviate negative feelings, and to muffle bad memories. I was like a heart with different parts—valves, muscles, ventricles, and atriums—or a country with disparate regions. I had a bunch of cubicles, slots, stalls, cubbyholes, and compartments where I could store that which I preferred to ignore. I even had tombs for the most disturbing experiences. I buried my deepest woes underground and tried to forget where I had stashed them. Two areas that had remained tightly shrouded were the tragedies that I called "childhood" and "the secret."

But that night, in a split second, my carefully constructed compartments disintegrated. They crumbled to the ground like a high-rise targeted by a wrecking ball. Coincidence and bad luck rolled into my life, unearthing "the secret" and laying it bare before my eyes. I descended into a tailspin—feeling frantic, angry, repulsed, grief-stricken, and vengeful. It was instantaneous.

The calamitous evening began in an innocent way. Larry— wearing his usual purple tuxedo—mentioned that John Travolta and Sylvester Stallone were having a private party at a nightclub called the Hollywood Palace (or the Palace) following the *Staying Alive* movie premiere at Mann's Chinese Theater. Guests for the event included Brooke Shields, Dolly

Parton, Ted McGinley, Peter Falk, Jane Seymour, and of course Travolta and Stallone. I perceived the festivity as another gate-crashing challenge and as an opportunity to peddle beaded creations, snag celebrity interviews for my book, and schmooze with movie producers and casting directors.

I got decked out, headed over to the Palace, and finagled my way into the affair—not once, not twice, but three times. I had to crash three times because I kept getting inside too early, before the party had begun. Thus, I got caught. Because the venue was mostly empty, I looked as conspicuous as a lemonade stand in the desert. I was told, in so many words, that no one was allowed inside yet, and then I was deposited back on the sidewalk. The third gate-crash was a winning move because the festivities were finally underway. Once safely inside the event, I mingled. I remember Jane Seymour telling me that her white gown had been made by the same designer who'd created Princess Diana's wedding dress.

That is when I spotted him. I couldn't believe it. My mouth was agape like an open bottle of pale ale. My heart slowed to a sputter, and I could barely breathe. It was my attacker—a vile man named Richie. He was Larry Holmes's trainer and semi-famous in the boxing world. He was a vicious and violent creature whom I hated with every follicle on my head and every tissue in my body. Since the attack, I'd plotted my revenge, over and over. My plan was simple. I would wait until his death—which I hoped would come sooner rather than later—and then I would sneak into his funeral and hand out pamphlets to guests, exposing what he had done to me. His loved ones would learn the truth, and his memory would be forever tarnished. His rotting reputation would be an unsightly mess, just like his rotting corpse.

Richie did not see me gawking at him, and I had no stomach for confrontation, so I dashed to the Palace restroom in tears.

There were various women milling about, applying makeup and chatting, but only one noticed me. Mucked up by smeared mascara, red eyes, and tear-stained cheeks, I announced to her. "He's out there. The man who raped me is out there." Then I stated his full name.

This woman froze with an expression that could only be described as mortification combined with fear. Her reaction was clearly more than sympathy for a stranger. "Oh, my God!" she replied. "I'm his secretary!"

Of the hundreds of people at the Palace, what were the odds that I would come into contact with my attacker's employee? Why had this happened? Was the universe angling for revenge?

On the other hand, perhaps the coincidence had nothing to do with me or my attacker. Maybe the cosmos was warning the secretary to be on her guard or to flee from her criminal boss. Maybe it wanted her to alert the authorities or to spread the news to the press. Whatever the case, I could do nothing beyond feeling abused, helpless, and desperate.

I fled the restroom while the secretary yelled, "Wait. You can't leave me like this. What do I do?"

I could not give her advice. I could not even give myself advice. I ran to my car, knowing that I could not compartmentalize the pain, at least for a while. The anguish was intense as I relived the trauma of the sexual assault, which had almost led to my death.

~

On the night I was sexually assaulted and almost killed, I had been living in Las Vegas. It was the early 1980s, and I was in my early twenties. I'd just dined in the coffee shop of a major resort on the Strip when I was approached by a hotel executive who informed me of a "well-paid job opportunity." It involved selling isolation tanks, also known as sensory deprivation boxes. These are contraptions in which people float in salt water with hopes of relieving muscle tension, chronic pain, or arthritis.

The executive told me to follow him to a guest room to view a sample of the device. I saw no red flags and had no off-putting premonitions, because I'd known this executive for many years, beginning when I was a seventeen-year-old visitor at the hotel. He was scrawny, over seventy, and used a cane. He had always been amicable and polite. The room containing the isolation tank belonged to a portly man named Richie, who was a fixture in the boxing world, a high-profile guest at the resort, and a friend of the executive.

Richie explained how the isolation tank worked, even kneeling beside the device to demonstrate its features. While soaking in the details, I heard the door slam behind me and pivoted to see that the executive had departed.

I turned back to see that Richie had sprung to his feet. It was as if the slammed door was a starter pistol, triggering "go" and attack. He leapt at me, grabbing my shoulders. He chucked me onto the bed as if I were as light as a feather and as insignificant as one. I was terror-stricken and in total disbelief. I attempted to get up, but he rammed me back into place.

"What are you doing?" I tried to squirm off the bed, but Richie became angrier and applied more pressure.

"Don't move, bitch."

"What are you doing? Please let go."

Richie began undressing himself with one hand as he kept me pinned. His massive arm was unyielding and kept me immobilized like a roller coaster restraint.

I knew I could not overpower this weathered-looking, street-savvy tough guy, so I tried to trick him. "I need to use the restroom."

He studied my face, searching for traces of deception. Then he growled, "Okay, but don't try anything funny. I'll be holding on to you the whole time."

He allowed me to get off the bed, but his mitt of a hand felt like a clamp around my bicep. We moved slowly across the room.

When we reached the bathroom, Richie released me for a split second, and I saw this as an opportunity for escape. I darted into the bathroom and barricaded myself while he frantically tried to turn the locked knob. Eventually, he moved away from the door—snarling, grunting, and hurling profanities.

There was a telephone in the bathroom. I pushed the zero, which connected me to the hotel's operator. "I'm trapped in the bathroom," I screamed into the phone. "This man is trying to rape me." I said Richie's full name as best as I could remember, but I figured the room number was displayed at the operator's desk.

Richie realized that I was on the phone. He also realized that the line in the bedroom was identical to the one in the bathroom, so he hit the hook or disconnection button, over and over. As a result, the call was broken up. It was hard for the operator to hear my words because of the constant interruption of off, on, off, on… click, click, click.

"Get off the phone right now," Richie screamed at me, "or I will break down the fucking door and kill you! You piece of shit!"

I truly believed this monster was capable of busting into the bathroom because of his massive build and tough-as-nails temperament. But I was not willing to surrender.

"Okay! I'm hanging up," I shouted, but this was actually another ploy. I put down the phone but then picked it up sixty seconds later. My goal was to make Richie think that I was speaking to him while actually communicating my message to the operator. I said things into the receiver like "Why are you trying to rape me?" and "Please just let me out of this room" and "I wish hotel security would come up here."

Richie quickly figured out what I was up to, probably due to the light on the bedroom phone, indicating that it was in use. So he interrupted the call once more by pressing the disconnection button, again and again. Half an hour passed while we were embroiled in this cat-and-mouse contest.

Finally, Richie yelled, "Just get out of my room. I want you the fuck out of my room. Now!"

"I'm not coming out, because you will grab me."

"I won't. I just want you out! I just want you fucking out of here!"

"I don't trust you."

"Just get the fuck out! I will leave the door open and stand on the far side of the room. I just want you the fuck out!"

Like an idiot, I believed him. I slowly opened the bathroom door and noticed that he was standing, as agreed, on the far side of the room. But once I got several feet out of the bathroom and peered around the corner, I could see that the door to the hallway was closed. I decided to try to make a run for it anyway.

I sprinted, and Richie nabbed me. He heaved me onto the bed and pounced on my petite frame with his massive weight, causing me to writhe in agony. Then he placed his hands around my neck and squeezed. His grip got tighter and tighter and tighter, until it seemed clear that he planned to strangle me. His face was a hideous collage of sweat, grit, misshapen blotches, beady eyes, scars, facial hair, aging lines, and seething hatred for a girl who had innocently inquired about a sales job. Why? Did he have a loathing for all females, or was there something particularly repugnant about me? I squirmed and gasped for air as I felt my throat close. I figured there was a good chance this monster would kill me. I could visualize the horrific scene. He would hide my corpse in the isolation tank and then he and his buddies would casually haul the contraption through the casino to a waiting van, which would be driven to an isolated area in the desert where I would be buried.

I tried to speak through my tears with the little oxygen I had. Richie let up on the strangling in order to hear. I choked out the words, "Don't kill me. I'll do what you say."

To my surprise, Richie removed his hands from my neck and replied, "Good."

Like before, he kept me pinned with one arm while using the other to undress. It seemed like this was his rape ritual, his favorite misogynistic routine, his way of feeling superior to females. I wondered how many other girls he had sexually assaulted and whether any of their corpses were decomposing in the Mohave.

Richie not only took off his clothes but let go of me temporarily while demanding that I lift up my skirt. I was sobbing uncontrollably and afraid to disobey. He then tried to put his penis into me, but couldn't. It was limp and floppy like a little baggie of mud. Richie became incensed all over again—now about his own incompetence, about his inability to complete the rape.

"This is your fault, bitch.... All your fucking fault." He shoved me away, grabbed my pocketbook, and dumped out the contents on the bed. He rifled through my wallet until he found my driver's license. "What's your real name anyway? I know it isn't 'Laws,' you fakey, lying bitch." He read the license to see that my real name was indeed "Laws" and threw the empty purse at me. "Get the fuck out of my room." I quickly stuffed everything into my bag and fled.

I hurried to hotel security in tears and explained what had happened.

"We went up there after getting your call," one security

officer said. "We stood in the hallway for a little while, but we didn't hear anything. So we went back downstairs."

"What? You left? Why would you do that?" I was incredulous.

"Because we didn't hear anything!" He shouted out the words in a callous and defensive way.

It seemed incomprehensible and willfully negligent for hotel security to ignore a distress call. Plus, I had phoned multiple times, pleading for help. I thought it was particularly bizarre that they had come all the way up to the room and then decided not to knock. Why? Were they intimidated by Richie, a high-profile guest? Were they lazy? Were they incompetent? The failure to investigate made no sense.

A second security officer laid into me. "What were you doing in the hotel anyway? You're not staying here."

It felt like I was being victimized all over again. These men were siding with my attacker. They were acting like the ordeal was my fault, like I was responsible for my own nightmare, for the worst experience of my life. They were treating me like a villain, a nuisance, an irritating girl who was interrupting their otherwise leisurely evening. I was a troublemaker who was putting the hotel at risk, making them legally liable. The officers clearly wished I would disappear.

The question was repeated. "What were you doing in the hotel?"

I felt abused and defeated. I was in emotional tatters as I cupped my head in my hands and sobbed. But this did not soften the officers.

The heartless question was asked a third time. "Could you explain what you were doing in the hotel?" I knew what he was getting at: He thought I was a prostitute. There was a sexist assumption in those days that any young woman at a Las Vegas resort was a call girl.

I figured I should reveal the truth. "I'm a friend of Tom Jones... and his group. I'm supposed to go backstage after the show." The officers suddenly looked frazzled, formed a huddle, and whispered to each other. Tom was, in fact, onstage at that very moment. He had been performing during my assault and near-asphyxiation. Ironically, he might have been belting out "Delilah," a song with lyrics about a woman's murder.

One officer called backstage, and ten minutes later the warm-up act, comedian Freddie Roman, appeared, saying, "Tom's onstage right now. What's going on?" I was distraught because I did not want Tom to know about the incident. I was embarrassed and disgusted, and I had turned the knife inward, blaming myself for going to Richie's room in the first place. Freddie was a nice fellow but in no way tight-lipped. He would surely tell Tom. The security officers conferenced with the comedian out of earshot, and then Freddie left.[4]

The officers confronted me again. This time, they segued from victim-blaming into telling me why I had better be a good little girl and keep my mouth shut. "Richie has a lot of money. Mr. Roman tells us that your father does, too. But Richie has more."

What was this supposed to mean? Why were they talking about cash rather than the crime? Why weren't they calling the cops? They had not once criticized my attacker. The officers seemed to fear a civil lawsuit, and they were playing a game called "court case." The winner, from their perspective, was the individual with the biggest, baddest, and priciest lawyer—a lawyer who could huff and puff and blow the house down. They had raised Richie's arm in their lawsuit and declared him "champ."

One of the officers leaned in close. "You're banned from this hotel. Unless Tom Jones is in town, we'd better not see you here."

Another one chimed in, "I think you should run on home."

Run on home like a child? Run on home like I am at fault? And they were banning *me*, not Richie, from the resort? Would he be allowed to operate unfettered, to tan at the pool, to gamble at the craps table, and to assault other females? I was in disbelief over the condescension, callousness, and male chauvinism, but by this time I had lost the will to fight. Combating Richie and the security officers had drained me. I felt weak, battered, despondent, and invisible. I knew the verbal victimization would continue unless I did as they suggested—unless I "ran on home."

I did not go to the police or file a lawsuit, because I didn't want anyone to know about the assault—not my friends and certainly not my dad. I designated this as "the secret" and sequestered it in the isolation tank of my mind—the tomb. If my old-fashioned father had learned the truth, he would have hauled me back to Georgia. He would have blamed me—a third victimization—and branded me with an *S* for slut. I would have been tainted and besmirched—a disgrace. I would no longer be respectable, decent, or "his daughter." Getting sexually assaulted is the opposite of being a debutante.

I later learned of Richie's ties to the underworld.[5] He had once worked as an enforcer for the mob,[6] and the FBI believed he was committing crimes,[7] mostly related to arson. He had a reputation for violence and had killed a man in a barroom brawl.[8] He'd also sexually attacked another woman, but she was rescued by boxer Larry Holmes.[9] (In fact, I spoke with Holmes on the phone in 2018 and asked him if Richie had sexually assaulted any other women. His all-too-telling response was, "I plead the fifth!")

If I had pursued Richie, criminally or civilly, would I have been in danger? Had the security officers known about his tawdry connections and homicidal tendencies[10] on the day of the assault? Was this why they declined to knock? Did they decide that it was better to railroad me than become the target of this monster's revenge?

Days, weeks, and months passed. But the sexual assault kept popping out of its compartment. It was the unspoken agony of my life, a gnawing sadness, a silent and persistent ache. Las Vegas had become an unhappy spot. It was a place that gave me anxiety and queasiness. I had come to see the entire city as blemished, as an oasis of burnt-out lights. So I decided to move to Los Angeles—to escape from the pain of remembering.

Richie died in 2016. Although I did not pass out pamphlets at his funeral, there was a feeling of relief. The clouds seemed to be a little less dark. The tumbleweed in my gut became slightly less prickly, and my heart frowned a little less. Perhaps full closure can come now that the secret is out of its tomb—now that it belongs to the world.

Chapter Five

WESTWOOD BOUND

I jammed the memory of the sexual assault back into its tomb and got on the phone with my father to discuss the real estate purchase in Westwood (an area situated between Beverly Hills and Santa Monica). Dad was being uncommonly pleasant. His hostility toward me and his upset over the gun, the Volkswagen, and my California residency seemed to have faded. Perhaps he had deposited them into his very own tomb. Although I knew they would eventually rear their heads and tower over me again—as had happened so many times in the past—I was happy to get a reprieve, to enjoy a break from stress and unkind words.

"I found a couple of places around a hundred thousand dollars, but they aren't in Westwood," I said, hoping Dad would spring for something cheap. One was an impeccably decorated townhouse on Sherman Way in Van Nuys owned by Dwayne

Hickman, who had starred in the TV show *The Many Loves of Dobie Gillis*. Hickman and his wife had advertised the property in a classifieds-only newspaper called *The Recycler*. The other was a cute condo on Barham Boulevard near Burbank, which I'd found in the *Los Angeles Times*.

"If you get something inexpensive," I reasoned, "maybe I can buy it from you in a few years?"

"Nope," Dad said. "It has to be Westwood. Narrow it down to three places, and I will make the final decision."

His final decision was a two-bedroom in a remodeled building on Kelton Avenue. The units were condo conversions. In other words, they had previously been apartments. They were situated only a few blocks from the University of California, Los Angeles (UCLA), which meant they conformed nicely to the "location, location, location" rule. Like most structures in the area, the building had a dormitory look with plain beige stucco and brick accents. A green awning stretched over the security entrance, and miniature trees sprouted from planters near the curb. Today these condos sell for $750,000. Dad paid around $250,000. I figured it would take a whole lot of sleazy club performances to come up with that kind of cash, and since I was no longer in that biz—or any other biz—I knew I could never own the place myself.

Moving took place in two parts. A humble U-Haul trailer accommodated the few items that I had in my one-room flat in Van Nuys, while the Jolly Green Giant transferred possessions from my Las Vegas storage unit. I had given the truck this name because it was puke green and so excessively large that it could barely squeeze between the parked cars on my street. I watched professional movers carry my "gaudy, gaudy, gaudy" dresses into my new "location, location, location" condo.

I was not alone at my new place. I had Paws, an Old English sheepdog mix, whom I'd adopted from a nonprofit called the

Doris Day Foundation. Paws had been tied to a tree and left for three days without food or water by previous "owners." Paws was everything a perfect being should be.

But there was also an imperfect being in my life. Dad forced me to get a roommate to offset mortgage costs, and I ended up with a grouchy UCLA math student who had as much personality as a zero. Just as the digit is used as a placeholder, my roommate was a placeholder in the equation called life. He had only two activities: studying or spying on me and Paws. It creeped me out when Zero peered at me from the kitchen while making a sandwich or from the dining room while rearranging his book bag. But I figured it was a vast improvement over strip club gawkers. Maybe Zero had never dated and was curious about this unfamiliar thing called "girl." Either that or he had a crush on my dog.

With the condo came the use of a brand-new car: a silver Ford Tempo. Dad had brought automobiles in and out of my life as if they were entries in a stock portfolio. Luckily, he had not stuck me with another stick shift. I had never gotten the hang of the five-speed Volkswagen, especially on steep inclines where I feared rolling backward into a car. Plus, it gave me a perpetual calf ache. It took more leg strength than the treadmill at the gym. The Tempo had the benefit of being automatic, but it had one minor drawback. It almost led to my death.

It was two a.m. on the third day after the dealership had handed me the keys to the new Tempo. I was barreling down the relatively empty freeway when I heard a jarring sound. There was a clang and then a jangle, and then a thunderous rattle. At first I thought I was losing my mind. But, in reality, I was losing my body—the body of my new car. The Tempo was falling apart before my eyes. It was leaving a trail of car parts up and down the 101 freeway.

I sputtered to the side of the road while shedding pieces

of the engine, and the vehicle stalled. I was unsure what to do. This was prior to cell phones and roadside emergency call boxes. For a few seconds, I sat in the blackness, alone, worried, wondering, and scared.

I became even more scared when a car stopped in front of me. The driver shut off his headlights. Was this a serial killer or a Good Samaritan? Would the next few moments lead to my death or to a repair shop? Would Paws be an orphan? Or would he and I grow old and redeem our senior citizen discounts?

A behemoth man climbed out of the vehicle and headed toward me. He did not look friendly, but he also didn't look unfriendly. He was indistinct, just a mammoth frame marching in the filtered moonlight. I was terrified and in a quandary. I didn't know whether to lock the doors and duck or greet this stranger with gratitude.

Possible scenarios whizzed through my head. If he was a killer, securing the doors would be fruitless. He would break the glass. Climbing into his car would make me completely vulnerable, so this could not happen under any circumstances. However, if he managed to drag me into his vehicle, I would have to force a crash rather than allow him to take me to an unpopulated section of town. The final option would be to make a run for it on the freeway. I pictured myself in high heels trying to outsprint a long-legged man with a gun. It did not seem like "smart talent" or craftiness could get me out of this predicament. There was no clear option.

The faceless stranger stepped closer and closer. But suddenly, there was salvation. I was illuminated by a white light from behind. I looked in my rearview mirror and saw the headlights of a police car that had parked behind me. I was relieved, especially when the approaching man, upon seeing the cop, darted back to his vehicle and sped away as if he were late for a date with a corpse. I figured someone with good intentions would not have panicked this way; thus the policeman may have saved my life.

After a tow truck dropped off my Tempo at the dealership for repair, I went home to be with my beloved Paws and to play another zero-sum game with my roommate.

⁂

"Hello, I'm phoning from Dr. Freud's office." This was my silly attempt to dupe an employee named Doris who worked in the Georgia Baptist Hospital records department, located in Atlanta.

"Sigmund Freud?"

"Of course not. He's dead," I replied. "Rudolph Freud—Sigmund's great-great-grandson on his father's cousin's side. Rudolph is a very important psychiatrist."

It sounded preposterous—even to me. But I'd been lazy. I'd failed to contrive a script in advance. I'd just picked up the phone the way a drunken sailor might pick up a hooker. I was flying by the seat of my pants. It was a ludicrous strategy but one that I hoped would prove fruitful in the end.

"How... uh... how can I help you?" Doris was clearly unsure whether I was being candid or whether I was a candidate for the loony bin.

"Well, we have a patient in our care," I continued with my goofy story. "She was born on May 11, 1960, at your hospital. Unfortunately, she has amnesia and cannot remember her name. So we need you to give us the names of all the baby girls born on that date."

"The baby girls?"

"Yes. She's definitely a girl." I laughed.

"Just a moment." She put me on hold. I figured a senior employee would get on the line and excoriate me as a trickster and a fraud. But instead, Doris returned and read out four names from the "Book of Deliveries," which I scribbled onto a sheet of paper. They were Tammy Carter, Mary Adams, Rachelle Wilpan, and Tracey Southern. I couldn't believe it! I had the names of the baby girls born on *my* birthdate at *my* hospital. One of these names was most likely mine! I scrutinized each of them closely, digging into the bowels of my being, and decided that "Rachelle Wilpan" was my real name. *Yes, that must be it*, I said to myself.

"Who was the doctor for Rachelle Wilpan?" I asked Doris.

"Umm… That would be Dr. Amatriain."

I thanked her and hung up. I was elated. It was one giant leap for me and one small step for adoptees around the world.

༄

Time passed while I strategized about what the next step should be in the birth family search. I also settled into a routine, taking classes at California State University, Northridge (CSUN) in an effort to earn a bachelor's degree. My father's financial contribution of $200 per month did not cover expenses, so I had to land gigs on the side: detective work, small acting roles, and respectable dance and hostess jobs (mostly at convention halls). Plus, I sold beaded clothing, here and there and worked assiduously on *Meet the Stars*, which I hoped would generate income down the road.

One afternoon, my friend Gary and I were in the hallway at CSUN, chatting with a pretty female classmate. I was in a giddy and teasing mood. I'd never consumed a glass of alcohol, but when I was in good spirits, I sometimes seemed intoxicated. This was one of those times.

"This is my philosophy object." I giggled, pointing at Gary. "I just *use* him for philosophy."

The classmate seemed perplexed. I explained our strange

but true tale. Gary and I had met in an ethics course. When the teacher asked whether it was morally right to use someone merely as a sex object, we decided it was fine as long as it was by mutual agreement. Then we extended it to our situation. We decided to *use* each other for philosophy, fulfilling each other's cerebral needs—discussing epistemology, metaphysics, and ethics well into the middle of the night.

"I was into utilitarianism," I said to the classmate. "He claimed to be a contractarian like the teacher. I think he was just trying to get a good grade." Gary and I cracked up, leaving the classmate even more puzzled as she wandered away.

"Wait!" I hollered. "Don't you want to go on a date with Gary? He's available!" My voice echoed through Sierra Hall, but it was too late. She had vanished. Gary and I howled with laughter.

Gary and I were close friends. We were never romantically involved, but I was very much involved in his romantic life, playing matchmaker. If there was a woman I knew who didn't get set up with Gary, she was as creepy as the stranger on the freeway or as ugly as the Jolly Green Giant. Gary was tall, dark, handsome, and ten years older than me—and most important, willing to be "used" for his Socratic method, a rare commodity in a man. He had been a singer and musician, but at the time he was working as an engineer at Rocketdyne in Canoga Park. The company produced engines for NASA.

Although Gary was a catch in many ways, he was subconsciously unwilling to be caught. He had a knack for finding something—anything—wrong with a woman. Then he would break up with her, just like that. I clearly remember the complaint, "I don't like her laugh," and thought to myself, *Then why do you keep dragging her to the Comedy Store and Laugh Factory?* Gary was a Seinfeld episode. He always had an excuse for why he couldn't commit, but I did not realize this about him until I had been his eHarmony link for years.

Gary had a complaint about me as well: "You are too much from your head and not enough from your heart." He suggested I attend a five-day self-realization seminar called Insight that had greatly enhanced his life.

Insight was a convergence of love, sweat, and tears. It was making me sick. There were more than a hundred people crowded next to me in a multipurpose room on Wilshire Boulevard in Santa Monica. Probably 90 percent of them would be like Gary and derive benefit from the experience, but I was rarely in the majority when it came to anything.

I was a cynic. I had never fashioned myself as a let's-all-love-each-other type. I saw myself as an independent thinker who investigated a situation and reported the truth, regardless of whether the answer rocked the communal rowboat or made others want to oar me in the face.

I was not alone. There was a handsome cynic across the room named Jed. I could tell that he felt as I did due to his quips, antics, and overall mischief. He was polite and well-behaved. On the other hand, he never missed the opportunity to make sport of a group exercise or angle for a laugh. He was classy and rugged with a beard, green eyes, and curly brown hair. He was five years older than me, originated from Chicago, and took lithium for manic depression. He was a comedic genius, which is probably why I started falling for him. I loved funny men.

One of his jokes prompted laughter from only one person: me. My lone chuckle within a sea of solemn faces prompted him to turn and check me out. When the Insight moderator suggested a group exercise in which each person was asked to single out a stranger, I chose him and he chose me.

This was 1984. I was twenty-four and had not been sexual with anyone except Tom, but I very much wanted to be married.

I'd enjoyed serial platonic dates with Jerry (an advertising executive and boat fanatic), Conway (a salesman with a bad attitude about losing games), and Tony (a Native American musician from the band *Redbone*), as well as singers Tony Bennett and Mac Davis, among others.

Jed was someone with whom I could fall in love, and I did. He was a screenwriter, writing teacher, and wannabe director with an out-of-the-box way of viewing the world. He named his black cat Whitie; sent me a sympathy card for my birthday; and hung pictures of his favorite icon, Betty Boop, in his avant-garde West Hollywood apartment. His ancestors had been Russian. He had affection for Ernest Hemingway and loved moussaka—some kind of meat casserole. Although I was a vegetarian and an animal rights advocate, I didn't expect Jed or any other prospective boyfriend to give up meat. I knew if I forced the issue, I'd die a spinster with too many romance novels and a blow-up Ken doll.

It was not only cynicism that prompted my rejection of the hug-your-nearest-stranger agenda that Insight offered. I was a nonconformist and had always been ill at ease following the crowd. There was a cult feel to group hand-holding sessions. I felt they led people astray, away from personal value systems and toward harmful absolutes. When attending crowded functions, my greatest pleasure had always been to stand in the corner and observe like an outsider. I could get a better understanding of the overall picture from afar. Plus, the empty corner lacked claustrophobic vibes. It was the proper place for a rebel.

A significant portion of the Insight agenda was geared toward helping seminar participants become fearless, and I didn't feel this was my weakness. I was always first to raise my hand when volunteers were needed onstage, and I was generally up-front about my life and feelings. My heart was not as melodramatic or as bulky as *War and Peace*, but it was mostly an open book. As Gary had rightfully pointed out, my emphasis had been on the brain, which I was hoping to convert into an encyclopedia in order to combat feelings of intellectual inadequacy. I'd always felt stupid.

Jed and I had been dating for ten months. We were in my car, and he'd been pumping me for clues, trying to find out where I was taking him. "Romeo and Juliet?" "The Bel-Air Hotel?" "The Polo Lounge?" He threw out the names of high-end eateries.

"We're there." I flashed a coy smile and pulled the Tempo into a crumbling parking lot adjacent to an unkempt apartment building. It was Jed's birthday, and I had arranged an unusual dinner surprise, but "unusual" was the norm when a guy was dating me. Jed eyed the run-down structure, thinking we'd be spending his special day surrounded by peeling paint and granny underwear on a clothesline.

"Are we going to Skid Row Seafood or the Ghetto Grill?" He laughed in his usual laid-back way. "I hear Public Squalor Subs has a great deal on baloney."

"Come on." I exited the car. "I want to show you grandma's bra. It's an antique."

Jed had a dancer's walk. It always made me grin. His hip swings and cadenced steps were at odds with his mountain man looks and masculine personality. Jed accompanied me past the apartment structure and clothesline and into Westwood Recreation Center, located off Sepulveda Boulevard in West Los Angeles.

This was essentially a gigantic park with trees, jungle gyms, tennis courts, grassy spaces, winding walkways, park benches, and a soccer field. A sign read, "Park Closed 10:30 p.m. to 5 a.m. No loitering." It was seven p.m. and getting dark. Since "loitering" was officially defined as "remaining in an area for no obvious reason," I figured we wouldn't be in violation. I had a distinct reason for being there, although a peculiar one.

As we passed a bed of philodendron plants, the birthday surprise started to unfold. On a carpet of lush green grass in the center of the soccer field, I had situated a small table and two chairs. There were candles, fine silverware, real china, linen napkins, and a white tablecloth. It looked as if a crane had lifted the romantic setup straight out of a Beverly Hills bistro and placed it in this dissonant setting. Two individuals, wearing perfectly ironed black-and-white waiter attire, posed next to the table. The woman had two menus, and the man held a small tray.

"I don't believe it!" Jed exclaimed. "This is great!"

The waiters were not strangers. They were my friends, Cheryl and Tim, who had recently moved to Los Angeles from the Midwest. They attended Fuller Theological Seminary in Pasadena. Although Christianity was their usual focus, that evening they planned to focus on serving dinner to me and my boyfriend.

"This is hysterical." Jed chuckled when he read the menu. There was only one entrée: Jack in the Box bacon cheeseburger. The only drink was Coke, and the only side dish was French fries. I had chosen these items for one reason: It was Jed's all-time favorite meal. Although I had a personal objection to providing meat for Jed, I had decided to overlook it on this occasion.

"At your service, sir. Are you ready for dinner?" Tim asked, feigning an uppity French accent.

"This wouldn't have worked if you'd had real food." Jed laughed. "The Jack in the Box is perfect."

Cheryl and Tim placed his sandwich, still wrapped in paper from the fast-food joint, on his porcelain dinner plate and poured Coke into his crystal goblet. Then they brought me my meal: a fast-food salad in a cardboard box and Jack's orange juice. It was a delightful and romantic dinner until the mishap occurred. It was eight p.m., and we had just finished eating.

There was a loud clicking. All four of us froze, scanning the pitch-black landscape in bewilderment. Then there was another loud clicking, and then a third. We were nervous and scared. We scoured the darkness for gun-wielding gang members and masked terrorists... until *bang*—the soccer field sprinklers erupted into cascades of water. All four of us and the dinner setup got soaked. Laughing, we quickly transferred the props to a dry spot.

"I hope you enjoyed the water park," I joked as Jed and I climbed into my car. "I thought the log ride was especially fun."

"Yeah," he replied. "I only wish we'd had time to ride the Granny Bra Roller Coaster."

"There's always next year."

Not long after the birthday dinner, I would get soaked again. This time it wouldn't be an amusing mishap but a full-fledged catastrophe. And Jed would be the cause.

※

It was "catastrophe day," and Laura and I looked ridiculous. We wore disguises: sunglasses, hats, and nondescript clothes. We were geared up to tail Jed, to find out whether he was cheating on me. We had even removed the license plates from the Tempo. I'd suspected infidelity for some time because my supposedly "exclusive" boyfriend had been mysteriously unavailable on too many weekends, especially for a man with few work obligations and even fewer hobbies. On this particular night, he had provided an inadequate excuse for cancelling our date, saying merely that he needed to meet a guy friend at a playhouse. They were purportedly going to see a production of *Tamara* at the American Legion Hall on Highland Avenue in Hollywood. Laura and I wanted to verify that this lame excuse was indeed true, although this would not alter the fact that it was lame.

We waited in the shadows of a mostly empty parking lot at the Pasadena Art Center where Jed taught a weekly screenwriting class. He had told me that he was attending the play after work.

"Oh, my God, there he is," Laura said. "Quick, duck!"

Because I was pinned in by the steering wheel, I could not crouch. Instead, I whipped my head to the left so only the back of my hair was visible. It was dark, so I hoped the interior of the Tempo would look like a palette of fuzziness. We waited thirty seconds in silence.

"Be ready to start the engine," Laura whispered. We waited another thirty seconds. "Is he in his car yet?"

I did a quarter turn and saw his black Alfa Romeo Spider exiting the area. "Oh no, he's leaving!" I screamed, and started the engine. We hightailed it out of the parking lot.

Although I'd staked out homes and businesses as a private detective, I had no experience following a car. I thought it would be easy. I was wrong. I had to zip through red lights and stop signs just to stay with Jed. To keep a reasonable distance from his vehicle, I had to slow to a crawl on busy streets, almost causing an accident. And to avoid arousing his suspicion, I had to periodically shut off my headlights, making the road ahead of me imperceptible. It was challenging and frankly quite dangerous, but luckily I did not lose sight of the Alfa Romeo, which entered the Hollywood Hills and turned onto Camrose Avenue and then High Tower Drive. Jed parked in front of a Spanish-style duplex. The Spider was about to be caught in a web of lies.

"Where are we?" I asked, realizing this was no playhouse.

On second thought, maybe it was. It was a place to play when "girlfriend" wasn't around.

Laura and I rolled slowly past the front of the building. It was charming with a huge, thimble-shaped window that opened into a grand living room. I could see inside the residence, and Jed was kissing another woman. I was devastated and heartbroken. The sting went deep.

I drove past the "playhouse" and fifty yards up the road. There was a dead end. Perhaps it was a sign from the universe that our relationship had reached its own dead end.

"Let's park and see what they're doing," Laura suggested.

After wading through potted plants, we tiptoed over to the picture window so I could get a good look at my rival. She was thin, with short auburn hair and freckles. She looked like Peppermint Patty (or PP) from Charlie Brown's *Peanuts*. She was dressed casually and seemed to have a lot more confidence in herself than I'd ever had. PP had a sassy, I'm-too-sexy-for-my-jeans way about her.

"Oh no!" Laura pointed. "The neighbor!"

I looked up and was spooked by a zombie. Actually, it was an old lady across the street. She had opened her second-floor window and was staring at us with a "you-naughty-girls" expression on her face. We must have looked like crazies. Part of me wanted to scamper to the Tempo and barrel away, but another part of me wanted to see what would transpire between Jed and his PP. I figured the old lady might call the police, but I knew it was a chance I'd have to take.

In an attempt to put this lady at ease, I flashed a toothy smile and waved as if all was fine. But she was not dissuaded. She leaned farther out of the window, threatening me with her snarling eyes.

"We'd better go," Laura said. "She might have the phone number for that girl."

I knew Laura was right, but I was just too curious. Laura waited in the Tempo while I lingered at the window. Ten minutes later, there were still no cop cars, but there was a second passionate embrace between Jed and his PP. It depressed me so completely that I gave a tearful nod to the old meddler in the window and left.

I never told Jed about the nutty caper or the busybody neighbor, but I did ask if he was seeing another woman. He confessed. He said that she knew about me as well, and he refused to end it with either of us. In a desperate and pathetic attempt to win his heart, I continued seeing him for another month. There was a lot of pain and sadness during that time, and even a few catty remarks.

"This is where all the prostitutes live," I said to Jed one day as we drove past his PP's street. He didn't realize I knew her address. I could barely keep a straight face because the comment was so ludicrous.

"No, it's not," he replied.

"Well, that's what I heard. I think they did a study."

Later, I related the story to Laura, and we laughed hysterically.

After the relationship ended, I made a hand-beaded blouse for Jed's mother in Chicago and mailed it to her with a nice note. As for the "playhouse," its tenants were evicted and the building was sold.

Jed's PP moved out of state.

Chapter Six

THE SEARCH FOR MY BIOLOGICAL FAMILY

The desire to find my biological family stemmed, in part, from a need to understand my true self, to comprehend why I had been a B-flat while my peers in Atlanta had been C-sharps. But it also sprang from my analytical nature. I enjoyed investigating, delving, burrowing all the way down to the truth—despite the fact that my adoptive family had not raised me in this way. In addition, I had a philosophical mind and a specific curiosity about the influence of biology upon a person's interests, beliefs, behavior, ideals, and moral values. Could genetics predispose an individual toward a certain clothing style, a certain political party, or a certain ethical code? Twin studies indicate the answer is yes, and many experts, such as renowned cognitive scientist Steven Pinker, claim that traits are almost completely heritable.[11]

This was my hunch as well, but I wanted to confirm or disprove this theory with my own case study as an adoptee. I was the experiment, the specimen, the human research project. I was eager to locate my blood relatives and put data about them into a test tube, heat the mixture on a Bunsen burner, blend it in a petri dish, and examine it under a microscope. In other words, I hoped to be as scientific as possible, concluding in an honest fashion whether I was similar to my kin or as different as grease in a glass of water.

My experiment would be subjective rather than controlled or repeatable. But this was fine because evidence often requires tasting, touching, and seeing for oneself. It sometimes relies on personal interpretation and a pinch of intuition. I knew if I was lucky, the reunion with my birth parents would culminate in a body of evidence on hereditary traits, a feeling of connectedness, and an epiphany—all at the same time.

It was 1985, and I was tired of toying with the "parent search" in my mind. I had carted around the mystery for too long. It was time to get sleuthful and dive into action. So I flew to Atlanta with the goal of marching into "The Agency," also known as the Child Services Association. I planned to confront staff and demand that they hand over my complete file—not a bunch of black blobs. However, in the end, I didn't demand.

I *did* end up conspiring in a crime.

◆

Felony day began in a legitimate way. I showed up at "The Agency" and met with an employee—a congenial older lady who worked in a typical office filled with an atypical number of baby photos. There were at least three hundred snapshots affixed to walls and crammed onto bookshelves as well as other surfaces. It put me on edge. There were bug eyes and tiny faces shooting out from every direction like a creepy house of mirrors. I wondered if my mug shot—my chubby, little cheeks from 1960—were among the lot.

"You certainly have a lot of pictures."

"Aren't they lovely?" Baby Lady smiled. "Can I help you?"

"I was adopted. I'm looking for my birth parents."

"I can only provide information about their ages, heights… you know, that sort of thing. I can't give you any names. Sorry."

Adoption records in Georgia were closed. Unless a birth parent submitted written consent or there was a court order, it was illegal to provide an adoptee with identifying information. It was contrary to 19-8-23 of the Georgia Code and punishable by civil and criminal penalties. When an adoptee made a formal request to the court, judges tended to be unreceptive unless there was "good cause," such as pressing health concerns. In 2003, only four states—Alabama, Delaware, Oregon, and Tennessee—had open or partially open records. In 2018, there were twenty-five. Georgia's records are closed to this day.

I told Baby Lady that I had already received documents from her agency with basic information. I knew, for example, that my mother was twenty and my father was twenty-four when I was born. I knew their heights and some of the ailments that ran in the family.

She pulled my file from a cabinet and studied it. "They married when your mother got pregnant but did not plan to stay together. Your father was in seminary school, and your mother was in college. Your father cried when he signed the papers. Your mother was Italian. There were religious differences between your parents. Your mom was a liberal. Your father was studying to be a Baptist minister."

Hmm, a preacher man who got my mother pregnant, I thought to myself. Even as a zygote, I was on track to be a TV movie.

I extracted a miniature notebook from my purse. "I have a name here... Rachelle Wilpan. Could that be my real name?"

Baby Lady looked alarmed. She glanced around the room, as if seeking advice from her three hundred tiny tots. It was clear: I was *not* Rachelle Wilpan.

"I'm going to leave the file open on my desk with the names on top," Baby Lady said. "I will be gone for exactly ten minutes. You will be in this office alone. Do you understand?"

This was my signal to jot down the *correct* information from the file. Baby Lady was no doubt worried that I would contact the wrong couple, a formula for disaster and disappointment. She'd apparently decided that breaking the law was better than traumatizing the Wilpan family, throwing my life into turmoil, and embroiling "The Agency" in a mess.

I did as Baby Lady expected. I wrote down my parents' names. I had not been born "Charlotte Anne." I was "Sherry Lee."

∽

I was climbing down the family tree toward my roots, but Laura disapproved. "What if your parents are murderers, drug addicts, or child molesters?" she warned me over the phone. "What will you do then?"

"They're not," I replied.

"You were wrong about being Rachelle Wilpan."

"Hey, my name wasn't on the hospital list. And you have to admit... Wilpan is similar to my real last name." (I later learned that my name was not on the list because my mother had given birth through the hospital's free clinic.)

"The point is... you were wrong, and you could be wrong again. Plus, your parents will probably reject you... for a second time. Is that what you want?" She suggested that I end the search, especially now that my adoptive dad was no longer treating me like an itchy rash or a chipped gnome.

"I'll call you after I talk to my birth dad."

"What if you have the wrong guy?"

"Then I'll just have to keep looking." I hung up.

Zero was in class, so it was a good time to call my birth father, who I believed to be a university professor. I settled on the couch at the Westwood condo with Paws in my lap. I placed a glass of water, a pad, and a pen at arm's length. I wished I could assemble talking points, but had no idea whether our conversation would go straight, veer left, or crash into a steel beam. Would my father be rejecting or receptive? Was he a lout or a saint? Would he complain about me to "The Agency," or praise them for ignoring the law? I took a deep breath, picked up the phone, and dialed the number. He answered.

"Hello. My name is Missy Laws. I was born on May 11, 1960. I was put up for adoption. I think you're my father."

"I'm *not* your father. Sorry." He hung up. It was like a branch had snapped under me. I was baffled. His name had been in Baby Lady's file. It had to be correct.

Regardless of whether the professor was my birth father, he had been easy to locate. I had initially been concerned about the commonness of his name. There are 1.7 million listings today on Google for those with his exact spelling. At the time, an online search was not feasible. The Internet did not exist for ordinary Americans until the 1990s. But Baby Lady had presented a key clue when she mentioned his ministerial studies. I knew Emory University had a first-rate school of theology. A simple call to their alumni association had given me what I needed.

I called the professor back five minutes later. "I think you *are* my father."

There was a beat of silence and then he replied, "You're right. I am. Let me pick myself up off the floor."

It was as if he'd anticipated my return call and waited patiently by the phone. He told me that he had been "a partial person, walking with a limp." For twenty-five years he'd coped with the nagging ache of wondering where his daughter might be. When he walked down the street and saw a child my age, he thought it could be his. He said, "It tore me apart."

Baby Lady had been right. He was an emotional parent. When my birth mom got pregnant, he said he'd abandoned his ministerial studies and wandered into the ivory tower of academia. He had a doctorate in history, had authored books, and worked as a tenured professor at a university.

"I knew you would contact me someday," he said.

It was my turn to speak. I explained how my identity was a pile of incoherent puzzle pieces. Key sections were missing. I was not simply curious about my ancestry. It seemed crucial to understanding who I was. I had been a black sheep in Atlanta and thought that locating my original flock could bring self-awareness, philosophical understanding, and the familial connection that I'd always lacked.

"I'd like to meet you," I said.

He stuttered. "I-I would need some time to tell my family. My wife knows you were put up for adoption, but my two kids don't know anything."

I was unsure whether "some time" meant two days, two months, or two years. So I let him off the hook. "You don't have to tell them before our visit."

"Okay," he replied. "I guess you could come in two weeks."

❦

You can never have too many parents. This was my personal philosophy, but it did not appeal to Bill Berle.

Bill Berle is comedian Milton Berle's adopted son. We became friends in a western civilization class at CSUN. I sat at the desk in front of Bill with my body turned so that my ear was in proximity to his wisecracks. Our whispers and snickers provided a backdrop for the teacher's biweekly lectures and blackboard demonstrations. It is not that the class was boring. For history, it was as good as it gets. The professor, Julian Nava, was masterful in bringing the Minoans, Mycenaeans, and ancient Romans to life. Historical time lines and battles were punctuated with discussions about bizarre customs, including unconventional sex practices.

"Were you in a Nazi concentration camp?" I tentatively asked Dr. Nava after class one day. For two months, I had been horrified by the tattooed numbers on his forearm, assuming he was an Auschwitz survivor. During the Holocaust, Nazis had labeled Jews and other "undesirables" according to their race and fitness for labor. Certain digits had a particular significance. The complicated system was devised by IBM.

"No. I was a pilot in the navy. The numbers were for identification purposes, in case a plane crashed. A pilot's hands and forearm might be found attached to the steering wheel while the rest of the body's gone."

I recoiled at the thought.

Dr. Nava was more than a professor. In 1980, he had been appointed by President Jimmy Carter to be the U.S. ambassador to Mexico. He had been born to Mexican immigrants and had served as the first Hispanic on the Los Angeles Unified School District Board of Education. In 1993, he was a pallbearer at Cesar Chavez's funeral.

Bill had no desire to track down his natural parents, and

I figured if intuition told him that it was a bad idea, maybe it was. An adopted child might inherently sense unhappiness and disease festering on her family tree. Branches could be rotting from the weight of alcoholics, convicted felons, or suicidal kin. The family tree could have withered entirely. It could have been dead for years. It is possible that an adopted kid intuits such things.

On the other hand, I felt that even bad news about one's relatives might be enlightening. It might help an adopted child better understand herself and improve her lot in life. Knowledge can bolster personal happiness, and some researchers have come to a similar conclusion. They say that adopted kids often search for their natural parents due to an emotional split from the community in which they are raised. The reunion with the genetic mom or dad can aid in solidifying personal identity.

"I never felt the need to find my natural parents and don't have any baggage from being adopted," Bill told me. "As the child of Milton Berle, I got to live like a little prince. Out of respect for my adoptive parents, my mom in particular, I haven't felt the need to search."

I heard Bill's words but didn't altogether believe him. There was a glint of sorrow in his eyes and a sense that he struggled to live up to the expectations of his dad. On some level, he may have enjoyed luxuries as a little prince of Beverly Hills, but on another level, he seemed isolated and jaded about the world. Bill's world was bizarre compared with that of the average American. Bill had lived on the fast track of glitz and sexual promiscuity with a father who surely loved him but who was self-absorbed, dictatorial, and disliked by many.

I was about to be brought into the unpleasant world of Milton Berle.

The 18,945-square-foot Friars Club looked like a windowless, grand yacht. It was anchored on Santa Monica Boulevard in Beverly Hills. Milton Berle and other old-time celebrities had started the private show business club in 1947. They frequented the venue for lunch and events. The ceiling was shaped like a rolling wave, and the dining room was a spacious cabin at the stern of the mighty structure.

Bill and I were seated at Milton's private table in the center of the room, and that is where I met the famous comic, who wore a blazer and gray slacks and treated me as if I were a deck chair rather than a person. By the end of the meal, it felt like I had been thrown overboard or walked the plank.

"I fucked Nancy Reagan, Lucille Ball, Rita Hayworth, and Marilyn Monroe," Milton bragged as if trying to impress me or somehow be funny.

"Nice… to meet you," I stammered, truly disgusted by the vile and misogynistic language. The man totally lacked class, and although I had rejected much of my Atlanta upbringing, I was unimpressed with people who cursed a lot or made an effort to be offensive. The comedian brought out the "debutante" in me.

"I bet you've heard about my dick." Milton slid into a monologue about his gigantic penis and then segued into kinky details about recent sexual exploits with women whom he clearly did not respect. I felt sorry for Milton's wife and glanced at Bill. He looked embarrassed.

"She gave me head and I ate her snatch.… Me and that broad. We shtupped for three hours…" Milton suddenly noticed a patron on the other side of the room. "Oh, I gotta give that cocksucker a cigar." He jumped from the table for one of his many flits to converse with diners on the other side of the room.

The menu was predetermined. A waiter appeared with a tray of dishes, which prompted Milton to dock himself at our table for a bite.

"I'm a vegetarian. No meat, please," I told the waiter as he spooned portions of food onto our plates.

"No. Give her some of that," Milton said, pointing to a beef dish.

The waiter seemed torn but ultimately decided to obey Milton.

"No, no," I pleaded. "No meat, please."

"Give it to her." Milton motioned again at the beef dish. "And give her some of that chicken, too."

The waiter flashed an apologetic look but did as Milton commanded. My pleas had been firm, but the comedian did not care. He seemed to be on an ego trip or think he was at war with me. I had lost the battle of the Friars Club lunch, and my plate was contaminated. My innocent peas and crisp salad had lost the battle as well. Meat sauce oozed onto them, encroaching upon their purity and deliciousness. Tiny chunks from terrorized chickens tainted my once-pristine rice. Bill looked ashamed but stayed silent. It was as if he knew from experience that he could not confront his dad. He had no doubt lost countless skirmishes himself. His spirit had been wounded.

I ate nothing for lunch, but Milton — still obsessing over sex stories — failed to notice. When the comedian bolted from the table to continue his romp around the room, Bill told me that his dad had sent a prostitute to his hotel room when he was sixteen to provide him with his first sexual encounter and that his dad had once suggested the two of them be "serviced" by the same woman.

"I hate your dad," I told Bill at the end of lunch.

"I know," Bill replied, as if this sentiment had been expressed as often as Milton's vulgarities.

Milton later told Bill that his only mistake in life was adopting him in 1961. Devastated, Bill placed a gun to his head, but in the end did not pull the trigger. Today, Milton and Bill's adoptive mother are dead. Bill still has no desire to search for his birth family.

∽

After my unpleasant lunch with Milton Berle, I finished up the last week of classes at CSUN, earning a bachelor's degree. However, a funny thing happened on the way to my college graduation.

Despite the downers related to my Tempo—such as losing the engine on the freeway and discovering Jed's cheating ways—graduation day was an *up-tempo* experience.

I was driving, and my adoptive dad was in the passenger seat. We were headed to CSUN, where I would don my cap and gown and parade on the Oviatt Library lawn with other B.A. graduates in the commencement ceremony for 1985. I told Dad that I'd filled out an application for a two-year master's program in Professional Writing at the University of Southern California (USC) and that I'd been accepted.

"Would you be willing to let me stay in the condo a little longer? And would you keep covering some of my monthly expenses... until I get a master's degree?" I asked.

"Yeah. I could do that," he replied.

I was relieved and put on my turn signal.

"Don't get on the freeway!" Dad hollered. "There's too much traffic. Turn around! Turn around! Turn around!"

His hysteria alarmed me, and I made a U-turn in exactly the wrong place. Then I heard the sound of a siren. A police car set out in pursuit, flashing its annoying little light. I pulled over to the side of the road and lowered my window, fully aware that I had not once talked my way out of a ticket. I had not quite grasped how cops tick. They did not seem to be in sync with me. They were clocks of a distant time zone, watches on a different wrist. I'd tried rattling off excuses, pleading for mercy, even feigning anger and indignation, but no cop had ever given me a pass.

"Give her a ticket," Dad shouted when the police officer reached the window. "Give it to her! Give it to her! Now!"

"Okay," the officer said. "I'm just going to give you a warning. Be careful next time, ma'am."

And that was it. The officer got in his car, turned off his annoying little light, and left. I figured Dad was a genius. He clearly had some "smart talent" of his own.

❧

I went from saying "farewell" to one dad to saying "hello" to another.

Following the graduation ceremony, my adoptive father returned to Atlanta while I took a flight to my birth father's hometown. I checked into the Quality Inn at forty dollars per night. The area had a rich history. It was the ideal location for someone such as the professor, who harbored a fascination with the past. I had clearly not inherited this trait. I found history to be tedious and burdensome.

After putting my suitcase in my hotel room, I made my way over to the university, where I waited at the prescribed time and at the agreed-upon place. It was an anteroom adjacent to the history department but open to the hallway. My birth father had said he would meet with me following a faculty meeting.

I fidgeted. I checked my watch. I crossed my knees to the right, to the left, and then back to the right. I picked at my fingernail polish and twirled my pinky ring. I was jittery, insecure, and unsure what to expect. Would my father have dark hair, light hair, gray hair, or no hair? Would he be introverted and pensive, or outgoing with a hearty laugh? Would he be funny like Jed, creepy like Zero, or perfect like Paws? Would he give me a bear hug and ask me to be a part of his life? Or would he mutter, "Nice to meet you, kid," and send me on my way?

Eventually, a distant door opened, and thirty professors poured into the hallway. As I scanned the crowd, I immediately knew which one was my dad. I was submerged in an oedipal weirdness because this man was cute, and I hardly ever thought anyone was cute. It was shocking to realize that if I had not known he was my father and had run into him somewhere, I might have suggested a date. It was an uncomfortable and unfamiliar feeling (although a common one, according to experts[12]). I had never found my adoptive dad to be remotely attractive.

The professor's blue eyes were distinctive, despite the fact that his dark suit, oyster white shirt, and plaid tie did nothing to accentuate them. His short gray hair, balding hairline, and stocky build suited him well. His heavy eyebrows were a plus. I had always found this to be an appealing feature despite magazine ideals to the contrary.

As my birth father introduced himself, his secretary appeared. "Who's this?"

"This is Missy," he replied to her. "We're just leaving." He hustled me out of the anteroom before she could inquire further.

Although the professor was traditional in some ways, he was refreshingly liberal about accepting different cultures and beliefs. When we discussed my conversion to animal rights, he did not criticize me or say that I was "well suited for living in California with the fruits and nuts," as my adoptive dad had suggested on numerous occasions.

"I pay attention to animal arguments. I don't eat much meat. In Singapore, where I taught, society was not responsive on animal issues. In East Asia, it's hard for them to understand why clubbing seals by Japan is a big deal."

When I told him that I was not a Christian, he did not denounce me or say I would go to hell, as so many Atlantans had. And despite his personal commitment to the Baptist faith, he smiled approvingly when I revealed my unorthodox beliefs. He seemed to think it was critical for a person to contemplate these issues and come up with her own perspective, rather than stumble through life as an automaton. He proved himself to be deep, intellectual, philosophical, and unprejudiced. He immediately garnered my respect. I was proud to be his daughter.

On the following morning, I played "student" by auditing two of his history classes. Afterward, we headed to the cafeteria for lunch, where we again bumped into his secretary. She seemed curious why a mere student would be spending two full days with the professor.

"Ah, it's you again," she said. My father whisked me away.

The third encounter with the secretary occurred later that afternoon. She saw me and the professor on a bench at the center of campus. Even from fifty yards away, I could tell she was suspicious.

My dad's upbringing had been quite ordinary. His father, who died of typhoid at age thirty-two, had worked as an engineer, while his mother had earned a living as a social worker. He met my mom, Sharon, at church, and they started dating. When she got pregnant, they married, but with plans to divorce after I was born. The professor did not want to stay with my mom largely because of her secular leanings. He had given her a book for Christmas about God called *To Live Again* with hopes of transforming her into a religious devotee.

"I think she was trying to trap me by getting pregnant."

Frankly, I doubted this was the case. The "trapped feeling" is fairly common among unmarried men facing fatherhood.

Women are rarely the beguilers they are assumed to be. The professor prearranged the adoption three weeks prior to my birth, and my mom abided by his decision. This would have been illogical if she'd been a trickster.

"You were born in the back seat of the car. I was driving. Your mother was in labor for fifteen minutes." He sounded tense just mentioning it.

I could imagine his stress. He would have been more emotional and ruffled than most new dads, although outwardly restrained.

"They took you out of the car at the hospital, and we never saw you again."

"Where's my mother?"

"I have no idea. I have not seen her since the divorce."

Digging up roots on my mom's side of the family tree would take more than a flimsy garden shovel and a phone call to an alumni association. It would take a team of archeologists, heavy excavation equipment, and some serious perseverance.

Chapter Seven

THE NEW YORK BABY DADDY

"How do you fix a broken pizza? With tomato paste."

I was a sucker for corny jokes. Maybe that's why I fell in love with Eric the day we met.

I was not on vacation in New York. I was there to get a publisher for my eight-thousand-volume how-to book on party-crashing. Actually, *Meet the Stars* was only nine hundred pages, but it might as well have been eight thousand volumes, because no publisher was going to take me seriously with that kind of verbosity. This was my first work, so I wrongly assumed editors would be thrilled to snip it down to size. Turned out they were more thrilled about snipping me out of their offices.

"Hmm, it's a bit long, don't you think?" A big shot at Simon & Schuster flipped through the corpulent tome and then showed me the door. "Give me a call after you shave off seven hundred pages. Thanks for coming."

But there was a Pyrrhic victory in all this. I was proud of finagling my way up to the executive offices in the first place. This was no minor feat, because I had arrived in Manhattan without appointments or connections. Publishing houses are virtual fortresses. Special permission is needed just to board the ground-floor elevators. I had to put my gate-crashing gift to work.

My strategy was to meet publishing house underlings downstairs as they ventured off to lunch. After a sandwich and a bottle of Evian water, they were putty in my keyboard-worn hands. We became friends, and they agreed to take me upstairs to pitch my book proposal to company executives. This worked three times running. Unfortunately, the nine-hundred-page manuscript was like a tanker without fuel. It was flotsam in a best-selling sea full of ocean liners, snappy Jet Skis, and marathon swimmers.

I had been churning out pages while taking classes at CSUN. I was twenty-five and aspired to have a signed, sealed, and delivered book contract prior to starting my master's program at USC. But this was not in the cards. A new boyfriend, however, was in the cards.

I smiled at Eric. He smiled at me. We were not at the Leaning Tower of Pizza, which was down the road, but some other Italian joint with checkered tablecloths and a burly chef in a poofy white hat. Eric was also twenty-five and cute with slightly curly, dark hair, and hazel eyes. I was surprised that I was attracted to a guy my own age. "You look like Richard Gere" was a comment he had heard more times than there are *Pretty Woman* reruns. He loved Nutella hazelnut spread and photography. He never threw anything away and collected paperweights and glass objects of art. You may wonder how many paperweights he had. If his apartment had been the state of California, it would never shake from an earthquake again.

Eric saw me across the room and motioned for me to sit at his table. "Americans, on average, eat eighteen acres of pizza each day. I know tons of useless facts."

"Useless facts are good." I smiled and joined him. "I'm trying to compile an encyclopedia in my head."

"How many acres do you eat?"

"Five in the morning and five in the afternoon," I replied.

"That's good. I like a woman who cares about the environment and her figure."

Our conversation at the restaurant led to a conversation just outside the Brill Building at 1619 Broadway, which led to three more hours of conversation in the hallway of that very structure.

The Brill Building has been called "the most important generator of popular songs in the Western World." Since it opened in 1931, it has been a prestigious address for entertainment professionals. It contained an astounding 165 music businesses in the 1960s. Paul Simon and Lorne Michaels still keep offices there today, and it was where Eric worked as a special effects engineer for a motion picture post-production firm. His dad was the president and chairman of the board. Eric gave me a grand tour of the offices and studios, including the windowless room where he worked. It housed audio tracts for every imaginable sound.

"This is a tractor." Eric pushed a button, and I could hear a John Deere in action, and then he hit another button. "And this is a tractor running over a plastic cup."

Both sounded the same to me, but Eric had a finely tuned ear.

"I guess you get a lot of call for these. There are so many movies about tractors and plastic cups."

Because my flight was departing that evening, Eric took off the rest of the afternoon to hang out with me. Mostly we stood next to the elevators in the lobby, where associates reprimanded him for playing hooky. I told him about my nine-hundred-page tanker and sloshing around to find a publisher. He told me about feeling inferior in a family of ambitious professionals. Eric was a success, in my view. But he felt mediocre in comparison with his highly accomplished dad and two older sisters, one of whom was a doctor.

"I have a blind date tonight," Eric revealed. "I'm not looking forward to it."

"Hope it doesn't go well." I laughed.

Eric gave me a good-bye kiss on the cheek, and by the time I arrived back at my Westwood condo, he had left a message on my answering machine saying his blind date was a disaster. Our physically distant relationship was emotionally close. We chatted on the phone regularly and exchanged corny jokes and sweet nothings. Sometimes we tucked them inside Hallmark cards, imaginative letters, or gag gifts.

In February, I wrote "Happy Valentine's Day" on an eight-by-ten photo of myself, made 250 copies, and mailed them to the receptionist at his workplace. She had secretly agreed to scotch-tape them all over the walls and ceiling of Eric's private office so that when he arrived on Valentine's morning, I would be *everywhere* to greet him.

"It looks so overwhelming," the receptionist whispered into the phone. "He'll be here any moment. I can't wait to see his expression."

Eric was blown away by the surprise, and in return, he mailed me a Xeroxed copy of his face in a frozen scream. Although the pained expression was not exactly romantic, the idea was.

I told Dad on the phone, "I invited Eric to join us in Florida for a week." Dad had a vacation planned at his condo on Marco Island, which is an hour west of Miami by car.

Dad replied, "You don't know anything about this guy. He could be a mass murderer."

Meanwhile, back in New York, Eric's mom was saying, "You don't know anything about this girl. She could be a mass murderer."

And just like that: the date between mass murderers was arranged.

We were thick as thieves in Florida. We played tennis, walked on the beach, made seashell earrings, enjoyed the island's famous key lime pie, and even rode on the motorboat with Dad. However, when Dad flung his fishing pole into the ocean, I became teary-eyed. And when he got a tug at his line, I felt the tug of my emotions. Scientific studies have confirmed that fish feel pain. When they are pulled from the water, they begin to suffocate. Their gills often collapse, and their air bladders—which are evolutionarily homologous to human lungs—can explode due to the abrupt change in pressure.

As Dad reeled the mackerel into the boat, he realized I was crying. He floundered because he had seen me tear up only twice during my adult life. In deference to me, he pried the helpless fellow (who I figured would die anyway due to mouth injuries) from the hook and cast him back into the ocean. He refrained from killing fish for the remainder of the trip, and for that I was grateful. But I was not grateful for the cruel comment he threw at me on the following day. Luckily, my new boyfriend was not within earshot.

"Eric can do better than you!" Dad roared with laughter from his easy chair in front of the TV.

Why did my father say such things? Was it because I had "adopted blood," as he put it? Or was I defective in some other way? The vicious remark reminded me of the time I had told my aunt that I wanted to get a date with Tom Jones. I was seventeen years old. Dad overheard our girl talk and blurted out, "Why would *he* want to go out with *you*?" Then he chuckled as if I was a pathetic creature and sauntered down the hall. The sideswipe had been confusing because my father loathed entertainers, calling them "low class" and "inferior." I was apparently more loathsome than they were.

In March 1986, I spent a week with Eric in New York. I was still a fan of mischief-making; I liked concocting outlandish surprises for my boyfriend. I suppose you could say it was my trademark as a girlfriend.

"Welcome to the Shakespearean treasure hunt," I announced when Eric returned to his apartment from work.

I'd spent the day diligently preparing the adventure. Eric studied the instructions, which contained his first clue. His mission was to read each quote from Shakespeare and to figure out which play it came from and where the next clue lay. He was allotted three guesses per quote, but I provided him with the list of the comedies and tragedies and told him that he could ask the "flaxen-haired maiden"—me—for assistance if he got stumped.

Eric read the first one out loud: "Let me tell the world." He figured out this had to do with communicating, which had to do with the telephone, which was where the next clue was hidden. It took him only three tries to predict it came from *Henry IV*.

"A man of my kidney." He mouthed the second quote, then ran to the toilet to find the next folded piece of paper. *The Merry Wives of Windsor* was the play.

Eric continued in this vein until he got to the final clue: "Lest too light winning, Make the prize light." It came from *The Tempest*. This naturally led to the bedside lamp, under which contained a certificate entitling him to a free gourmet meal at

Lutèce. This popular French establishment opened its doors in 1961 and played a pivotal role in the culinary development of America. In the 1980s—when Eric and I were there—Julia Child, Zagat, and numerous food critics had named it the best restaurant in the country. After dinner, Eric said he enjoyed the treasure hunt so much that he wanted me to design a new one for the following evening. So I did.

I met Eric's friends and family during my stay and was introduced to his sprawling childhood home on Long Island, including his former rough-and-tumble little-boy bedroom which had not been touched since the day he moved out. I was thanked for the gifts I'd sent weeks earlier: a pillow that I'd needlepointed for Eric's dad and a blouse that I'd beaded for his mom. I adored Eric's family, especially his father, who was an accomplished artist in addition to juggling several businesses.

Although Eric did not go to temple except on High Holy Days, he was proud to be Jewish. This was something we had in common. I had officially converted to the religion only months prior to hearing his first corny joke.

·৵·

Months before meeting Eric, I was at Stephen S. Wise Temple in Los Angeles. I had attended this synagogue on a weekly basis for two years, even though I was not a member. I wanted to become a Jew, and I was eager to initiate the conversion process. I knew the rabbis at the synagogue personally and hoped one of them would sponsor me. I was wrong!

"I will *not* help you convert!" the rabbi barked at me from behind his desk.

"Oh… okay." I backed toward the door of his private office. "Thanks for your time." I bolted from the building.

Was this a game? Was he pretending to be angry? After all,

tradition dictates that a rabbi reject a potential convert three times before accepting her into the religion. It was hard to imagine that this normally mild-mannered man, whom I considered a friend, was actually upset with me. On the other hand, there was *the essay*. This rabbi had asked me to write a paper for him, discussing Judaism and animal rights philosophy. I'd proudly handed it over a week prior. Rather than cheerlead for the religion, I'd produced a scholarly and balanced piece with footnotes and a fair amount of criticism. He may have been unimpressed with the criticism part.

Rather than risk further fury and repudiation, I sought out a different rabbi to help me with the conversion process: Rabbi Maller of Temple Akiba in Culver City.

Maller had been the spiritual leader of the synagogue since 1967, and he was one of three rabbis who had instructed me during a year-long Introduction to Judaism class that I'd completed.

"Take what means something to you and reject everything else," Rabbi Maller had said during class. "I believe in reincarnation, for example. You don't even have to believe in God to be a Jew."

I found this open-mindedness and flexibility appealing. It was nothing like the blindly-accept-the-word-of-Jesus form of Christianity that I had been force-fed as a child. I was a baby boomer who believed religion should be a consumer choice, no different from selecting options on a new car. Just as I could refuse splash guards and a spoiler, I thought it made sense to reject those parts of the Torah (or Bible) that seemed to rely upon isms: sexism, racism, and speciesism.[13] Religion was simply one aspect of a person's value system, and I felt it should be treated as such.

I considered myself a cultural Jew. I felt connected to the Jewish people and their heritage, and I liked attending Stephen

S. Wise because the sermons were interesting and congregants were urged to offer opinions.

"I don't agree with you, Rabbi" was something I heard more than once during a Friday night Shabbat service. This made me smile. Debate and disagreement were encouraged in Judaism. They were arguably fundamental components of the faith.

My conversion ceremony at Temple Akiba involved memorizing Hebrew passages and reciting them in front of the congregation. Afterward, I was handed the all-important certificate. I was officially a Reform Jew.

Days later, I sheepishly approached the Stephen S. Wise rabbi who had rejected me. I muttered, "I've converted."

I expected him to recoil in horror or vow to undo the process. Instead, he welcomed me with a warm hug and blurted out, "That's great."

He seemed to have amnesia about our previous encounter, or maybe it *had* all been a game. The rabbi and I remained friends, and Stephen S. Wise continued to be my favorite Friday night date.

※

I had an appointment at the USC student health center a couple of months after visiting Eric in New York. I had just turned twenty-six.

"I have some bad news." The doctor had a long face. "You're pregnant."

The doctor was not alone. Virtually everyone I knew was alarmed. I had not tried to get pregnant, but now that I was, I was pretty excited. I felt I could handle the situation. I was not a teenager. I was in graduate school, and I had supported myself for several years, both in Los Angeles and in Las Vegas.

"My dad only gave me one instruction in life: *Not* to get a girl pregnant," Eric said on the phone. "You're getting an abortion, right?"

"Of course not."

He expected this answer. We had discussed the scenario on more than one occasion. I'd said that abortion was not right for me, but Eric had tried to convince me otherwise. We'd never resolved the issue but had continued to see each other.

"We probably would have ended up getting married if you hadn't gotten pregnant," Eric said.

This statement made no sense. I figured Eric was trying to punish me or seduce me into an abortion. He knew I was in love with him and that I would have been ecstatic about getting married. I didn't propose to him, because I didn't want to be manipulative. If he'd wanted to step in the direction of commitment, he would have said so.

It was not just Eric who hurled bunker busters in my direction. Attacks came from all sides. I was bombarded by naysayers and their doomsday predictions. Virtually nobody could handle the notion that little Missy Laws—the former Atlanta debutante who was unemployed, husbandless, and practically broke—was going to have a baby out of wedlock. The impracticality was only part of their horror. From their view, my situation was sinful.

"I'm disappointed in you," Dad said on the phone. "You'll have to terminate the pregnancy." When I refused, he said he was putting the Westwood condo up for sale and would support my schooling only until the end of the year. "You'd better figure out a way to finish your two-year program in one. After that, you're on your own. No more money from me."

I was calm and upbeat. My father's promise to yank the financial rug out from under my feet was of little concern. I was in a motherly state of mind and fully trusted in the universe. I believed it would protect me. Every negative remark that entered my awareness ricocheted off of my excitement, positive attitude, and confidence that I could go it alone.

Upon reflection, I noticed something else profound. I'd felt insecure and inadequate all of my life, yet I rarely behaved as if those feelings were real. It was a paradox, a contradiction. My actions came off as sassy, fierce, and confident. My life had never been about conforming to the wishes of my father, Atlanta society, or my friends. My life had been about acting in accordance with my own essence.

So was I *really* insecure? I chewed on this for a while and realized that the answer was yes and no. I was composed of two sides, like a two-headed turtle. One noggin was tucked away in its shell wallowing in self-doubt while the other was exploring the terrain. One head symbolized the inner me, and the other represented the outer me.

The inner me was tentative, shy, polite, careful, and hard on myself, while the outer me was a bulldozer, flattening anything in its way. The inner me often felt stupid, ugly, fat, and inadequate, while the outer me was brassy, gutsy, fearless, and driven by high-minded ideals. The inner me wanted to be accepted and loved. The outer me was a renegade and did not care about the opinion of others. I was both parts, and I needed to deal with both parts. I needed to allow each side to shine from time to time, and the pregnancy provided an opportunity for the outer me to take the stage.

I shifted into superwoman mode, taking an excess of classes at USC so I could earn my degree in half the allotted time. School was much more difficult because I could not take migraine medicine due to possible side effects to my baby. There were lots of week-long headaches, and I looked like a hospital patient, wearing cold packs wrapped around my head to class and the grocery store. Plus, I was the upchuck queen, tossing my cookies in the strangest places. When it happened in the car on my way to school, I had to turn around and go home to change clothes. When it happened at the DMV, nobody noticed because, of course, it was the DMV.

I was so nauseated that I immediately lost fifteen pounds. I felt quite svelte and wondered why no one had packaged pregnancy as a weight loss plan. Three platonic male friends proposed marriage to me during that period, probably because they thought I needed a husband, but also because I looked so slender for an expectant mom. I never needed maternity clothes and did not appear to be "with child" until my final month.

Pickles and ice cream were not on the menu. I became obsessed with chocolate, which had not excited me in the past (although I tried to resist it because it had been linked to miscarriages). I was suddenly captivated by strangers' babies. They all seemed so adorable and perfect. This was an unusual reaction because I had never been one of those females who coo over children. I was, by nature, more of a career type.

I had two doctors with two opinions. Dr. Fussy Pants (as I called him) was worried about my tendency to overexercise and insisted that I reduce my extreme workouts to a more moderate level. Dr. Party Hearty (as I nicknamed him) felt that Dr. Fussy Pants was overreacting. I stepped in as the third medical opinion and sided with Party Hearty. At eight months of pregnancy, I won a five-hour-long tennis tournament at Santa Monica College. I was pretty impressed with myself, but Dr. Fussy Pants wasn't. He was concerned about the health of my child.

"The heartbeat doesn't sound right," he told me in mid-December. "I think there's a problem. I want to induce labor."

"You don't need to be worried," I assured him. I could not consult with Dr. Party Hearty, who was in Belize—probably partying hearty.

I agreed to let the hospital induce labor, even though I believed my baby was fine.

Chapter Eight

KAYLA: MY PRECIOUS TWIG

Trivial Pursuit and childbirth don't mix. I had thought playing the board game would be the perfect distraction while in labor at UCLA Medical Center. Boy, was I wrong. The contractions were just too powerful. I quickly learned that my brain goes blank when my abdomen is burning. Of course, this makes perfect sense. During a fire, they always evacuate the top floors first.

"What does an anthropophagist eat?" Laura read a Trivial Pursuit question.

"Aggh," I wailed in agony. "I don't know."

"People," she replied. "It's the same thing as a cannibal."

"Stop talking about food!"

Throb, jab, ache, and pang. The pain was

colossal. It was as if I had an alien being inside my tummy or had consumed a bowl of Elmer's glue, moldy blueberries, and thumbtacks.

"What bird lays the largest egg?" Laura ignored my distress.

"That's an inappropriate question, too." I writhed along with a spasm. "I can't even think. Put the game away."

"Ostrich." She tossed the card into a box on the floor.

Other than my friend Sarah, who lived out of state and was keeping Eric apprised of the baby drama by phone, Laura was the only person I'd told about my hospital stay. I had invited her to assume the role of Alex Trebek but shooed her away before the final round of the delivery process because I didn't think having a studio audience would be desirable.

I'd tried to tell my two dads, but faced indifference. The professor had reprimanded me. "Don't call me at home." Then he hung up. He was more worried about spilling the beans about his secret daughter than learning about his grandchild-to-be. My adoptive father had cut me off before I could say anything beyond, "Hello. I…" He mumbled that he had no interest in my life. I ended both calls knowing that my baby's birth would be a solo performance rather than a family affair.

Dr. Fussy Pants—who was still worried about my baby's heartbeat—wanted to induce labor. Although I thought he was getting his stethoscope in a bunch over nothing, I was glad to experience a frenzy-free car ride to UCLA Medical Center. I was able to drive myself in keeping with my self-sufficient nature.

I was assigned room 236 and visited by more doctors than dollar signs on a hospital invoice. I figured the numerous white coats who roamed into my room with clipboards were really turncoats with an allegiance to their professor rather than to me and my fetus. They seemed like medical students. I was probably the semester project or an essay question on their final exam.

When one of them asked if I wanted a tissue to wipe my

drool, I replied, "No. That would probably cost fifty dollars." It was my first hospital stay, but I was aware of the gouge-the-patient policy at hospitals. A person could come in with a gouge to the thigh and walk out with additional one to the wallet.

Although I was ecstatic about having a baby, I was sad about losing Eric. I had tucked away my tears because I wanted my baby to feel "happiness molecules." I believed negativity could be absorbed through the placenta wall and place stress on a fetus. Plus, I felt it was narcissistic to be upset over a guy. Although I had spent many weepy nights paddling around in puddles of self-pity over former boyfriends, such as Tom and Jed, my goal was to be thick-skinned and rational. There were serious problems in the world. Focusing on a mere breakup seemed self-centered. It was a foolish place to invest my energy.

Throughout my life I had umpired the battle between my heart—which often obsessed over personal woe—and my head, which urged me to be high-minded and outward looking. I felt that my value system and essence required siding with my head and moving beyond the trivial. I wanted to teach myself how to live in the big picture, always remembering there are others in greater physical and emotional hurt. If this meant I was "from my head" (as Gary liked to say), then so be it.

Besides losing Eric, I had lost the Westwood condo. My jiffy pop of a dad had hired a Realtor, obtained a buyer, and closed escrow before I could say, "Don't put me out in the street." At eight months pregnant, I'd packed dozens of boxes, lifted heavy furniture, and found an apartment that would accept pets on Aqua Vista Street in Toluca Lake.

There was more bad news. Some of my gorgeous Vegas furniture had been stolen when the professional moving company left pieces on the sidewalk unattended. Their insurance company reimbursed me $200, so I was only out $9,800 instead of the full $10,000. At least the lost pieces had been purchased with chip chatting cash rather than income from a low-wage, back-breaking job. The only good news related to the upheaval was that I proved myself worthy of being jiffy pop's daughter by finishing my master's program at USC before my baby's due date. Plus, I was finally able to zero out my creepy roommate.

The modest stucco apartment building was called the Pink Flamingo, although it bore no resemblance to its posh Vegas namesake. My two-bedroom unit with mottled brown carpet was lean on windows and not much larger than a birdcage. It was like residing in a Public Storage unit. There was too much stuff and too little space. I felt like a speck among skyscrapers: Tables, chairs, boxes, and other personal effects were stacked up to the ceiling in each room.

I had carved skinny paths from my computer—where I was painstakingly whittling down my 900-page book to 210 pages—to my bed, the kitchen, and the crib where my baby would eventually sleep. Because there was no heat or air-conditioning in the bedrooms, the crib was positioned in the living room adjacent to the refrigerator. The fridge was too fat to fit through the kitchen doorway. The whole place was a discombobulated mess. To retain a semblance of order, I had unpacked only what was necessary for survival and hoped I could afford a bigger place soon. But the prognosis looked grim. My bank account was empty, plus I had no job. It seemed like Paws, my newborn, and I would be facing lean times.

"It's a girl." Dr. Fussy Pants placed my tiny daughter on my stomach in the delivery room. She was precious and a bundle of beauty with dark brown hair, investigative blue-gray eyes, and a prominent chin like her dad. She weighed seven pounds one ounce and was born at 11:19 p.m. Despite the doctor's constant nagging about her irregular heartbeat, she was healthy. His announcement about sex had not been a surprise. Sonogram photos taken during my eighth month of pregnancy had already determined that my baby was a girl. I had decided on the name Kayla, based on the word *caelum*, which meant "sky" in Latin.

"It only took five pushes for her to come out. That's a record at this hospital," Dr. Fussy Pants said.

Popping out quickly was Kayla's first major accomplishment. I suppose one would expect nothing less from jiffy pop's granddaughter.

Two days after the birth, Laura gave me and my daughter a ride home from the hospital. I planned to go back later to get my car. On the way, we picked up Kayla's brother, Paws, from the dog-boarding facility. It was a sunny Sunday.

"On which weekday do illnesses usually begin?" Laura vaulted into Trivial Pursuit mode.

"Perhaps you haven't noticed, but I'm not in labor anymore."

"The answer is Monday," she continued. "I think Kayla will get sick tomorrow. You should keep her away from drafts."

Kayla turned out to be a robust little dumpling, and she got along just fine with her nippy neighbor, the refrigerator.

∽

Dad had ignored me since the sale of the condo, and he seemed disinterested in his one-and-only grandchild. But he did phone to give me the big news. It was sixty days after Kayla's birth.

"Your mother died last month. She came down with pneumonia."

"What? Last month? When's the funeral?"

"There was no funeral. I didn't tell anyone."

I figured he had not told anyone due to embarrassment. He'd been (to his horror) the husband of a woman who had attempted suicide and, for all practical purposes, succeeded. As mentioned earlier, Mom had cut her wrists and neck and popped pills in the bathtub ten years prior. She'd ended up in a semi-vegetative state. I could visualize Dad hiring shadowy figures to creep into the cemetery in the dead of night with my mother's coffin. I could imagine them lowering her into the ground and refilling the hole with dirt. All would be completed before sunrise. Only the ghosts, crickets, and night owls would witness the clandestine event.

Dad had always made it clear that he didn't want anyone to know about the (attempted) suicide, even though that genie had escaped from its bottle years prior and was still doing a striptease in the street. In other words, everyone was aware. Gossip still circulated through upper-class Atlanta. The stares were uncomfortable. The whispers were deafening, and my father's directive to me and my brother—only hours after the (attempted) suicide—had been bizarre and, frankly, heartless.

"You are *never* to mention your mother's name in this house again. And you are *never* to visit her. Am I understood?" Then he'd stomped out of the room while my little brother and I stared at each other in disbelief.

Dad went to see Mom only once. And on that occasion, she apparently flailed around, screamed nonsense, and glared at him with hate. He filed for divorce shortly thereafter.

Although I had never been close to my adoptive mom, I sneaked off to visit her, usually with my brother in tow. We saw her regularly, first in the hospital where she was hooked up to life-sustaining machines and later in the convalescent home. She never flailed around or yelled at us. She had brain damage and could control only one side of her body. Her memory was like an electrical cord that had been partially chewed by a rat, and she slurred her words to the point of incomprehensibility. She remained a quasi-vegetable until her death.

After my father informed me of my adoptive mother's passing, he said that I would be inheriting furniture and household effects from her portion of the estate rather than desperately needed money. I would be getting our family's couches, tables, ashtrays, and lamps, as well as worthless items such as the rusty can opener and the broken Christmas ornaments. Standing in my tiny Public-Storage-unit apartment, I could feel panic kicking into gear. It seemed Kayla, Paws, and I would have to hit the streets so our stuff could have a roof over its head. I envisioned the three of us huddled under a freeway overpass, mumbling to strangers about how we were evicted by a footstool, an end table, and a plaid wingback chair.

"I talked to an auction company," Dad continued. "They said they could give you ten thousand dollars for everything."

Although I was relieved that Dad was talking cash rather than burying me under the $10,000 pyramid of possessions, the proposal seemed inadequate. I knew there were numerous antiques—which had been passed down from both sets of my grandparents—as well as sterling silver pieces, oriental rugs, and fine china.

"That doesn't seem like enough."

"I think you should take it," he said. "It's the best you're gonna get."

I refused, so he generously offered to help me secure a retail property in an Atlanta mini-mall where I could open an antique shop. As a contractor, he had "connections," and one of them was willing to let me occupy a 2,000-square-foot space free of charge for a month. I phoned Laura, and she agreed to babysit Paws at her place while I played "shopkeeper" and Kayla played "junior assistant." I bought plane tickets for our trip to Atlanta.

Good news came on the following day. I received a letter from Ross Books in Berkeley, California, offering to publish *Meet the Stars*. I accepted the deal, even though the advance was small. The offer had not come out of nowhere. I'd spent months trimming my book. I'd flooded publishing houses with my query letter and sample chapters. I'd made phone calls to editors, hobnobbed with industry professionals at nonfiction conferences, and generally refused to take no for an answer. I credited my daughter with this success.

In the months surrounding Kayla's birth, I had transformed from a paper airplane casually gliding through a master's program into a Boeing 747. I was in supersonic mode, and Kayla was my propeller. Without her, I might have accepted Dad's meager $10,000 offer for the household furnishings. Without Kayla, I might never have found a book publisher. And without Kayla, I would not have gotten the idea to buy my first home. Although I cannot say with certainty that my daughter saved my life, she clearly reduced hemorrhaging. She rescued me from falling into a mind-set of underachievement.

"Our book is going to be published," I told little Kayla, who was in her bassinet chewing on her fingers. "And we are going to buy a house because you and Paws need a yard." Of course, I had no idea whether I could come up with the needed funds.

Despite my doubts, I contacted a Realtor and asked her to show me properties. I was specifically looking for a house that was spacious enough for my excess of possessions and that was laid out in such a way as to permit me to convert a section to a rentable guest unit. Plus, the place had to be in the inexpensive $130,000 price range, which could be found only in moderate-income areas of the San Fernando Valley, such as North Hollywood, Van Nuys, and Reseda.

"I'll be heading to Atlanta to collect the down payment. I'll be back in a month," I told the Realtor, hoping I would be able to live up to my word.

My next call was to the AIDS Project Los Angeles office, where I'd been volunteering for the previous three years. I needed to let staff know that I'd be out of town. I'd been assisting this nonprofit not so much out of a passion to combat the illness as much as a passion to combat prejudice. At the time, the societal trend was to victim-blame, to assert that it was the gay community's fault if their members got sick and died from the disease.

This upset me so much that I decided to volunteer. I possessed what seemed to be an innate loathing for isms—racism, sexism, anti-Semitism, speciesism, and homophobia—and had even come to believe that the universe was beckoning me to work toward their defeat.

The epiphany had come to me during my teen years while reading a philosophy book on a hill across the street from my parents' home with my dog at my side. A feeling of purpose washed over me, and I made a decision that going forward I would try to make a difference in the world by fighting discrimination. It was likewise clear that happiness and personal fulfillment stemmed from othercentrism (or helping others) rather than focusing on the self.

I was vocal about my newfound mission and encountered backlash from family and friends. I was called "grandiose," "silly," "egotistical," and "delusional" for my "stupid goal" and "goofy belief" that the universe cared what the heck I did. My life in upper-class Atlanta—which already dwelled in the third circle of hell—spiraled further downward. One classmate teased me as a "nigger lover," and my brother bombarded me with racist jokes after school. My mom explained the "inferiority of Negroes" and revealed that our family's ancestors had been slave owners—a fact that horrified me and confirmed, to my mind, that nature outweighs nurture.

"Some things from the black culture tend to lower our culture," my father told me. "Like the degeneration of marriage. That comes from blacks. All four of your grandparents were prejudiced."

When it came to gay and lesbian rights, opinions were also skewed. A family friend lectured me on how homosexuality was "against God's will," while my dad called same-sex relationships "repugnant," adding that "nobody is born queer." He further said, "Gays hurt the family unit," and "I wouldn't want to associate with *those people*."

In addition, my father's musings about the inferiority of females was a staple of my existence.

"Men are nothing like women. They are put on this earth to make money, protect, and provide for the family," he said. "Women are put on this earth to clean the house and raise the children. Women who have a career or don't use their husband's last name are weird." Of course, there was a bright side to Dad's sexism: There was less pressure on me to succeed than my little brother, since I was only a girl.

This had been my life in Atlanta. This was the life I'd escaped. This was the life to which I never wanted to return. But this was also the life that arguably transformed me into a tougher and more self-sufficient person. My childhood was like boot camp. It was a foundation that helped me to acquire grit, spunk, debate skills, and an independence of spirit. And it readied me for a lifelong battle against bias.

※

Kayla and I arrived in Atlanta. Dad had kindly agreed to let us stay at his place while operating the antique shop, but he had not informed me that he would be residing elsewhere.

"Where are you going?" I said after pulling into my father's driveway on that first day. He was tossing suitcases into the trunk of his car.

"I'll be at the lake house."

"You're not going to stay here with us?"

"Nope. You and I lead different lives."

Since becoming pregnant, "you and I lead different lives" was Dad's standard line before hanging up the phone, that is, if I could get him to talk to me in the first place. Perhaps this was code for saying we had irreconcilable value systems. I was like Mom. I was an embarrassment. He needed to keep me out of sight. It seemed Dad's moral code would not permit him to have a relationship with an unmarried mother and her born-out-of-wedlock child.

Kayla made a gurgling sound from her car seat.

"Would you like to meet your granddaughter?" I asked.

"Nope." He barely glanced at her. "She sounds like a cat." Dad slipped into his Mercedes and sped out of sight.

I did not see him again during my month-long stay in Atlanta. In fact, he would refuse to see me or Kayla for the next twenty-one years.

Dad was an odd mixture of coldness and generosity. He refused to spend time with his only daughter and only grandchild, yet he'd inquired about getting $10,000 for my inherited treasures, and he'd secured the mini-mall space for my antique shop. He was outright cruel to my face, yet friends and strangers said he bragged about me behind my back.

Dad was a paradox.

⸙

Operating an antique shop was like running a marathon while being beaten with a stick. In other words, it was exhausting and unpleasant. As a child, I'd thought I might someday want to own a gift shop, but now that I knew what it entailed, I abandoned that idea. While Kayla slept next to the checkout counter, I spent sixteen hours each day organizing, getting merchandise appraised, affixing price tags, hiring employees, placing ads in the local newspaper, and eventually selling. I was as tired as an old highway. It felt as if I'd been worn down by a million Michelins, Bridgestones, and Goodyears.

Thieves made it worse. Because of my "smart talent" and "private eyes," it was impossible to steal without my knowledge. When several girls pocketed sterling silver cups, I considered phoning the police. Of course, approaching them was inconceivable because I hated conflict. I wished I could be confrontational, but in the end I just scowled at them, sort of like the old lady at Jed's playhouse. The crooks knew "I knew" and did not return. The possibility of theft added another layer of stress on my already high level of anxiety and exhaustion, and I was so paranoid about losing other items from the large and sumptuous collection of sterling silver that I locked the rest in a storage room to take to Los Angeles.

The silver was not alone in that storage room. It was surrounded by some very fancy friends, such as my adoptive grandmother's (Nanny's) gorgeous sixty-piece set of rose china and her antique blue vases. I had been a fan of her "rose and blue" since I was a toddler and old enough to say the word "pretty." The vases alone had been appraised at $5,000 each, which of course totaled what the auction house had offered for the whole lot in the first place.

The odd thing about being in the antique shop all day, every day, was that the stuff grew on me. Items that had once been so-so became keepers. I would haul them back to the storage room to await the cross-country journey back to L.A. Things that I had once dubbed ugly started to look okay. I was a jagged rock undergoing attrition. My edges were becoming rounded and smoother. My taste was broadening, and I was beginning to feel protective over and sentimental about my ancestors' treasures. I realized that I wanted to pass on a significant number of possessions to my little twig Kayla and her twigette kiddies someday.

"I love this platter. I think I'll buy it," a customer said. "But I'd like to use the restroom first."

He trotted away. I stared at the orange-and-navy platter that I remembered seeing on Nanny's coffee table as a child. It had never really spoken to me, but now its little platter voice seemed to be saying, "Keep me. Keep me." I was spellbound by its delicate porcelain nature and distinct markings, and I suddenly realized it matched a set of dinner plates I already owned.

I scanned the store to make sure no one was watching. When the coast was clear, I sneaked the platter inside my jacket and bolted to the storage room, where I locked it up. Then I wandered back into the merchandise area.

The customer returned from the restroom. "Where's the platter?"

"Oh, it's gone"

"Wow, it sold fast," he said.

I nodded and smiled.

"Oh no!" a sales clerk screamed.

I looked over to see that baby Kayla had rolled off a two-foot-high platform, where she had been sleeping. I rushed over, picked her up, and held her tight. Luckily, she was not injured, but she did shed a few tears over the incident.

"The perils of being a junior assistant," I said to the sales clerk so she would not feel guilty about failing to keep an eye on my girl.

By the end of the month, I'd made $42,000 in profit, which was enough for a down payment on a house. Plus, I'd retained the sterling silver pieces, two oriental rugs, the blue vases, the rose china, the orange-and-navy platter, and another five moving boxes full of collectibles and antiques.

On the final day that the store was open, an executive at Dad's company bought the remaining items on the floor so I would not have to lug them back to L.A. or arrange for charity to take them. It was a much-appreciated gesture. Kayla and I boarded the U-Haul for an arduous cross-country journey back to our jam-packed apartment.

※

The road trip from Atlanta to Los Angeles in the jiggly U-Haul was grueling. I stopped at motels along the way because with a baby, I was not about to sleep under hotel conference room tables as I had done in my teens and early twenties. After arriving at the Public-Storage-unit apartment, I unloaded the family heirlooms and called the Realtor to tell her that I had acquired the down payment funds. We looked at properties.

I found a perfect five-bedroom, two-bath home. It was 2,000 square feet, cost $138,000, and was located in Van Nuys adjacent to an alley. I knew the back section of the home could be converted into a guest unit, which could rent for $500 per month. My plan was as follows: I would convert part of the garage and turn one of the two washer-dryer hookups into a kitchenette. Then the tenant would have a living room, bedroom, efficiency kitchen, and bath, while Kayla, Paws, and I would be able to enjoy the rest of the home, consisting of an enormous living room, kitchen, breakfast nook, bath, and four bedrooms. It would give us approximately 1,500 square feet of living space.

Luckily, there were no-qualifying loans in those days, because I could not have obtained "full doc" funding with a brand-new baby, no job, and slightly more than a down payment in the till. Today, Congress has outlawed government-backed no-qualifying loans, even though this product existed successfully for decades without high foreclosure rates. When I purchased my house, no-qualifying buyers had to put down a full 25 percent and have excellent credit. In addition, the property had to appraise for the purchase price. My debt-to-income ratio was obviously out of whack since I had no job, but I knew I would be stupid if I did *not* buy. Others did not see it that way.

"You can't afford a house," Laura said. "It's way too risky."

"You're gonna end up in foreclosure." Dad chuckled in his typical make-her-feel-guilty-so-she-will-do-what-I-want way.

The "pessimism patrol" (as I called them) were once again collecting at my doorstep. They were serenading me with ominous predictions and dire warnings. As usual, I ignored them.

I had been paying $650 per month to live in the cramped apartment, yet the monthly cost (including mortgage, tax, and insurance) for the new house would be only $800. With the $500 income from the guest quarters, my family could enjoy a spacious four-bedroom home for a mere $300 per month. From my perspective, there was *more* risk in remaining a tenant. I bought the home, which doubled in value the first year, giving us a degree of financial security and independence. I am forever grateful for no-qualifying loans. They are the reason why I was never again a boarder in cramped quarters, scrambling to come up with monthly rent.

It felt good knowing that I had moved to Los Angeles with a mere $500 and now owned much-prized California real estate. It felt good ignoring naysayers. And it felt good proving to my family and friends that I could succeed, despite the cynicism they lobbed my way.

❧

Being a single mother was relatively easy. This was partly a testament to Kayla and partly a testament to the babysitting co-op I joined. The thirty-family child chaperone exchange worked on a point system, which meant I never had to fork over hard-to-come-by cash when I wanted to work or go on a date. I simply phoned a co-op member—of which two-thirds were single moms—and asked if Kayla could come over for a playdate with her kid. For extra points, members would do pickups from school or watch a child overnight. In return, I would charge points to babysit their youngsters. It was a convenient way to save money and to provide regular play pals for my daughter.

I was also thrifty in other ways. Because kids quickly outgrow their clothes, I bought cute outfits at garage sales. A church held a charity event on their front lawn and charged a dollar for each grocery sack filled with apparel. They had adult duds as well, and I bought a raincoat that cost me a whole dollar because it filled the whole bag.

In addition, I became the Barter Lady of Van Nuys, using antique-shop leftovers and designer clothes (that I'd bought in Las Vegas years prior) in exchange for goods and services. Kayla's doctor accepted sterling silver dessert plates in return for routine medical exams, and a stranger swapped her piano for my hot-to-trot halter top. When my cash got low, my creativity shifted into high gear.

Kayla was an easy child, and her two favorite foods were spinach and carrots. She slept through the night from day one, breastfed with a smile, and did not develop a sweet tooth until elementary school, when she was corrupted by classmates who introduced her to Snickers and Little Debbies. Two of her friends' parents were particularly despicable when they laced her food with meat while assuring her it was vegetarian. When she found out, she broke into tears and became less trusting of others. Apart from these unfortunate incidents, Kayla was a vegetarian until she became vegan in adulthood.

Kayla's first season of babyhood included despising socks and meeting Tom Jones. She also participated in a local beauty pageant called the Baby Cupid Contest. Although she did not win the grand prize, she was "two thumbs-up" in comparison with her thumb-sucking competitors.

Kayla's second season of babyhood involved delivering breathy laughs that turned into hiccups and attending her baby-naming ceremony at Stephen S. Wise synagogue. She was officially dubbed Rivka, in remembrance of her recently deceased grandmother on her dad's side of the family. Kayla also posed for *People* in the backyard of the Van Nuys house. The magazine was doing a story on *Meet the Stars* and wanted to know the tot behind the party crasher.

"Is she part Chinese?" the *People* magazine photographer asked during the photo session.

"No," I replied. "But I hear that a lot." As an infant, Kayla looked part Asian, although neither Eric nor I had any Far East ancestry.

"You are going to marry an Asian man in two years, and it will be a disaster," a psychic lady had told me backstage at *The Oprah Winfrey Show* a month prior. This woman had asked to see Kayla's photo before giving me a free reading.

The psychic and I were appearing onstage with assorted occultists. The segment was about celebrities who return from the dead or who give messages from beyond the grave, a fact that I did not realize until my interview began. How I got thrown in with this crowd I'll never know. My book was about crashing parties and award shows, not about crashing the life-death divide. *How to Meet Deceased Stars* would have been an entirely different book.

"I've never dated an Asian," I told the psychic. "You're just saying this because you saw the photo of my daughter."

"No, that's not the reason," she replied. "I work with the FBI to solve crimes. I know the future." Needless to say, I did not marry an Asian. I hope she had better luck with the FBI.

Oprah's show was the first of over a hundred television and radio programs on which I appeared to discuss *Meet the Stars*. Ross Books had no publicist, so I had to set up the guest spots myself. I felt comfortable in front of the camera because I had rehearsed for years, beginning in childhood. My brother had teased me about playing "talking head" with a hairbrush as a microphone. He liked to say, "You're getting dandruff in your mouth!" Finally, those embarrassing moments were paying off.

During Kayla's third season of babyhood, she learned to walk, attempted to eat dog food from Paws's bowl, watched me do a book signing at the mall, and trick-or-treated with singer Lou Rawls at his Hancock Park estate.

Her fourth season of babyhood was really toddlerhood. When Kayla was almost four, we decked out in our finest duds and knocked on a Long Island front door. "Hi," I said when Eric's parents answered.

I was unsure whether we would be embraced or tossed out of New York like a stale bag of bagels, but his parents invited us inside their sprawling estate for a three-hour conversation. I figured that by showing up on their doorstep, I was doing them a favor, because they would be able to meet their grandchild for the first time (which I think they wanted) yet not be blamed for it by Eric. I would be the fall guy, the villain who forced the encounter. Eric, who had also never met Kayla, had his own apartment in Manhattan, and I did not pop in on him.

Each year, I'd sent one or two letters to Eric's parents with photos and updates on Kayla. As matriarch and patriarch, I figured they would disseminate the information to the rest of their kin. I continued this letter-writing practice for years after the Long Island visit—until I received a stern letter in the mail. Kayla was seven years old at the time.

"Please stop sending these updates. You're upsetting our family," Eric's mom wrote.

Although I had always liked her (she thought her letter was perfectly fine, by the way), I was outraged because Eric and his family had not participated in Kayla's life for seven years. Kayla had never received a card, phone call, or present. Yet she had the nerve to tell me that *I* was upsetting *them*! In my view, *they* were upsetting *Kayla* by depriving her of family. I didn't want my daughter to grow up like I did, feeling isolated and unloved.

Even more galling, I had chosen not to ask for child support, despite the fact that Eric had trust funds and his parents were superrich. It would have been nothing for them to set aside a few bucks for their grandchild each month.

There were three reasons why I had not sued for child support. First, I cared about Eric and knew that asking for money would depress him and make him look bad in front of his parents. Second, Eric had wanted me to get an abortion, so I felt it was unfair to ask him to contribute financially when I had not taken his advice in the first place. Last, I wanted to prove to myself and the world that I could raise Kayla alone without help from Eric or the well-to-do folks in my life: Dad and Eric's parents.

However, the you're-upsetting-our-family letter changed everything. Now I was angry and figured it would not be right to deprive Kayla of her legally entitled funds. I had already proved I could go it alone, plus I'd heard that fathers who pay support tend to become invested in their children. They are more apt to form relationships, and I wanted Kayla to have that connection.

Not long after the first child support check came rolling in, Eric came rolling into Kayla's life. She was ten years old when they first met. He began flying her to New York twice a year. I am happy to report that my little twig has become close with her dad's side of the family tree.

~

Despite my efforts to close off my heart, curl up in my head, and focus on the big picture, I had many tearful moments missing Eric. I would sit on the couch with Kayla asleep next to me and stare out the window. In the daytime, I would see gardeners zigzagging across lawns with their mowers. They were going on with their lives, doing their chores, yet I was obsessing in a wholly unproductive way. At night, I would watch headlights from the occasional passing vehicle and memorize the dark outline of the crepe myrtle tree adjacent to my driveway. I would sit there for hours like a statue, lacking vitality. It was as if Loss had carved me into a motionless and despondent creature.

Eric contacted me only once during pregnancy in a futile attempt to try to get me to agree to an abortion. And during Kayla's first seven years, Eric did not call at all. I was sad, but I was not angry, partly because I believed in the determined universe (that Eric was a product of cause and effect rather than free will) and partly because, deep inside, I knew him to be a good guy. I loved him and hoped he would change his mind. He never did.

Financially, I struggled off and on after Kayla's birth, even going into $20,000 debt on credit cards. Thank goodness I had bought the Van Nuys house. It kept my mortgage payments well below rental rates.

I had too much pride to ask Dad, Eric, or Eric's parents for financial assistance. I wanted to prove that even though rebels don't adhere to society's instruction guide, they can be self-sufficient. They can persevere, devising an instruction guide of their own. I was determined to succeed financially, spiritually, emotionally, and romantically.

In the area of love, I'd always ignored conventional advice, which instructs women to play "hard to get." I'd dated on my terms, and I planned to continue in that way. I hoped to find a husband by being a maverick, by being assertive and bold, by being myself. Of course, there was no assurance that I would ever find a permanent partner, and virtually everyone I knew predicted failure. Yet I plodded forward. I was hopeful for the future. I had to succeed in this—and all facets of my life—because my little twig Kayla was counting on it. Her life was at stake as well. And there is nothing like a child to motivate.

Chapter Nine

THE GUNMAN AND SHEENA'S SCHEME

Kayla and I could have been held hostage, shot, or even killed. Luckily, we had four dogs.

It was the middle of the night at the Van Nuys house. I awoke to pounding rain, thunder, and a mysterious sound in the backyard. I slid out of bed and peered out the window. A metal trash can had tumbled over, and some of its contents—a banana peel, watermelon rind, crumpled papers, and empty jars—had spilled onto the muddy landscape. The container was too heavy to have been toppled by a stray cat. I knew there was an intruder on the property.

I crept down the dark hallway into Kayla's bedroom. I gazed out her window. Scenes from *The Amityville Horror* and *The Texas Chainsaw Massacre* played in my head. I could see nothing except drenched shrubs and spooky blackness, but I knew someone was out there. My four dogs did as well. I could tell by their low-pitched growls. (In addition to Paws, I had adopted three dogs from animal shelters.)

Suddenly, there was a banging. Someone was at the front door. I moved into the living room and past my dogs to the peephole, where I could see six Los Angeles Police Department officers crammed together under my porch overhang trying to dodge the downpour. I cracked open the door.

"Ma'am, a dangerous man jumped over your fence from the alley. He's in your backyard," an officer said. "Can we go through your house to the back?" A sliding glass door in the living room led to the rear yard.

"Sure," I replied. "What did he do?"

"Armed robbery and attempted murder."

By this time, my four pups thought the fortress was under siege. They were snarling and barking. The police officers froze at the sight of my agitated canines.

"Will they attack us?"

"No, they're fine." I knew they were all talk and no teeth.

The police marched in and out of the sliding glass door. I moved into the backyard behind them and watched them tiptoe toward the rear of my property with their weapons drawn. The front door was still wide open.

When I glanced back, I noticed the villain trying to hide behind a post inches from the front entrance. He was eyeing my pissed-off pups and holding a gun. He did not notice that I'd seen him, so I reacted just as I had when finding Mack's rifle pointed at Lynn's head. I tried to outsmart him. I casually meandered back into the house, pretending all was fine. I calmly closed the front door and locked it without glancing in his direction. Thankfully, he did not try to stop me. I didn't want to leave the door unattended even for a moment while I alerted a police officer, for fear this guy might sneak inside. Frankly, it was unprofessional of the Los Angeles police to put me in this position.

I informed an officer of the situation. The police rushed to the front, knocked the man to the ground, and arrested him. Had there been no dogs, the living room would have been unattended. It is possible the gunman would have crept into the home, hid in Kayla's bedroom, and waited for the cops to leave. Kayla and I might have been alone with him.

The same four dogs protected Kayla a year later when she was a toddler. The six of us were playing in the backyard when the phone rang. I went into the house to answer the call. It was my friend Sheena from the babysitting co-op.

"I'm trying to get Mary into an exclusive school," she said. "And I want you to go with us to the interview."

"I didn't think you could afford a private school."

"It's not private. It's charter, and they're super picky about students."

Sheena was a dark-skinned African American and so was her daughter, Mary. They had applied to a Los Angeles charter school that had quotas for the types of students they would accept. Because the institution comprised 90 percent black students, the school claimed they would accept only other races. Sheena had been told by an administrator that blacks need not apply until the racial distribution was more balanced. To circumvent this ludicrous rule, Sheena had checked the application box that read "Caucasian." At the time, she had not realized that an in-person interview would be required.

While I was on the phone, Kayla somehow managed to open the gate at the back of the property and get into the alley. Apartment buildings with underground parking garages lined the north side of this thruway, and garages attached to single-family dwellings bordered the south side. The area was unkempt with graffiti, abandoned shopping carts, and garbage.

Suddenly Paws bolted into the house and barked at me. It was odd behavior. I hung up the phone and went outside to find Kayla and the other dogs gone. The gate was open. I hurried into the alley and saw them a hundred yards from our house. It was a frightening sight to see my little girl so far away, but it was a relief to see that the other three dogs had not run off as I would have expected. They took baby steps alongside Kayla. They were at her side. They seemed to understand it was their duty to serve and protect.

⁂

I accompanied Sheena and Mary to the charter school interview. The place was well organized. Every stack of papers had its own shelf. Every knickknack had its own cubicle. Sheena and Mary sat in front of the principal, an older African American woman. I took a seat at the back of the room, trying to be inconspicuous and hoping not to be questioned.

The principal reviewed the application, furrowed her brow, and then stared at dark-skinned Mary. She moved her eyes back to the application and then back to Mary. After a beat, she spoke in a slow and puzzled way.

"You say your daughter's *white*?"

Sheena barreled back like a nightclub bouncer. "Yes. She *is* white. You got a problem with that?"

The principal was taken aback. Her eyes became wide, and she started sweating. She glanced at me as if I was a lifeline, but I flashed an expression of "Hey, don't look at me!"

Sheena spoke again in her tough-guy voice. "You got a problem with that?"

"Um... no... no problem," the principal replied. Perhaps

she feared the god of political correctness or anticipated a lawsuit and a newspaper headline: "Racist Principal Questions Student's Skin Color." In any case, it was the shortest interview since a reporter asked a deceased disaster victim "Are you dead?" Mary was accepted into the school.

A few years later, I had my own experience with "Sheena's scheme."

I wanted to earn a doctorate in philosophy and had even come to realize that philosophy should have been my major in the first place. To my mind, it was a Rembrandt while all other subjects were cheap velvet Elvises sold on the sidewalk outside the Shell station.

Although I already had a bachelor's degree in theatre arts and a master's degree in professional writing, I had returned to CSUN on a part-time basis following Kayla's birth to take undergraduate classes in philosophy. The school did not offer an advanced degree in this field, so UCLA was my first choice for furthering my studies. I chose this university because it was closer to my home than USC or Claremont College and less expensive. Prior to filling out the application, I spoke to a UCLA secretary on the phone. She informed me of a bizarre rule: Doctoral students in philosophy had to live on campus.

"Our program is competitive, ranking seventh in the nation," she said. "Students who refuse our accommodations are simply not accepted."

I told her that I had a baby, four dogs, and a four-bedroom home. Cramming the six of us into a dorm room like gumballs was illogical. And philosophy was supposed to be about logic, wasn't it?

"Well, you could get rid of your dogs," she suggested. "Then you could accept on-campus housing and compete for a slot in the program. You might get accepted."

"I could get rid of the kid, too," I replied sarcastically.

There was silence and then a dial tone. The secretary was a speciesist. She was prejudiced against nonhumans. She believed that they were inferior to humans. Dumping canine family members onto the street to fend for themselves is one reason why more than two million dogs and cats are killed in U.S. shelters each year.

My four dogs knew the meaning of "disposable" and "dumped." Paws had, of course, been tied to a tree and left for three days without water or food. Plum and Lucy had been dropped off at a Los Angeles animal shelter, where they were slotted for death. Angel had been abandoned at a vacant house without food or water when her family moved. She ended up at the Burbank animal shelter. These dogs were part of my family now, and they were more important to me than the UCLA Philosophy Department.

I shifted gears, selecting a different major at UCLA—one without a housing requirement. I chose education, although I was unsure whether I had sufficient interest in the field. I also worried about getting accepted into this program or *any* program at UCLA. The school had rejected my undergraduate application years prior despite the fact that I had a 4.0 grade point average from one of the most prestigious high schools in the nation. Had "being white" been the problem? Could this have been my fatal mistake? I was unsure but decided to take advantage of my newfound information: my birth mother's Italian heritage. I ignored the "Caucasian" box on the UCLA application and checked "Other." Then I scribbled "Italian American" in the margin of the form. I had no idea whether Italians were a minority group or underrepresented at UCLA, but I knew they had been victims of prejudice in the nineteenth and early twentieth centuries. The largest mass lynching in the United States had not been against African Americans but against Italian Americans in New Orleans in 1891.

Like Sheena, I was summoned to an in-person interview. Unlike Sheena, I was not worried because I'd been forthright on the application. When I entered the room, I quickly realized there was a huge misunderstanding.

The interviewer dashed over to me. "I'm so happy to meet you! I'm Native American, too!"

"What? I don't underst—"

"Come on in." He pulled me into the room. "You've been accepted into the program." He winked at me with a big smile. "Sit down. What tribe are you?"

I was hesitant but took a seat. "I'm not Native American."

"You're not?" He looked puzzled, pulled out my application, and pointed. "You wrote 'Indian American.'"

The phrase "Italian American" looked a little like "Indian American."

"Oh, no." I laughed. "I'm Italian American."

"Oh, I see." He continued to study my application.

"I'm excited about being accepted."

"Actually, it's not a full acceptance. It's conditional. You have to make a B average or better the first quarter. If you do, you'll be in the program."

I accepted the offer. Although I made the grades, I dropped out after the first quarter, realizing what I already knew in my heart: that philosophy was my true love. Education, on the other hand, was that nerdy son of your mother's friend who will never be more than a friend but you give him a chance anyway.

I resumed my part-time undergraduate courses at CSUN while I chewed on where I wanted to go for a PhD: USC (expensive and far from my house) or Claremont College (expensive and really far from my house).

True love is not always geographically desirable. And it can cost a pretty penny.

∽

I was signing autographs, taking pictures with fans, and doing interviews about my book. I was the center of attention and loving it. It felt as if the Anaheim Convention Center were an 8,000-square-foot party and I was the birthday girl. This was the American Booksellers Association fair—an annual gathering and a promotion vehicle for publishers, bookshops, and authors. Ross Books had a table in the center of the shindig to promote *Meet the Stars* and its other titles.

I'd just finished talking with a *Publishers Weekly* reporter when Arnie, a longtime acquaintance, came up to me. I wondered what he was doing here. He was from Atlanta. Arnie was a few years older than me and worked for an independent bookstore that had a booth at the convention. As we started to catch up with each other's lives, he told me that he had run into my father a month prior.

"I know what you've been doing," he said in a coy way. "Your dad's been bragging."

"Really?" I was surprised, because my father would barely talk to me on the phone and refused to see me or meet his one-and-only grandchild.

"He told me you're married, driving an S-class Mercedes, and living in a Beverly Hills mansion." He beamed. "And you have a baby girl."

I suddenly realized that the bragging that I'd heard about for years through the grapevine had nothing to do with my accomplishments. Dad was not proud of me. He was trying to make himself look good. He wanted high society to think he'd raised a winner. To his mind, I was still a failure. His fabrications were devised to enhance his own reputation, to fend off embarrassment and scandal.

"I do have a baby girl." I changed the topic to my book

and did not admit that the rest of Dad's tale was fictitious. I figured there was no point in setting the gossip train in motion and causing the truth about my semi-insolvent, out-of-wedlock life to get passed around Atlanta like a spoon of crack cocaine. Not only would the old-money crowd deem me a "loser of a daughter," but my dad would be viewed as a laughing stock and a liar.

My next conversation at the convention was with a woman named Jen. I'm pretty sure she stole my business cards.

Jen was an author and psychologist who sat at a booth adjacent to the Ross Books table. She was promoting a dating book and seemed bothered by the attention I was getting. Jen and I chatted, off and on, about the frivolous and superficial. "It's such a nice event." "You are wearing such a nice dress." "The cover of your book looks really nice." Everything was nice, nice, nice, or really nice.

During the course of the day, I was approached by three separate television producers, and Jen noticed. I could see the invisible steam coming out of her ears and the frown plastered under her fake smile. All three men handed me business cards and expressed an interest in turning my book into a TV movie. I was unsure why the content was unworthy of a theatrical release, but I was excited nonetheless. I stacked the three cards on the table next to a pile of my books and glanced at them lovingly from time to time.

At the end of the day when it was time to leave, they were gone. They were not on the table. They were not on the floor. They had vanished. Poof. It was then that I caught Jen eyeing me while pretending she wasn't, thus proving beyond a reasonable doubt that she was the thief.

"Have you seen the business cards that were on my table?" I asked her.

"Nope" was her reply.

Although I was upset with her, I was more upset with myself for failing to secure the cards in my purse. I could not recall the producers' names or the companies where they worked. My less-than-reliable memory was leaving me in the lurch. I went home feeling down. But within a week, I'd concocted a daring plan—a way to crawl out of the dumps.

※

Sheena babysat Kayla while I embarked upon my most brazen party-crashing scheme to date. I planned to sneak into the Emmys with hopes of meeting TV producers who could turn my book into a movie. I knew the address for the intimidating high-rise offices for the Academy of Television Arts and Sciences (the headquarters for the Emmys), and I knew the award show would be taped at the Pasadena Civic Auditorium on a particular date.

Unfortunately, I was a nobody. I lacked the prestige necessary to phone the Academy and reserve a seat. So I pretended to be a reporter, saying that I wanted to cover the event. I invented a nonexistent publication called *Creative News Magazine* for my press pass request.

"Skepticism" is the word that best described the reaction from the man on the other end of the phone line, and "We'll get back with you" were his dispiriting words.

For days, I answered my personal phone like a *Creative News Magazine* receptionist under the assumption that the Academy would deem me a fraud if I merely said, "Hello." I also learned from my friend Larry that those who were getting passes would be able to pick them up at the Academy's office on a particular Monday. Naturally, on the one occasion when I failed to answer the phone properly, a woman from the Academy called.

"Sorry, we won't be able to give you credentials. We have so many requests this year. We can't oblige everyone."

As the Rocky Balboa of the gate-crashing world, I was not about to throw in the towel. I shifted into tenacity mode and planned my scheme. I would pretend to be from the media outlet *Entertainment Tonight* and try to convince the Academy that I was there to pick up the show's press passes. I assumed the program would be on "the list" and that there would be no harm in the end because "approved" reporters would still be granted access even if I was able to confiscate their credentials.

On the proper day, I rode the elevator to the top of the intimidating high-rise, where there was a spectacular view of the city. I was entering the kingdom of the privileged, the castle of the celebrated, the throne of glamour and power. In the credential-granting chamber was a prim man in a suit and tie. Mr. Prim seemed proud of reigning over Emmy credentials. He scrutinized me when I entered the room.

I was nervous, but became less so when I noticed that sealed envelopes were stacked on a desk, and I could read the name printed on the envelope closest to me. I quickly scrapped my *Entertainment Tonight* plan.

"I'm here to pick up credentials." I feigned confidence.

"What's the name?" Mr. Prim asked.

"J. Adams," I repeated the name on the envelope.

"Oh, I tried to call this morning. Are you Janet Tompkins?"

Oh no, I thought. J. Adams is not some faceless entity. I imagined a ticking and a fatal boom. "No, I'm just a messenger." I tried to sound nonchalant. "I was just hired to pick up an envelope. I don't even know what it's for." Then I tried to divert Mr. Prim's attention to the window. "You have a great view. It must be nice working in this building."

Mr. Prim was a combination of doubt and desperation.

Although he didn't seem convinced that I was trustworthy, he was more preoccupied with finding that darned envelope.

"I can't remember what I put it under," he mumbled. "I didn't do it alphabetically." He plowed through the stack of credentials and seemed to be embarrassed about taking so long. I kept my eyes and the conversation focused on the view.

He was still riffling through the credentials when he asked me, "What company did you say you work for?" Panic set in, and I figured I'd better point out the elusive envelope rather than answer his question.

"Is this it?" I said in an innocent voice while pointing to the "J. Adams" envelope. I figured Mr. Prim would call me out as a charlatan now that he knew the name had been visible from the start.

"Yes, that's it." Mr. Prim stared at me suspiciously. "Hmm." He looked me up and down and then handed me a sign-out sheet. "All right. You need to put your signature here."

I signed with a fake name, and Mr. Prim reluctantly handed me the envelope. I left as quickly as possible. Inside the envelope was a general photo pass. It was numbered. I was worried that security would nab me at the show, so I only used it to finagle my way through the main door. Once inside, I dodged the press area and sat in the second row surrounded by Michael J. Fox, Ted Danson, Louis Gossett Jr., Joan Collins, and Tom Selleck. I even schmoozed backstage and sneaked into the after-party.

The bad news was: I didn't meet a producer who could turn my book into a movie. The good news was: I didn't get arrested or run into Mr. Prim.

Chapter Ten

DESPERATELY SEEKING SHARON

While at the mall, I spotted him. At least, I thought it was him. I crept down aisles and peered around clothing racks, secretly tailing Mall Man, determined to confirm his identity. When he exited into the parking lot, I followed, ducking behind a Subaru to stay inconspicuous. I waited for him to pinpoint his vehicle.

Did he have a Mercedes? That was the big question. Was this the dirty rotten scoundrel who had pilfered my seventeen bucks just after arriving in L.A.? Were Mall Man and Mercedes Man one and the same? If not, the resemblance was extraordinary. Both had straight blond hair, blue eyes, dimples, and a rounded jaw. Both wore designer clothes and had the same nose—long with a slight uptick like the graph of a rising stock.

I remembered the encounter six years prior. I had been window-shopping on Rodeo Drive when a man parked his Mercedes at the curb and approached me. Mercedes Man was not my type romantically speaking, but he had that pretty-boy, babe-magnet look that my gal pals would have liked. Maybe he thought I was loaded since I was browsing in L.A.'s high-rent district. Maybe he thought I was a wallflower in need of some gigolo love. Maybe he thought I was an easy mark.

Whatever the case, I mentioned that I was a newcomer in town, and he offered, "You need a tour guide." He suggested that we lunch at Canter's deli and then see the town. I accepted the invitation. I had always been open to making new friends and figured there was no harm in playing tourist, especially as I had just arrived in Los Angeles.

An hour later, we met at Canter's with its 1950s decor and waitresses in brown-and-yellow uniforms. After we ordered sandwiches, I excused myself to go to the restroom but left my purse at my seat. It was uncharacteristic for me to be so careless, and to this day I have no explanation for this lapse in judgment. When I returned to the table, I noticed that my pocketbook was still there, but Mercedes Man was gone.

"I think he left," a waitress whispered to me. "He cancelled the order."

"What?" I hurried onto the sidewalk, where I observed him in the distance scooting into his vehicle and zipping away. That is when it dawned on me to check my wallet, and I found that he had pilfered my cash—all seventeen bucks. Had he realized that I wasn't Richie Rich but was instead a down-and-out in Beverly Hills? Did he fear getting stuck with the lunch bill? Whatever the case, he had swiped a full 3 percent of my bank balance—money that he probably used to buy something trivial, such as fuzzy dice for his rearview mirror.

So, here it was six years later, and I was spying on this guy in the mall parking lot, determined to appease my curiosity. However, my thirst for answers went unquenched because Mall Man climbed into a BMW, not a Mercedes. I was left wondering whether he had bought a new car. Was there a connection between Mall Man, Mercedes Man, and BMW Man? The riddle has never been solved.

✥

It was Saturday at the Van Nuys house. Kayla was watching a movie: *The Great Mouse Detective*. I was in the breakfast room scarfing down a big salad and plotting the next move in the search for my natural mom. I was too exhausted to do anything more than make phone calls, because on the previous day I had been standing for ten hours as a greeter at the Los Angeles Convention Center. Luckily, I had not needed to be tall, pretty, or thin to be a greeter at this event. The job simply required smiling, looking presentable, and passing out pamphlets to visitors. The gig had earned me a much-needed $200.

My plotting and salad-eating segued into a ploy called the "county hustle." This involved phoning libraries in the states of Maryland, Georgia, and West Virginia and asking reference desk clerks to check the local phone books for people who went by "Moroose." I knew this was an unusual surname and figured my mom (Sharon Moroose) might be in one of those states because she'd given birth to me in Georgia, and the professor had told me that she'd lived in Maryland and West Virginia. I dialed and dialed. I asked and asked. I was placed on hold more frequently than blouses at Macy's. I spent hours speaking with over two dozen libraries until I achieved a partial victory.

A woman at the Marion County library in West Virginia told me that there was a "Moroose" in the phone book. I called the number, which turned out to belong to my cousin. He informed me that no one in the family knew the whereabouts of my mom; her twin sisters; or my grandmother, Ginger.

"They vanished in the late 1940s. No one has seen them since the murder."

"The murder?"

"Yeah. Your grandfather was murdered in 1948."

It turned out that my grandpa, Tucker Moroose, had been killed by a devil worshipper in what was described by newspapers as one of the most shocking incidents in West Virginia history. My cousin recounted the incredible tale and mailed me copies of detail-rich newspaper clippings. I spent weeks digesting the story about my grandpa and the killer. The section of this book called Bonus Story II offers a compressed version of the events, while my 2018 nonfiction novel *Devil in the Basement* details the full story.

&

A few months after learning about my grandpa, it was once again time to get serious about locating my birth mother. It felt as if I were stumbling down a dark corridor. Although I had clues about Sharon, I knew little apart from her height, her Italian heritage, and her age at my birth. She was five feet tall and had been twenty years old. Architecturally speaking, my birth father was an ivy-covered historical building. But what about Sharon? Was she a cute cottage, a swanky high-rise, or a trendy loft on the Lower East Side?

I got on the phone. My birth father had told me that her last known address was in Baltimore and that my grandmother, Ginger, had been a teacher. But the Baltimore County Board of Education had no record for Ginger, and a local Towson, Maryland, school where she had taught had only an outdated address, which they released to me. Ginger had been listed in the Baltimore phone book until 1964. I called neighbors and current residents of any property remotely associated with my mom, as well as nearby schools.

"Hi, I'm calling from California," I told stranger after stranger. "I'm adopted and looking for my birth mother."

Those who answered my call were receptive. They searched old records, talked to neighbors, and even made inquiries themselves. I had an army of little detectives in Maryland; Washington, DC; Virginia; and Georgia helping me with my mission.

At one point I placed an ad in the classified section of the *Towson Times,* which cost $13.22 for twenty-two weeks. I mentioned my mom's sisters because I figured twins would be memorable. I received no response.

Sharon had lived on Donegal Drive in Towson, Maryland. I had a pleasant but unenlightening conversation with the current owner, Mr. Kisner. My mom had lived on Stevenson Lane, Shadyside Road, and Twenty-Fifth Street in Baltimore and on Candler Street in Atlanta with my birth father. I was two steps behind her, but it felt like I was gaining momentum.

A common reply was, "Yes. She lived here," followed by, "I don't know where she is now."

From 1966 to 1967 there was a "Sharon Moroose" on N Street in Washington, DC, and on Second Road in Arlington, Virginia. I was inching further down that dark corridor and finding encouraging flickers of light.

A woman named Robyn Quinter from Brookeville, Maryland, was especially helpful, prying open the first locked door.

"Maybe she went to the University of Maryland," she said. "I'll check the yearbooks."

Days later, I received my first photo of Sharon in the mail. Her face was perfectly symmetrical, which is a sign of good looks according to experts who research beauty. Sharon looked like a young Elizabeth Taylor, but with brown eyes and fewer curls. Promo shots of the actress with Paul Newman from the 1958 movie *Cat on a Hot Tin Roof* convey a similar facial expression and vintage feel.

Robyn had found Sharon in the University of Maryland yearbook called the *Terrapin* as a 1962 graduate. In addition to the requisite senior shot, she was included in a Psychology Club group photo. I sent a letter to Leonard Adler, the student who stood beside her in the group shot, guessing he might be a friend. He wrote back saying he had no recollection of my mom.

I hit a wall when I called the university's alumni association. They had no updated file for Sharon or her twin sisters. The secretary could tell me only that she had received a "social dismissal from college" in December 1959 when she was pregnant with me. She had withdrawn from classes "with good academic standing" and had graduated later.

I had already checked with the alumni office for Towson High School and found nothing. But as a last-ditch effort, I telephoned the school's main office to see if Ginger had been an instructor.

"I'm calling to find out about a possible former teacher who went by the name of Ginger Moroose or Ginger Morris," I told an office assistant.

"Moroose?" she asked.

"Yes."

"Just a moment, please." The assistant sounded secretive and hesitant and put me on hold. "Why are you looking for her?" she inquired when she got back on the line.

"I'm trying to find my birth mother, Sharon," I explained. "Sharon is Ginger's daughter."

The assistant placed me on hold again, then returned a minute later. "The Moroose daughters went to this school.

We're in touch with Sheila Moroose. I'll give her a call and tell her to contact you."

Persistence was the torch that had lit the dark corridor. Although I was elated, I was also nervous because I did not know whether my mother would be receptive to a meeting. I also did not know whether our reunion would be a positive experience if we were to meet. Research was on my side. Ninety percent of the reconciliations between natural mothers and their children are good.[14]

My aunt, Sheila Moroose—who had since married and went by a different surname—telephoned ten minutes later and suggested a family "meet and greet" at Ginger's house in Florida. The timing was excellent because my *Meet the Stars* publicity tour was taking me to the East Coast. I could easily coordinate my schedule to see my mom. Barring a disaster or change of heart, all was set for a spring reunion. It looked as if it could be a rebirth of sorts.

※

I was at a television studio, doing an interview on *Meet the Stars*. This was part of my nationwide book tour. I had been traveling from city to city, appearing on local television shows where I would give party-crashing advice, tell about humorous celebrity escapades, and encourage people to pursue their dreams.

During this particular interview, the host asked, "Did you ever fail to get into an event?"

"No," I replied. "But once I had a problem getting *out* of an event."

This prompted laughter from the studio audience, and I delved into a funny experience that I'd had with the flamboyant master pianist Liberace, who, according to Wikipedia, was the highest paid entertainer in the world from the 1950s through the 1970s.

I first met Liberace—who went by "Lee"—at the Sunrise Musical Theatre in Fort Lauderdale when I was a student at the University of Florida in the late 1970s. This was the same venue and dressing room where I'd had my first date with Tom Jones. Getting to know Lee and his friends was easy. I just appeared backstage and was quickly welcomed into their circle. Seymour Heller was Lee's manager, and Scott Thorson was his chauffeur and boyfriend. Terry Clarkston was Lee's personal assistant; he was always reattaching sequins to the entertainer's glittery stage attire. A couple of years later, I beaded a gift for Lee's birthday: a rhinestone jockstrap in the shape of a piano.

"The perfect gift for the man who has everything," Liberace exclaimed with a full and gracious smile.

Liberace would go to lengths for a friend. He enjoyed being a perfect party host and showing off the extravagant one-of-a-kind furnishings and accoutrements at his home. Like me, he was a Taurus, so we shared that illogical bond that two people have when they share the same astrological sign.

Lee invited me to a party at his Las Vegas estate, and I asked my friend "Pirate Pete" to be my escort. Although Pete had no parrot or eye patch, his friends had informally christened him with this seafaring title because he barreled his red Porsche down the freeway at over 100 miles per hour as if he were Blackbeard on the high sea.

"The government watches me," Pete said. "I am part of a select group of fast drivers. They let me speed because they want to see if I will slow down on my own. I have never gotten a ticket in all these years."

Although I did not normally believe in conspiracy theories, I did not know Pete to be a liar or a mental case. It sounded preposterous, but maybe his tale about a "secret test group" was true.

Pete was good looking, but I'd never had any interest in

him. As I often did with celebrities and other male friends (such as Gary), I set him up on blind dates. I enjoyed playing matchmaker, plus it was a way to stay on friendly terms with famous men who'd expressed an interest in me. When they'd ask for a date, I'd counteroffer.

"Sorry, I can't go out with you, but I know this really pretty girl..."

Their eyes would get big, and their grin would get wide. Of course, the situation was win-win-win. I was also doing a favor for the girl. Most women would jump at the chance to go out with a star. Being a millionaire matchmaker gave me control and staying power with otherwise inaccessible people. Although Pirate Pete was no star, he claimed to want a steady girlfriend, and I regularly offered to help.

On that festive night, Pete and I entered Liberace's six-foot-tall iron gates and then his lavish home. That is when we learned that this was not just a "people party." It was also a "poodle party." Some guests had been encouraged to bring their dogs. Canines flaunted their finery: bright-colored bows and bedazzled collars. Liberace's own pups were regal and refined. One would expect no less from Mr. Showmanship's "children."

Lee wore a dramatic, ground-length white coat and gave the guests a grand tour of the place, including the master closet, which was frankly inadequate. Clothes were smashed together and suffocating. It looked like an overstuffed mailbox.

After dinner, drinks, and conversation, some guests headed home. The pirate and I decided to leave.

"Thanks for having us." I gave Lee a hug.

"So glad you could come." The entertainer smiled and closed the front door.

Pete and I negotiated the front walkway just fine, but when we reached the iron gate, it seemed to be locked. At the very least, it was much too complicated to open. Pete suggested I ring the bell and ask Lee for help getting out, but I was too embarrassed.

"We've already left. We can't go back. It would make us look stupid."

We fumbled with the gate for ten minutes without success. It simply would not open.

"I think we should knock," Pete repeated.

"We've been out here for ten minutes. What are you going to say we've been doing?"

I hiked up my cocktail dress and positioned my foot on the bottom rung of the fence.

"You're gonna climb? Are you crazy?" Pete was shocked but boosted himself up alongside me. We went over the top of the fence.

Just as we landed on the sidewalk, the sound of police sirens flooded the street. We had set off a silent alarm. We dashed behind a neighbor's shrub. Two cop cars screeched to a halt and exited their vehicles. Liberace opened the front door with a puzzled expression.

"Your alarm went off," one officer said. "Is there a problem?"

"No," Lee said. "No problem. I don't understand how that could have happened."

After the cops left, we sprinted to our car. I was relieved that we didn't get caught. I'd hate to do time for "breaking and exiting." *Meet the Stars* said nothing about crashing *out* of celebrity events, but it turns out I'm an expert on this as well.

✎

"We're getting a divorce if you ever meet her," Sharon's husband, Ricky, stormed out of their Washington D.C. area home after she told him about my phone call with Aunt Sheila.

Ricky was fourteen years younger than Sharon, which put

him only six years older than me. Perhaps this accounted for his discomfort and upset. My birth mom had been married twice before Ricky, including the short-lived union with my birth dad. She had never mentioned having a baby and had no other children.

Sheila called to tell me about the blowup but concluded the conversation with, "We're all still getting together, right?"

"Yes. And I'm bringing my daughter, Kayla, as well."

"Oh, good," she bubbled.

I felt bad for putting a strain on my mom's marriage. I assumed the meeting was still "on" for two reasons: because Sharon was curious to meet me and because once the volcano had erupted, it was impossible to ladle the lava back into its throat.

A month later, it was time to meet Sharon. I finished a *Meet the Stars* interview in Miami and drove to Ginger's place in Punta Gorda, Florida.

Ginger's house on Macedonia Drive looked like a lemon drop in a community that some might call cookie cutter. I parked my rental car near her one-story residence, which had the same facade as the other lemon drops on the block. I wondered how these tract homes, which probably had hurricane truss straps and other state-of-the-art upgrades, fared in the winds of 100 miles per hour that can whip through the state.

On the front porch, five grins tumbled my way. Aunt Sheila, whom I had spoken with on the phone, wore a baseball jersey and an athletic look. She was in her forties, taught aerobics part-time, and had a husband and two kids. Sheila was the extroverted half of the fraternal twin duo, lots of fun, and best represented by the color bright orange.

The introverted twin, Aunt Shirley, was a pastel palette. Home was where her heart was. She was married with two kids and keen on cooking but not conscientious about staying in shape. Her daughter, Julia, who stood next to her mom, was an explosion of curly hair. Each ringlet looked like a 1950s phone cord. She was a few years younger than me and as mellow as her mom.

Ginger was hot pink like a party dress. Although she was slightly overweight, she had blue eyes, a lovely face, and perfect posture. She insisted that I call her "Grandginger" instead of "grandmother." She was similar to me in that she loved feminine and showy clothes, ornate furniture, and eccentricity, but she was dissimilar in that she had no interest in philosophy, politics, or the news. She was creative and an expert at clothing design, china painting, and ballroom dancing. She had once been recognized as the Mother of the Year by the governor of Maryland and had traveled around the world.

My birth mother, Sharon —who was thin with shoulder-length dark curls—was pine green like a lush forest of animal sounds. An earthy, practical, and outdoorsy woman, she enjoyed camping, canoeing, and planting flowers in her half-acre backyard. She was an environmentalist and as fascinated with politics and current events as the *New York Times*. Howard Stern's radio show reverberated through her BMW each morning during her one-hour drive to her job, where she assisted the elderly as a county social worker. Baby Lady was right. Sharon was not overly emotional. Matters were to be handled matter-of-factly. Sharon was a lot like me: She preferred problem solving rather than being gushy, touchy-feely, or weepy.

Hugs and hellos were followed by a tour of Ginger's home. In the kitchen, Kayla and I were introduced to Ollie, a red-headed parrot who was nibbling on a seed. He was oblivious to the excitement of the reunion. A financial show was airing on a toaster-sized television. My mother was a conservative investor but always curious about the latest industry advice.

"I love this program." Sharon galloped up to the TV and

broke into what looked like a dance. She jumped up and down and flicked her hands as if she had water on them. It was an odd sight. She looked like a little girl who had gotten a new toy. Apparently, this funny-looking jig was routine whenever Sharon got excited. (My daughter claims I do something quite similar, but I have no idea what she is talking about.)

During the weeklong stay, I learned my slight shoulder hunch was inherited. Sharon had the same problem. Like me, those in my birth family were big cereal eaters, board game players, dancers, and athletes. I also learned that my birth mother and I had ventured down the same religious path: We were both raised Christian, then attended a Unitarian church for a short time, and later converted to Reform Judaism. In more recent years, I have made Jainism a part of my religious journey, although my mother has not.

There seemed to be distinct links between my beliefs and interests and those of my natural family, and twin studies provide evidence for this perception. In Chapter 19 of *The Blank Slate*, Steven Pinker argues that traits—such as political leanings, personal philosophy, intelligence, and personality—are largely heritable.

Sharon did not own a fur coat. Although she was not an animal rights activist, she was not opposed to the ideology, and like the professor, she ate little meat.

I wanted to know more, so I peppered Ginger with questions, beginning with, "Where did you go after my grandpa, Tucker, died?"

She told me that she moved to Baltimore and that she cried every night for two years after Tucker's murder. She had been dealt an unlucky spade but vowed to turn that card into a diamond. It took her sixteen months to earn a bachelor's certificate and teaching credentials. She was not interested in education, but it was the only job that would permit her to care for three small girls. A few years later, she completed her master's degree in education at John Hopkins University.

She said, "The day we moved to Maryland, I told my girls, 'Don't tell anyone your father was Italian.'" Ginger did not want her children to face the discrimination that their dad had encountered. She wanted to build their new life from an aristocratic foundation. She emphasized her maiden name "Morris," and her upper-class ancestor, the distinguished Robert Morris Jr., who lived from 1734 until 1806. He had been a Pennsylvania senator as well as one of the signers of the Declaration of Independence, the Articles of Confederation, and the United States Constitution. Along with Alexander Hamilton and Albert Gallatin, he is said to have founded the U.S. financial system, and his portrait appeared on $1,000 notes in 1862. Morrisville, Pennsylvania, is named after him.

Ginger had many suitors and married several times after Tucker's death, although the unions were bumpy and brief. A man named Lee was Ginger's husband for twelve months, and Bill assumed the role for two years. She was engaged to an artist named Henry, who died of cancer. Then there was husband Chris, a chiropractor who saw clients in a back guest unit at their property in Denton, Maryland. Ginger had become a self-sufficient lady and had bought the place prior to the relationship. She had thrown weddings for my mom and Aunt Sheila in the backyard.

One afternoon, Ginger drove up the 150-foot driveway of the Denton home, which was lined with rows of irises stretching toward the sun. She parked. From the trunk of her car, she extracted a heavy bucket filled with mother-of-pearl buttons. The manager at the button factory down the street always had leftovers and defectives and gave them to Ginger for her driveway. Pebbles were plebian, she thought. But 150 feet of shiny buttons was utterly majestic. She emptied the bucket into an area that seemed a little thin and then grabbed her Lord & Taylor shopping bag, also in the trunk, and went into the house.

She could tell that her husband, Chris, had not left, and this infuriated her. He was supposed to gather his things and be out by noon. Her attorney would be serving him with divorce papers on the following day. He had cheated on her with some lady friend, and she did not want to see his curly brown hair or bushy mustache again. She had contributed to the problems in the marriage by being bossy and disagreeable, but she saw the breakup as entirely his fault.

She put a pot of soup on the stove and moved up the wooden plank staircase to her pink master bedroom. She glided past her canopy bed and her antique spinning wheel and into her closet, which looked nothing like Liberace's. Everything was organized to perfection and color-coordinated. It resembled my massive closet today, except Ginger had safety-pinned labels to each garment, listing the accessories that matched. Ginger took off her olive-colored jacket and hung it in the green section of the closet and then went back downstairs and relaxed in an antique parlor chair adjacent to the organ in her living room.

Ginger's two Siberian Huskies sat at her feet. She opened the lid to her sewing basket and pulled out plastic containers of sequins and beads. Then she did something I had done many times prior to meeting my birth family: She redesigned a brand-new designer outfit. From the Lord & Taylor bag, she pulled out an expensive dress with tags still attached. In her view, it needed ornamentation on the bodice. She stitched and beaded, confident that she could make a more beautiful garment than any French designer. She had done it many times before.

"You're home." Chris leaned against the doorway next to a china plate hanging on the wall.

"What are you still doing here?" Ginger said, barely

glancing up from her sewing. "And don't break that plate. I painted it."

Belongings occupied Ginger's thoughts, especially as she aged. Perhaps it was because objects beautified her world. They provided a getaway from an otherwise ordinary existence. But my best guess is that Ginger equated possessions with memories. Each item was chosen carefully, or created by her, and to relinquish it meant relinquishing a part of herself. That is how I feel as well. Just as members of Ginger's family felt she was too concerned with "things," I get the same criticism. I cannot bear to throw away things, partly because it seems ill-advised to do so. Many have "saved the day" years later. But largely my reluctance has to do with the fact that each item has special meaning and was chosen or created by me. I have many of Grandginger's outfits, plus vintage clothing from other female relatives. I cherish them all. When I buy things, I don't toss them into a shopping cart without thought. I put love into each purchase. I say to myself, "Does this go with my essence?" To surrender it later means I am discarding a chunk of myself.[15]

"I'm leaving now," Chris said. "My bags are already in the car."

"Good," Ginger replied. She didn't glance up from her beading, because infidelity was an unpardonable sin.

Chris left and married his lady friend. He died of a stroke two years later.

Ginger was like the ingredients in a kitchen cupboard. She was a mixture of bitter and sweet. She was wildly creative but often overly concerned with appearance and status. She could be hysterically funny, but she had little interest in the world outside her home, despite having traveled extensively. She was a self-starter and survivor but could also be preoccupied with possessions. She was the life of the party, was an excellent hostess, and could cook like a chef. But she had no interest in animal rights.

※

After Ginger told me about herself, I asked my birth mother to tell me about her relationship with the professor and how I came to be put up for adoption.

Sharon told me that she'd met my birth father at the University Baptist Church in Baltimore on Easter Sunday in 1958. Sharon was in her late teens, studying at the University of Maryland, and the professor was in his early twenties, attending John Hopkins University. They courted, despite the fact that they had no money for restaurants or movie theatres. They put marriage talk on simmer due to their starving student status. The professor wore tired blue-and-white-striped slacks, diluted his grape juice with water to save funds, tinkered under the hood of his twenty-year-old vehicle to keep it running, and was Mr. Let's Make a Deal. He loved locating underpriced books and other "finds" at thrift shops around town. He and I were similar in this respect.

"I'll put this vacuum cleaner together to see if it works," Sharon said one afternoon at the Salvation Army.

"No. I want to get it for five bucks. I don't want them to think it works," he replied, letting his smart talent kick into gear.

Afterward, they rode the street car back to his apartment on York Avenue with the newly acquired five-dollar Hoover.

When Sharon got pregnant, my birth dad's world shattered. He had committed what he viewed as an unpardonable sin: engaging in sex before marriage. He didn't want anyone to know that he had failed to live up to the moral and religious absolutes that he saw as the anchors of his life. They were his most treasured possessions. They had important meaning for him, just as pretty dresses and household objects were priceless to Ginger. The professor felt that losing his grasp on absolutes would leave him in a void, in shreds, in a subjective and relative world without God.

The world he dreaded was becoming Sharon's world. She had come to believe Christianity was a myth, and she had joined a Unitarian church. She was a postmodern before postmodernism was "in." Her acceptance of relativism and subjectivism ripped at the very fiber of the professor's soul. He was an ascetic, while she was into this-worldliness. He clung to personal guilt and self-flagellation, while she was into pragmatics and being lighthearted. Every time he lowered the moral anchor into the water, she yanked it out. Their relationship was a perpetual push and pull, a tug-of-war over philosophy, morality, and religion.

The professor rarely spoke of his childhood, which he called "disastrous." It was like sliding sand under his feet, and it is probably what propelled him toward revered absolutes. He never introduced Sharon to family or friends. She was a secret. The professor agreed to marry her under two conditions: She could not tell anyone about the marriage or pregnancy, and she had to consent to putting me up for adoption. She went along with his plan, thinking he would change his mind. He didn't.

Sharon and the professor were married by a justice of the peace on October 30, 1959, in DeKalb County, Georgia. This was seven and a half months prior to my birth. They moved into a private apartment in the back of a house on Candler Street in Atlanta. It had a sun porch. After I was born in their car in the hospital parking lot, Sharon and the professor remained married for over a year, although they lived apart most of that time. Sharon went back to the University of Maryland to finish her degree. Eventually, at his urging, they divorced. They could no longer build castles in the sand. Their relationship had become an ever-dimming light: murky, helpless, and broken.

Sharon met another guy and became engaged. This depressed my birth dad enormously. Although he could not live with Sharon, he could not live without her. He experienced nightmares when she was with him, but he was similarly tormented when they were apart. His life was a turbulent Catch-22.

The professor perceived morality as a reassuring anchor in his life, but this was an illusion. It had been a cumbersome and heavy slab of sharp metal. It weighed him down. It sliced through him. It was the reason he made Sharon into a scapegoat for getting pregnant, and it was the reason he felt anger and blame toward himself. It was the reason he thrashed his very being with shame, stigma, and culpability in a skunk world of black and white, or good versus evil. Worshipping "morality" had become a burdensome ritual in his life.

After Sharon told me the story, I thought about the irony. I subscribed to philosophical determinism (a metaphysic that left no room for moral truths), and I had spent years talking about the damage that moral absolutes do to the self and society. Unlike my birth father, I had a love for the subjective, for the relative, and for that which is of "this world."

I was the new Sharon.

※

I left Ginger's house feeling content. There was satisfaction in knowing Sharon and the professor. I had been searching for family all my life, first co-opting high school teachers to be stand-ins and then reaching out to entertainer friends. If I could not be raised by folks who loved me, my plan at an early age was to seek substitutes. Rebels do not sit in the corner and let life pound them to the ground. Rebels jump up, dust themselves off, and run. They are active, always persisting toward their dream, and finding family had been an important goal from the start.

In addition to my connection with Sharon and the professor, I felt close to my other natural kin. I was bombarded by "aha" moments. Through these revelations, I gained a better understanding of myself. I came to believe that nature outweighs nurture. Grandginger was a case in point. We shared the same unusual hobby: attaching beads and sequins to brand-new department store clothes. Plus, we had similar color-coordinated closets, and we owned identical pieces of rare carved furniture—items that I've never seen elsewhere. The limited-edition, carved claw-foot desk in my living room was identical to a desk in Ginger's guest room. These examples may seem trivial, but they were significant enough to shake me away from my adoptive dad's mind-set that children are born as a blank slate.

The last "birth family" hurdle revolved around meeting my real half brother and half sister (the professor's children), who did not yet know of my existence. I hoped someday to meet them, but I knew there were no guarantees.

※

After seeing Sharon, Grandginger, and my other relatives in Florida, Kayla and I stopped in Atlanta so I could appear on a local morning show and do a book signing at the mall. Then we dropped by my old high school, Lovett, where we ran into my former biology teacher, Carolyn. I told her that I'd meant to say something for years about dissection in the classroom and how it was unnecessary. She brushed off my words with "Your daughter's cute. It's nice to see you, but I'm in a rush." She hurried away.

My least positive high school experiences were in Carolyn's classroom, not because of her but because of dissection. I was not an animal advocate at the time, but I thought the requirement to cut open dead creatures was disgusting and unproductive. I remember wax trays, pushpins, forceps, scissors, section lifters, frogs, and worms. I refused to engage in the ghastly exercises, but I never got reprimanded, because Carolyn never knew about my lack of participation and how I sneaked out of the room when the smell of formaldehyde filled the air. Students were always split into groups for these projects, and my teammates never complained about doing my work in addition to their own.

"Sorry. I'm not doing this," I'd say to my group, and then head for the girls' restroom, where I would read until the end of class.

When I had not yet managed to duck out of the room, I would see students throwing dead animals at each other and giggling. The goal of one particular game was to heave the long, white worms—which looked like spaghetti noodles—against the windows and try to get them to stick. No student gained an ounce of knowledge from the experiments. It was a waste of time and of lives. Although Lovett was a Christian school with ethics classes, there was never any discussion about these poor creatures. Students were being indoctrinated with a blatant irreverence for life.[16]

꼬

After leaving Lovett, Kayla and I dropped by my former childhood home on River North Parkway. The place gave me a chill. I remembered how bad things had happened there. There was Mom's (attempted) suicide, the stolen horses, and the deaths of my dog and my brother. But that was only the beginning. The neighbor across the street told me that the calamities continued long after our family had gone. The next resident was a young dentist who died from a heart attack. His wife and three kids promptly moved. Then there was a creepy attorney and his wife who hated animals. They complained about barking and cut the vocal chords of their own pups. After they left, a painter found a dead cat in the freezer. A nonprofit bought the house and rented it to a psychiatrist who was accused of having an affair with a patient. The authorities came after the man, and he fled. The nonprofit lost the home in foreclosure, and the property became dilapidated. It lolled around untouched and unoccupied for well over a year.

That is when Kayla and I warily approached it again. The house was vacant and for sale. I got the lockbox code from the real estate broker. There was no power. I darted from room to room as if I were being chased by a ghost, and I avoided the pitch-black basement, where my father's radio room had been situated.

I telephoned Dad afterward to tell him that the house was up for sale.

"Maybe I should buy it again," he suggested.

"Absolutely not!" I did not tell him about the suspected curse on the place.

"How's your face?" he asked out of the blue.

"My face?"

"Yeah. You were disfigured when you were twenty."

"What are you talking about? I've never been disfigured."

"You had a big, ugly spot on your face. I had it surgically removed. Don't you remember?"

"No." I was unsure whether my father had dementia or whether I did. "I was not disfigured, Dad. I was dating Tom then. Plus, there are lots of photos of me at that age."

"What about your chest? Did you ever get it reduced? You've never looked classy."

"No," I replied. My father had nagged me since my teens about getting my breasts trimmed down to a more "sophisticated" size.

"Okay. Is that it?" He seemed anxious to get off the phone.

"Wait. Before you hang up, I need to talk to you about something. Maybe I could drop by?"

"Nope. Too busy."

I wanted to tell him about finding my natural family, because a reporter was doing a story about me and I'd agreed to discuss the birth parent issue. I wanted to be honest with Dad before he read about my *other* dad in an article. I figured he'd be upset. Dad had made it clear that he never wanted me to search for my biological family, and he had always insisted that the records were destroyed.

"I didn't want to tell you on the phone, but I recently got in touch with my biological parents."

"You found the wrong people."

We never discussed the issue again.

Chapter Eleven

THE WIFE RÉSUMÉ

My husband didn't need to be bald. He could have a few well-placed tufts or be as hairy as Cousin Itt of the Addams Family. He didn't have to be a particular weight. He could look like a pencil or a pomegranate. He wasn't required to be a certain height. He could be the size of a large midget or a small dinosaur. There was likewise no prerequisite for big muscles, high cheekbones, perfect teeth, or ocean-blue eyes. And he didn't need to dress like Pierce Brosnan.

In other words, external attributes were not on the list of must-haves, other than the fact that this guy had to have a handsome face. Of course, his face didn't have to be handsome to Laura, Sheena, or Angelina Jolie—just me. Plus, my perfect man had to be intellectual, funny, kindhearted, stable, and responsible, and he had to adore children and animals. I didn't think my demands were too high, but my girlfriends thought I was too picky and would never get married. They said I had a better chance of falling into a black hole. They also criticized my rejection of the time-honored game of "guy chases gal" and added that my need to be the "chooser" was akin to enlisting in the old maid's club.

"You're too assertive and too up-front with your feelings," Laura said. "You're going to die alone."

"The male is wired to be the trapper," Sheena argued. "You're supposed to be the fox."

Lynn chimed in. "You're supposed to be feminine and demure. You're not following the rules."

To my mind, this was sexism and conformity, pure and simple. It put a sour taste in my mouth and ignited my inner rebel. On the other hand, I figured there was a fifty-fifty chance that my girlfriends were right. I might end up a spinster.

෴

Ms. Fooker looked like a circus freak. She was an alcoholic and chain-smoker. She was disheveled and wore a flat, pink sandal on her left foot and a three-inch-high black pump on her right one. She wobbled like an off-balance washing machine. Ms. Fooker was Lynn—my former roommate who had survived the middle-of-the-night Mack attack with me—and she was playing an April Fool's Day prank on James.

James was the man to whom I would eventually propose marriage. He was the vice president of Proficiency, the private investigation firm where I worked in 1988 and 1989. I was enamored the second we met, largely due to his magnificent wit and adorable personality, although he was no slacker in the looks department.

On the first day of work, an executive named Dale introduced me to the crew, including James. I'd been recommended for employment by a former high school friend who worked at an insurance firm in Virginia. Her company commissioned Proficiency for investigative work.

As a private detective, my job was to examine insurance claims. I interviewed claimants as well as neighbors and doctors. I obtained medical records and pharmacy paperwork, and I wrote reports. The position was flexible timewise, which was advantageous for spending time with Kayla, for taking classes, and for promoting *Meet the Stars*.

"James hasn't had a date in ten years," Dale told me that first day while unwinding in the lunch room with coworkers.

"Really?" I said with subdued glee, not wanting to reveal my attraction for James.

Although everyone laughed at Dale's remark, I assumed it was a reflection of the jovial nature of the office. Employees loved kidding around. I left the lunch room thinking it would be a cinch to make James my boyfriend. Boy, was I wrong.

It turned out James had a girlfriend. He'd been dating her for years. She was older than him, was not interested in commitment, and had once worked as his secretary. She had a beefy build and short brown hair. She was cautious and conservative.

James claimed to be cautious and conservative, too, although he came off as spontaneous. He played golf and wore what he called a "nerd string" to hold his glasses in place around his neck. He was obsessed with peanut butter, always voted Republican, and resided in a modest home in a blue-collar Orange County neighborhood. James was Mr. Popular, and I could visualize him two decades earlier gliding around Notre Dame University (where he had gone to school) in a letterman jacket, although he was much lankier than your average football jock. He was from the Midwest and forty-four years old. I was twenty-eight at the time.

He was divorced. When his wife cheated and became

pregnant from an affair, James divorced her but took in the other man's child. He loved kids and felt the boy needed stability. His ex-wife was irresponsible and gladly relinquished custody. James was also raising a daughter whom he and the ex-wife had adopted while married.

Apart from being a single dad, James supported the traditional male-female roles in a relationship. He felt the man should be the aggressor. Although it came off as tongue-in-cheek, he routinely pretended to be Anne Landers, instructing me on how the romance game is played.

"You need to let the guy chase you," he advised. "You can't be so assertive with me. Now, when I ask you out, what do you say?"

"Yes?" I feigned ignorance.

"No. You tell me you are busy." He chuckled. "You are supposed to play hard to get."

"Oh, okay, I'm busy," I replied. "But when can we go out?"

James knew I was in love with him, as did everyone in the office, and he seemed to like it. He and I lunched together regularly and hung out in his office chatting for hours.

Proficiency was located in an industrial area on Bandini Boulevard in Commerce, California, which is halfway between downtown L.A. and Orange County. The offices consisted of cheap paneling; metal windows; and commercial-grade, gray carpeting. They were positioned around a center courtyard that had patches of grass and a leafless tree. By joining Proficiency and chasing after a relationship with James, I had embarked upon the middle-class phase of my life. I don't mean this in a pejorative way, but it was quite different from living hand-to-mouth or from spending time with old-money Atlantans and new-money celebrities, such as Tom.

Ms. Fooker's hair resembled a dirty mop, and her blouse looked like a wrinkled tablecloth. She had come to the office at my request. I still enjoyed concocting outlandish surprises for the men in my life. This was sixteen years prior to the *Meet the Fockers* movie, but the screenwriter and I were obviously of like mind. Everyone at Proficiency, except James, knew about the April Fool's Day prank.

Lynn had telephoned weeks earlier, pretending to be Ms. Fooker, a prospective client who would be visiting Los Angeles. She'd said her firm was looking to hire investigators, and she'd arranged a day to meet with James, which happened to fall on April first.

"Ms. Zucker, so glad you could make it." James immediately confused her name when she walked through the door.

"It's *Fooker*." Lynn was wholly convincing as a whack job. She'd been trained as an actress and had appeared in several movies. "Say it. *Fooker, Fooker, Fooker*."

James was taken aback but escorted her into his private office and closed the door. This was the signal for office employees to congregate, placing their ears against the wall in an effort to hear the hoax unravel.

As Lynn rattled on and on about her nonexistent firm in New York, her hands began to shake.

"Do you mind if I smoke?" she asked.

"Not at all," James replied. "Do you want an ashtray?"

"I brought my own." Lynn plowed through her purse—dumping most of the contents onto James's desk—until she found an extra fat cigar, a lighter, and an ashtray.

Lynn's shaking turned into full-body convulsions. James asked if she was okay. She snapped at him that she was fine. James was like a Boy Scout on a mission. He wanted to help this rattled woman and win the contract with her firm. At the same time, it was hard for him to choke down his chuckles. The whole thing seemed so outrageous.

"Do you want me to light your cigar?" James asked.

"Sure," she said.

James held the flame within reach, but Lynn's hand was so jittery that she failed to connect with it. "That's good," she replied, even though the cigar was not lit. She pulled the cigar in and out of her mouth pretending to smoke like kids used to do in the days when tobacco was cool. Periodically, she would feign a deep inhale and blow nonexistent smoke in James's direction.

"Maybe you need something cool to drink?" James was worried about her, plus he was hoping to finagle his way out of the room. He stood, ready to fetch her a beverage.

"No!" Lynn barked.

Once James settled back down in his chair, Lynn asked, "Do you mind if I have something to drink?"

Like a Pop-Tart in a toaster, he jumped up a second time. "Sure, we have coffee, water… What would you like?"

"I brought my own." Lynn plucked an airline-sized bottle of Vodka from her purse and downed it. It was actually water.

James settled at his desk again.

"You know, I'm a nervous wreck." Lynn grabbed a newspaper resting on James's desk and hurled it at him. "And did you see today's paper? My motto is 'You never miss the train.' That boy got hit by a train."

James was baffled and contemplating how he could gracefully pull the plug on this crackpot and eject her from his office.

"Oh, my gosh. It's getting really hot in here." Lynn started unbuttoning her blouse. James panicked.

"Dale. Dale. Could you come in here right now?" James shouted through the wall.

Dale was snickering with the rest of us and did not come to his aid.

"Dale? Somebody help me." James bolted from the office only to realize it was all a gag. He loved it.

Lynn emerged and did a striptease down to a granny bra and girdle. It looked like a getup from the vaudeville stage. I snapped multiple photos, in particular getting a shot in which James pretended to spank Lynn. A month later, I would have sneaky plans for this embarrassing photo.

*

A month later, I slithered into a camera shop and positioned the framed photo of James pretending to spank Ms. Fooker on the checkout counter. Then I crept back to Proficiency.

James received a mysterious package that morning from a man in a trench coat. I had given this guy a few bucks to play secret agent. He worked at a business in the neighborhood.

Puzzled, James opened the package to find a tape recorder, a tiny pink paper bag, and pair of red-heart sunglasses. He immediately listened to the cassette in the recorder. *Mission: Impossible* music filled the room, and my voice boomed from the device with the same inflections and gravity as the off-screen character from the TV series.

"Hello, James. Your mission, if you choose to accept it, is to find your birthday present. But first you must locate Freddie the Flasher, an exhibitionist of lengthy proportions."

The instructions were complicated. James learned how the devilish Dr. Dastardly would be using stealth bombers and slingshots in an effort to obstruct him from finding Freddie. To go undetected, James would have to wear the enclosed pair of goofy red-heart sunglasses. Plus, he would have to lug around the child-sized pink paper bag. After James located Freddie, he could remove the sunglasses, letting everyone know that he had singlehandedly saved the world. James had to be available on two dates for the mission: that day (May 11) during lunch and again on Saturday, May 14. at seven p.m.

"At noon today, your mission will take you to the Steven's Steakhouse pay phone, where your contact will call you with further instructions. You will also receive your first piece of the puzzle, which will be taped to the wall."

The final words were, "Good luck, James, and beware of Dr. Dastardly. This tape will self-destruct in five seconds."

I had concocted this outlandish scheme to celebrate James's birthday, which fell on the same day as mine: May 11.

James recruited me as his assistant gumshoe. He donned the silly sunglasses, and we drove to the phone booth at noon. The phone rang and Lynn—who disguised her voice—told him to go to the Commerce library and flip to page fifty of the children's book *The Dastardly Murder of Dirty Pete* by Eth Clifford.

A slip of paper in the book led us to the camera shop on Jillson Street, where he found the photo of his hand, reared back and ready to slap the scantily clad Ms. Fooker on her buttocks.

"Oh no!" He laughed, snatching the picture from the counter so customers would not see it.

Inside the picture frame, a paper revealed that there was an envelope waiting for him in the lost and found at the Commerce post office.

James and I zigzagged all over town, accumulating clues. One was hidden in a newsstand on Commerce Way. We found others under the seat of his car, in the lunch room popcorn machine, and inside a phone book under *M* for "Mission." The final clue of the day instructed James to wait on Saturday outside an informal sandwich shop called Millie's Country Kitchen in Anaheim. He was told to be appropriately dressed for dinner, to wear his "love" shades, and to bring his pink sack.

The puzzle pieces did not make sense to James. They were scraps of paper bearing medical terms for muscles and body parts, such as *rhomboideus major, teres minor, intercostales, infraspinatus*, and *spinalis thoracis*. When arranged properly at the end of the mission, they would reveal a simple message: that James was entitled to a thirty-minute back rub from me.

Saturday night came. Drivers stared at James as he waited at the curb outside Millie's Country Kitchen, which was down the street from Disneyland. He was becoming a popular tourist attraction in his fancy coat and tie and his not-so-fancy heart-shaped sunglasses and tiny pink sack. He looked a little like Freddie the flasher himself.

The white stretch limousine that I had commissioned appeared. The chauffer drove James to a 7-Eleven in a downscale part of Santa Ana and instructed him to buy a *Recycler* newspaper and to check the last page of the classifieds section for his clue.

The ad read, "Special Agent James. Go to the Las Brisas restaurant in Laguna Beach. Your final contact will meet you there."

I was naturally his final contact and hoped to be his final wife. I had preordered his favorite drink: Diet Rite cola. Plus, I had given the waitress a plastic Easter egg to float on top of his drink. Inside it was the last clue, which told him to contact the "attractive couple in the bar," who would tell him where to find "America's Most Wanted Flasher."

James arrived in the limo, received his drink, and walked over to the bar to find me—dressed in a sexy beaded cocktail dress—with the ever-so-elusive two-foot-high Freddie. He was propped up on the chair like a small child. I had purchased the charming one-of-a-kind doll at an art show.

"I'd like to introduce you to my date, the distinguished Mr. Flasher," I told James.

"He seems to be a quiet fellow."

"I don't think you should shake his hand," I said. "You don't know where it's been."

"I don't believe raincoats are in compliance with the restaurant dress code," James added.

James and I had a romantic dinner overlooking the Pacific Ocean while Freddie lay in a box at our feet. Although confidence is considered an alluring quality, the fact that James was insecure and probably intimidated by me did not make him less attractive.

"I'm too old for you," James said, clearly wanting me to object.

"No, you're not." I took the bait.

"You'd get tired of me." He acted as if he was kidding around, but I knew there was fear and self-doubt fueling these statements.

"No, I wouldn't."

"You'd eventually leave me. You're on TV all the time." Office employees sometimes gathered to watch my *Meet the Stars* interviews.

"I would not leave you."

I glanced out the window at the sea. James seemed eager to venture into deep waters and experience a fast-paced life with an energetic young woman by his side. But it was safer to stay in the shallow end with his older girlfriend, a conservative homebody. Each time James paddled past the lifeguard's stand to explore options with me, he'd become afraid and anxious and let the tide transport him back to the sand. He had already faced disaster with his first wife. He felt lucky to have rescued the two kids and paddled back to land.

His current girlfriend, on the other hand, was not risky. She was traditional, older, and predictable. I felt she would sink James, or at least make it hard for him to paddle into deeper waters. James's homebody could be satisfied assuming the role of a nondescript wife in a stucco tract home, preparing meals and doing laundry. But I could not. I wanted to venture out to sea. I wanted to make an impact on the world, clean up pollution from the waters, and even save the whales.

Since meeting James, he'd splashed around in knee-high waves with flippers and a face mask. He could not bring himself to don scuba gear and inspect the beauty beyond the shoreline. And from this night forward, he would regularly express worry that I would leave him or become disinterested with time. This was his excuse for why it could not work. There was nothing I could do to convince him otherwise, but I continued to pursue a permanent relationship because I believed in the power of persistence and because I loved him.

James gave me a kiss at the end of our lovely "Freddie the Flasher" evening. It was the first time this had happened, and I was elated. James took Freddie home with him that night and did not redeem his thirty-minute massage. The two of us continued to flirt, kid around, and lunch together. Many months later I would propose marriage.

❧

After the Freddie the Flasher evening with James, I traveled to South Carolina, where I found myself standing next to Ferdinand, crying.

"I'm sorry. I'm sorry," I whispered. "I wish there was something I could do."

Ferdinand was silent. He was not persuaded. He was pleading for my help with his big, sad eyes, and I was just standing there blubbering like a coward who was worried about social convention and rules.

"You know I would help if I could." Tears had blurred my vision, and I realized my perfectly applied mascara had turned my face into a Rorschach test.

Ferdinand looked at the tear stains on my cheeks, but he did not see sunshine, flowers, or happy thoughts. He saw impending torture. He saw his throat being slit, his body being hoisted upside down on a hook, and his head being sliced off. Then he imagined being chopped into two dozen pieces and eaten by folks who were nothing more than little Jeffrey Dahmers.

"I'm so sorry that I'm a human," I said to Ferdinand as I stared at his ear identification tag. It made him seem like a cheap stuffed animal from Toys "R" Us.

It was embarrassing being human, and it was painful feeling helpless. I wished I could be like Nelson Mandela and buck the law for my cause. I wished I could throw open the gate to the pen. I would, of course, go to jail, and Ferdinand and his friends would still die. But at least I would be making a statement.

Those sixty seconds with Ferdinand were some of the most powerful moments of my life. I had named him after the classic children's tale, but he was just one bull among many at a livestock exhibit and rodeo in South Carolina in 1988.

I was there for only one reason: to appear on the local morning show to discuss my book. Rather than broadcast from the television studio, the production was being taped that week from a platform in the middle of the fairgrounds. I would be working under harsh conditions, because from the stage I would be able to see pain emanating from coops, cages, and animal pens. Worst of all, Ferdinand the bull would be watching my every move, and when I grinned at the camera, he would think I had already forgotten about him.

I wiped the smeared mascara from under my eyes. I tried to be perky and smiley-faced. I was expected to perform. When given the cue, I rushed onto the stage and pulled off the facade. I spoke eloquently about hobnobbing with the rich and famous and pursuing one's dreams whatever they may be. I never mentioned how Ferdinand would not be able to pursue his dreams.

I was not so eloquent on the next morning show. It was the day after the Ferdinand encounter, and I was appearing on a television program in North Carolina. I was there to discuss the ups and downs of celebrityhood, review "hot" films, and pitch my book. When the host asked me about the Kevin Costner flick *Bull Durham*, I suddenly made a right turn and spoke about the horrific conditions that real-life cows endure on factory farms. The host tried to veer me back to "fluff," but by that time, it was too late.

Afterward, the producer was incensed. She called my cattle comments "disastrous" and screamed at me, "Our viewers don't give a rat's ass about the welfare of animals!" Although I had angered a bunch of humans, at least I'd made poor Ferdinand proud.

The Carolina TV interviews were just two of many. I was traveling around the United States and Canada appearing on television and radio shows, and afterward I was heading to local bookstores to sign copies of *Meet the Stars*. Apart from North Carolina, I stayed "on topic," so the other program executives were pleased with my performance.

There was an executive, however, who displeased me. She booked me to appear on *The Late Show* and later caused me to exploit—and embarrass myself with—singer Julio Iglesias.

It all started in Los Angeles with a woman named Lena—known to her friends as "Lena the liar." She and I had worked on an Anheuser-Busch commercial together. Lena bragged about how she had dated actor Warren Beatty—which may or may not have been true—and she invited me to accompany her to the Playboy Mansion under one condition: that I help her meet the man of her dreams. This man was Spanish singer Julio Iglesias, who is listed as one of the top ten best-selling performers in history by Sony Music Entertainment. He had recently become popular in the United States due to a duet he performed with Willie Nelson called "To All the Girls I've Loved Before."

Lena boasted about being a Playboy model—which may or may not have been true—and suggested we meet at the Beverly Hills Hotel and then head over to a Friday night party at Hef's. On the following night, she wanted me to use my gate-crashing skills to help her sneak backstage at Julio's Universal Amphitheatre concert.

"I can go to the Playboy Mansion whenever I want," Lena said. "Everyone knows me there. We are on the guest list for Friday."

Friday came, and Lena the liar was absent. She was not one of "the girls next door." She was not even on the street. I waited at the Beverly Hills Hotel bar. I phoned her apartment. I left a message. I ordered ice water. I phoned her apartment again. I left another message. I fiddled with my cocktail napkin and eventually pulled out the phone number for the Playboy Mansion, which I had gotten months earlier from Lynn. Lynn had attended a party there once. Hef had parties on Friday and Sunday nights.

"The names aren't on the list, and we've never heard of the Playboy model Lena," a woman from the social director's office said on the phone.

I was all dressed up with nowhere to go. I knew that the best way to get revenge is to attain personal success. What better way to give Lena the finger than to meet Julio Iglesias myself. And I figured that when she eventually returned my call, I could slither into my catty voice: "Too bad you couldn't make it. I ended up hanging out with Julio that night." (But in reality, Lena never got a verbal clawing because she never contacted me again.)

I knew nothing about Julio except that *Entertainment Tonight* had aired a segment about him, live from Chasen's restaurant near Beverly Hills. So I phoned the Universal Amphitheatre and asked to be connected to the backstage area, then to the singer's manager.

"I met Julio at Chasen's, and he told me to come by the show," I told a man who identified himself as Alfredo Fraile. "Do you think it would be possible for me to drop by this evening?"

He floundered for a moment, but then in his thick Latino accent replied, "I guess so. If Julio asked you to come by, I suppose it's all right."

The Universal Amphitheatre backstage area was accessible via a driveway and guard gate. The scenario looked intimidating, but the manager's name was all I needed to gain entrance. Alfredo was preoccupied with actress Angie Dickinson, so he distractedly handed me a backstage pass and told someone to help me find a seat in the audience so I could watch the show. I ended up sitting next to Merv Griffin, who remembered me from Tony Bennett's hotel suite in Chicago.

After the show, I hung out in the green room with Julio and some of his entourage, including Alfredo, Fernán Martínez (Julio's right-hand man), Tony de Corral (a guitarist), Tony Renis (a songwriter), and Ray Rodriguez (Julio's worldwide manager). Ray later became the president and CEO of Univision, the country's leading Spanish-language media company.

"Julio tells me you would make a good publicist," an associate said moments after the singer had wandered out of the room. "How would you like to work with us? Julio would like to hire you."

Although flattered, I replied, "No, thanks." I thought about how Lena would have sold her soul for the opportunity.

"You'd be stationed in the Fresno area or central California, but you'd travel a lot. You'd even come on the road with us sometimes."

"Thanks, but I don't think so."

The offer harkened me back to James. Although I wanted him to go into deeper waters with me, that didn't mean I wanted to move to Fresno or adhere to a grueling "night in every city" schedule, which I knew quite well from my days with Tom. In fact, my idea of "venturing out to sea" did not mean travel at all. It simply meant embarking on exciting experiences, usually close to home. I believed that moving around reduced the chances of making a positive impact on the world. It meant diffusing myself, perhaps having to learn new languages, new cultures, and new laws just to survive. It meant always starting from scratch. I wanted to build on what I had in Los Angeles. I had no desire to create a bunch of flimsy grass huts all over the place when I could erect a magnificent structure in one locale.

"Thanks for the job offer," I replied. "But I'm going to pass."

I exchanged contact information with the entourage and was even provided with Julio's home phone number in Miami. I was told to call if I changed my mind. I used this number to get in touch with the singer when *The Late Show* wanted a celebrity to participate in a gimmick with me.

The Late Show host, Ross Shafer, was going to pretend to flip through my "little black book" onstage and randomly select a famous person to call. It would be Julio. He would answer because, of course, he had been told in advance to wait by the phone. I appeared on the show and discussed my book with Ross and comedian Bobcat Goldthwait, but unfortunately, to my dismay and embarrassment, Julio was not called.

"I'm so sorry," I told Alfredo on the phone moments after we finished taping *The Late Show*. "I don't know why they cut the bit."

"Julio waited a long time," Alfredo said. "He has left now."

It is three decades later, and I still feel bad about making Julio go out of his way for me.

It didn't take three decades for me to learn that I didn't need Lena the liar to get invited to the Playboy Mansion. I attended functions there twice. The first time I had dinner and watched a movie with Hugh Hefner and twenty-five guests. On the second occasion, I was introduced to the menagerie of animals in the "zoo." Unfortunately, one introduction was a little too intimate, and Hef's monkey bit me on the finger. It was not serious and required only a Band-Aid. But it did prove one thing: There was most definitely monkey business going on at that place.

∽

Investigative work was barely paying my bills, so I decided to ease into real estate while working at Proficiency. I liked viewing properties and realized I could live vicariously through other people's purchases. I made the transition into the industry slowly, first enrolling in classes at Valley Community College and then passing the state exam and joining a real estate firm. As a Realtor, I specialized in helping average folks—teachers, nurses, police officers, sales clerks, construction workers, and others—get rich with rental properties and house-flipping. Some were able to quit their nine-to-five jobs. Most are affluent today.

∽

I'd enjoyed dozens of lunches with James, but the most memorable was marriage proposal day.

"Where are we eating?" he asked.

"You'll find out." I grinned and pulled the car into a Holiday Inn parking lot.

The hotel lobby had tile floors, brown walls, and a

grape-colored couch. Today, it is the Quality Inn and has even more of a leftover-Christmas-lights look than it did back in the day.

I pushed the elevator button—which led to the guest rooms—and James immediately got nervous.

"Where are we going?" he asked, worried that I was planning to take him to a room and try to seduce him.

"Just follow me," I said confidently, and stepped into the elevator. James hesitatingly followed.

The previous week had been eventful. There had been a three a.m. break-in at Proficiency, but the burglars had been frightened away by a security guard.

"It looks like they only ransacked one office," a cop said, pointing at James's work area. Papers were scattered everywhere.

"No. They didn't ransack anything," an associate replied. "That guy's just really messy."

Then there was the weekend football game that I had attended with James and his two kids. His sister was there. I met her for the first time.

"James says the middle child is the well-adjusted one in the family," I joked to the sister, assuming the entire family must have a sense of humor. (James had three older siblings and three younger ones, and he frequently ribbed me about how he was the well-adjusted one of the bunch.) The sister snarled at me as if I were on the opposing team.

"No, I said *maladjusted*. Not *well-adjusted*." James laughed.

"Ah, yes. That makes more sense," I replied.

Sis still did not crack a smile. In hindsight, maybe she was a supporter of "team girlfriend" and saw me as a relationship wrecker.

That week I also created a beaded blouse for James's mom

and sent it to her home in Sun City, Arizona, with a note thanking her for raising such a fine son.

The Holiday Inn elevators opened, and I sashayed down the second-floor hallway. James trailed behind apprehensively. I unlocked a door to reveal that it was not, in fact, a bedroom but a conference room.

I had set up a picnic on the carpet, complete with a checkered tablecloth, wicker basket, French baguette, fruit salad, and other goodies, such as an afternoon supply of Diet Rite. There was also a lone red rose in a vase. James beamed with excitement as he settled on the floor.

"This is not just a lunch, James. I'm asking you to marry me."

"You're kidding?" He shook his head in disbelief. "What happened to letting the guy chase you?"

"Oh, yeah, I forgot about that," I joked. "This is my wife résumé." I handed him the three-page document, which listed all the reasons why I should be his spouse. It was 99 percent comedy. "I'm much more qualified for the position than any of the applicants you are considering."

"There are lots of applicants." James laughed and read much of the document out loud, enjoying it thoroughly.

He touched on some entries from the Talents and Abilities section. "Late-night faxing skills." "Owns a house, which could one day be clean." "Can cook gourmet meals (often edible)."

"Edible is always a good start," he said.

Then he read a few of my "Promises."

"I will always let you think you are smarter than me." "I will give you priority on the couch (unless, of course, the dogs want to take a nap)." "I will like totally continue to be the cute, charming Valley Girl, that I am, like totally." "I will give you the respect you deserve (i.e., very little)." "I will keep a never-ending supply of Prozac on hand."

"Prozac is a good foundation for any marriage." He chuckled.

I pulled out a jewelry box. Inside was a Hells Angels motorcycle ring.

"This is a biker engagement ring," I said. "I know you're not a biker. And I know I'm not a biker. But a bike symbolizes exploring life together, and this is a stand-in until I can get you an appropriate ring."

James looked at me in a serious way and hesitated as if he was tempted to accept, but then he said, "You know I can't take it."

I had not really expected a "yes," although I had hoped for one. Despite likely rejection, I wanted to go through the motions because I was in love with him and felt we had more than a James Bond. We had a real bond. Plus, I had wondered what it would feel like proposing to a man. It was a gray area that I'd never experienced. It was one of my bucket list goals.

Soon after, I left private investigation work to become a full-time real estate agent.

One day I dropped by Proficiency, hoping to see James. I did not make it past the reception desk.

"Did you hear the good news?" the receptionist bubbled. "Just after you left the company, James asked his girlfriend to marry him. She had to think about it for a few weeks because she wasn't too sure about him, but she finally gave in."

My heart sank. I was devastated and could barely breathe. I felt another Rorschach test welling up in my eyes.

"That's great," I lied, and ducked out to the parking lot to cry.

I was disturbed by the fact that James would marry a woman who had to "think about it for a few weeks," who "wasn't too sure about him," and who finally "gave in." Frankly, I thought he deserved better. Then again, maybe she was just playing the romance game.

I never visited Proficiency again.

Chapter Twelve

THE DUD AND THE DEAD GUY

I met Lola at a baby shower in the late 1980s, and she became one of my closest friends. She told me that Charles Manson had slept in her apartment in early 1969, just before he and his "family" carried out the Helter Skelter murders.

Back then, Lola's one-bedroom Hollywood pad was a flophouse for drifters, druggies, and prostitutes. She was a devotee of the hippie lifestyle even though she had been raised by an upper middle-class family from the Northeast.

Lola opened the door to find her friend Bob and his new pal, Charlie Manson. They brought out beer and band gear and made themselves at home in the living room, unconcerned that Lola's frayed and beat-up furnishings came from garage sales and thrift shops. Free spirit types—many with percussion instruments—rolled into the apartment to listen to Manson preach, play the guitar, and sing.

Lola was under the spell of alcohol and drugs, but she was not under Manson's spell. When he made an advance, she rebuffed him, although she agreed to let him stay the night on her couch. She was accustomed to scuzzy types, but Manson seemed downright creepy. When she retreated to her bedroom, she did something she had never before done: She locked her door.

The next morning, she ushered Manson out of her apartment with other overnight guests and did not hear about him again until his crimes were emblazoned on newspaper headlines throughout the nation.

Lola was tall with long blonde hair and had a nurturing way about her. If she had lived in Salem, Massachusetts, in the 1600s, she would have been accused of witchcraft. She was an expert on homemade remedies. Some of her unconventional concoctions worked like magic. She had natural cures for physical ailments as well as tips for the house and garden. She was a cauldron of valuable advice.

When I first met Lola, she'd just had a one-night stand in an elevator with a homely circus performer whom she'd met that very day. A week later, she had sex in an Ahmanson Theatre broom closet with a man who earned his living as a gigolo. They got caught by management and were removed from the building. Both men were younger. Although Lola was in her late forties, she liked men half her age. She was a trendsetter. She was a cougar before cougar was cool. Her next conquest was a long-haired rock-and-roll musician who worked local clubs around L.A. She hoped the fling would turn into a long-term affair, but he was more interested in twenty-somethings. She bought him new boots, cooked him homemade pie, and made her body available. He used her for a couple of weeks and then cast her aside.

Then there was Adam, whom Lola met through an *LA Weekly* personal ad. He could have appeared on *Hoarding: Buried Alive*. His apartment looked like an overstuffed pawn shop. Adam was a handsome wannabe actor and young enough to be Lola's son. He slept eighteen hours a day in order to avoid life. When he was not sleeping, he was at the mall buying compulsively. He rarely removed merchandise from shopping bags. New purchases were piled upon old purchases, which were piled upon even older purchases, until he was gasping for air in the deep end of his dining room.

Lola liked playing lifeguard. She was a good rescuer. Adam was suicidal when Lola started cooking his meals, giving him allowance, returning his purchases (some of which had been made years earlier), and generally treating him like a dependent. The relationship was unhealthy, and I was Lola's confidant during her daily struggles with Adam. Lola eventually extricated herself from the situation.

Lola had become a born-again Christian in an effort to quit drugs, alcohol, and wanton sex. She hoped to compensate for her sordid past. In her view, the alternative was to spend an eternity fending off oversexed outlaws like Manson. When I met Lola, she had succeeded in becoming vice free, except in the area of promiscuity. With sex, she was like a Ferris wheel. Sometimes she was up in the air with her faith, and sometimes she was down on the ground, rolling around in the leaves with her latest squeeze.

She and I veered apart on religious ground, but we agreed to disagree. Although I was not a Christian, I could see how it had helped her move away from the treacherous edge of society to more solid ground.

I thought that many of Lola's Christian ideas were peculiar, such as when she announced that God wanted her to find a husband from Sweden. I am unclear how this message came to her. I don't think she'd visited Mount Sinai or seen a cloud in the shape of a Viking. Nevertheless, she scoured the Internet for a Nordic lad and, lo and behold, found Stefan, who was hoping to relocate to America. Stefan was the proper age for a now fifty-year-old cougar. He was twenty-four.

Although Lola did not have a job and lived off a modest sum from her ex-husband, she was able to scrounge together the funds to buy Stefan a one-way ticket to Los Angeles. They exchanged a couple of letters and had a phone conversation in which Lola revealed to him God's plan: that they were to be married. When Stefan arrived at the airport, Lola took him by the hand to a hole-in-the-wall wedding chapel, where they became man and wife. Other than a couple of strangers, who acted as witnesses, there was no guest list. I met Stefan for the first time a few hours after the ceremony. He was dazed and intoxicated. His bloodshot eyes told me that he had been caught in a cyclone, that it was unpleasant, and that he wanted to escape. But it was too late. He was married to a stranger and on his way to becoming an American citizen.

The marriage was problematic from the start. Stefan got a low-paying job renting out surfboards at Venice Beach, where he flirted with bikini-clad hotties. He also had an unpredictable temper and was physically violent toward Lola twice. The second time she kicked him out and filed for divorce. I guess God had been wrong about that marriage thing.

While I was consoling Lola, she was listening to complaints about my boyfriend, Pat.

∽

Pat was a pain. Dating him was like hauling around a wet sack of leaves. I should have tossed him into the recycling bin right off the bat, but I was loyal and devoted. Thus, I was always the one to get dumped.

I'd always hated dating. My childhood game plan had been to get married at a young age. My previous attempts—with Tom, Jed, Eric, and James—had failed. Although I went on tons of dates with tons of perfectly nice guys, I was a snap decision maker. If I was not enamored by date one and "in love" by date three, it was simply not going to happen for me.

When it came to dating, my decisiveness and knack for knowing what I wanted was viewed as a liability. I was in the "don't" column of relationship self-help guides, which advise women to let men pursue them. These texts state that males have an innate desire to be hunters and that women should go along with that instinct and accept the role of conquest or prey. Then, females are further counseled on how to "play the game"—as James used to say—or on how to manipulate men. This was deceptive. Plus, my face was a billboard for my feelings. No man was blind enough to think I was unattracted to him when I indeed was. That is, none except Pat. Actually, it wasn't Pat's fault. I'd told him that I couldn't go out with him for two months. This was not because I was disinterested or playing a game. It was because I was too darn fat.

It all began when I placed a personal ad in the *LA Weekly* and crossed my fingers. I knew it was easier to find a real estate buyer in Los Angeles than a *ready, willing, and able* man for commitment. Many men were *ready* for an acting career, *willing* to get a fake tan, and *able* to cheat. But I was looking for class, intelligence, humor, and a down-to-earth personality. Unfaithful orange-colored actors were not on my radar.

It was 1990, and I was thirty. I had been celibate since becoming pregnant with Kayla. I had been on numerous platonic dates with men whom I classified as "just friends." Just as guys despise that label, I despised characterizing them that way. I desperately wanted to find a fantasy mate and don a fantasy gown for my fantasy wedding. I was admittedly a typical girl and a conformist in that way. As mentioned before, my friends believed marriage would not happen for me. Laura said I had a better chance of being killed by a ready, willing, and able terrorist.

"This is you." Laura drew a large stick figure on a sheet of paper. "And this is the man you want." She sketched a microscopic male inside a tiny square. "You are too picky. You don't give anyone a chance. If they don't fit into your itty-bitty box, you eliminate them."

Laura was right. But doing anything else would have eliminated me. Loosening my standards would have been tantamount to ignoring my value system and essence. It was not an option. Although advice books warned that my sidekick—Perseverance—would be no help in romantic matters, I plowed ahead, hoping they were wrong.

The *LA Weekly* seemed like a reasonable place to find a boyfriend. This was years before it became inundated with sexually explicit ads. As Miss Careful, I wanted to be triple-sure to weed out perverts, so I tailored my ad accordingly. It read, "Seeking respectable, conservative man with morals who loves kids and animals." The fact that I did not believe in moral absolutes was irrelevant, as was the fact that I was not a traditionalist. I just wanted to find a good guy and thought this sort of language would give me the best shot. My ad ran for two weeks. Interested men could call a designated number for the newspaper and listen to a one-minute message that I had recorded. They could then leave a response with their contact data, and I could opt to call them or not.

I got a whopping 225 responses. I envisioned my own version of *Groundhog Day*, repeating the same dreadful dinner over and over. How many times could I cheerfully ask, "Where are you from?" and "What do you do for a living?" And God forbid the men wanted a second or third date. My photo could end up in the *Guinness Book of World Records* on the "small-talk burnout" page.

Rather than morph into Bill Murray, I came up with a solution. I invented my own version of speed dating. According to Wikipedia, the first speed-dating event took place in 1998, but my less formal version started in 1990. I arranged to meet men at different eateries up and down Ventura Boulevard. I would start at one end by popping in for a drink with bachelor number one before moving on to bachelor number two, and so forth.

I had gotten through thirty *LA Weekly* men before I met Pat. He was bachelor number three on one particular evening and the final date of the night. I was glad he was last, because the drink turned into dinner. I didn't mind the small talk, because Pat was a hunk. He looked like a rock star with blue eyes; shoulder-length, curly brown hair; and a diamond stud in his left ear. He was a psychologist, British, and ten years older than me. I thought the dichotomy between the radical look and the educated profession was sexy. Plus, I was shocked that through the personals, I'd found a stick figure that seemed to fit perfectly into my itty-bitty box. Of course, I did not yet know that Pat was insane.

"Would you like to go out on Saturday night?" he asked.

"I'm really busy for the next couple of months," I replied. "Could I give you a call when I'm free?"

"Sure." He seemed disappointed.

"I definitely want to go out with you," I added, but I could tell he didn't buy it.

I didn't know what to do. I could not reveal the truth: that I was really a fatso. I had selected my loose-fitting sweater dress precisely because it was tight-lipped about the excess flab on my hips and thighs. I knew the other outfits in my closet were blabbermouths. They would blow my ruse as a "cute chick worthy of dating a stud." I could not tell Pat that I would be spending the next sixty days grazing on rice cakes and sweating like a furnace worker in an effort to get pretty for him. That would go to his head. Plus, finding out about my pudgy parts would be a turnoff. It was better for him to feel rejected.

During the next two months, I dieted, obsessed over the *Buns of Steel* workout video, and bought a sexy red dress for my date with bachelor number three. Plus, I overdosed on step aerobics classes at the gym and even got credentialed as an instructor. (Years later, I would teach classes part-time at Bally Total Fitness.)

I telephoned Pat two months later. "Okay. I'm ready to go out."

"Really? I didn't think you were interested," he said.

"What possibly gave you that idea?"

And my romance with the crazy guy began.

My romance with the crazy guy was about to end. We had been seeing each other for six months, and our two-day vacation in Del Mar had been a disaster. We were driving back to Los Angeles in painful silence, listening to the hum of the air conditioner.

Not long after meeting Pat, I figured I should not let the other 224 *LA Weekly* stags go back into the woods, so I threw a bash for my girlfriends at the Sherman Oaks Hilton. Because I was lean on gal pals, Lola and I were reduced to picking up chicks at bars.

"Hey, want to come to a party with 224 men?" was my line.

"These are all guys interested in Charlotte," Lola would obnoxiously add. (By that time, I was being called by my actual name "Charlotte" rather than "Missy.")

Then I phoned each *LA Weekly* bachelor from my ad. "I'm already dating someone, but would you like to meet my girlfriends?" Most were receptive.

The bar at the Hilton looked like a singles cruise. The room was sleek with a black-and-beige color palette and walls of modern art. I had neglected to tell Hilton staff there would be hundreds of "under forties" ordering drinks, so they were frazzled and snarled at me regularly. Not one of the 224 was as cute as Pat, so I left the party feeling confident that I had made the right choice.

But now I was not so sure. Pouty-mouthed Pat would do nothing in Del Mar, other than sulk, scowl, and gripe. This was nothing new. My attempts to get Pat to smile were always met with a frown and the feeling that I was tiptoeing over shards of glass. One false move and I would be ripped apart by this psychologist who had actually diagnosed himself as crazy. He had informed me of this on several occasions.

"I'm clinically insane," he said at a café one morning.

"No, you're not." I laughed.

"Yes, I am…. Really, I am," he said in a serious tone.

Dating Pat was like dating a weather pattern, except there were only three forecasts: cloudy, rainy, or monsoon. He had snubbed my friends—Gary, Lola, Lynn, and others—when we attended the Bolshoi Ballet at the Shrine Auditorium. He had warned me to never—and he repeated *never*—plan any cute surprises for him like I'd done for other boyfriends. And he acted really shocked on our first date, saying, "You're so clean!" Had he been dating dirty women?

On our second date, he took me to a party where I met three of his old girlfriends. He was very tense and emotional about the ordeal and afterward looked at me shocked again. "I'm surprised. You handled yourself so well." Who exactly had he been hauling into his cave? The ex-girlfriends had seemed perfectly normal.

Pat's main problem was that he was overly emotional. In his world, there was no such thing as relaxing or laughing. Every second had super-duper significance and was linked with a childhood trauma or pivotal experience. It was frankly draining, and after six months of this, I felt like an old piece of elastic. I had been stretched to my limit and had lost my shape. I realized I'd rather be dating an insensitive brute.

Pat went bonkers when his therapist went on vacation. I seemed to be his only tie to reality during that period. Although he worked as a psychologist, he paid big bucks to be diagnosed by a Malibu therapist six days a week.

Pat was also mental when it came to money. He had two leased Mercedes and could not afford the payments on either. He had thousands of dollars in credit card debt and no equity in his condo. He explained that he could not live within his means due to the trauma of being impoverished as a child. I shook my head like his mommy but said nothing for fear of another cloudburst.

Now we were in his car sitting in silence. I wanted to climb inside the glove compartment. My tears could have filled up his bucket seats, but I no longer had the desire to cry. Every off-ramp reminded me that it was time to exit the relationship. I imagined people in other vehicles having pleasant conversations, but "pleasant" was simply not part of Pat's vocabulary.

Back in L.A., Pat dropped me off at my car, and I screeched away in anger. I had never screeched before. It was a little scary, a little odd, and a little satisfying.

An hour later, he phoned. "I thought that went pretty well.

What did you think? That was the best vacation I've ever taken with a woman."

"What?" I exclaimed. "It was terrible. Are you crazy?"

Since I was allergic to initiating breakups, I stayed in the mental ward with the thunderstorm for another month, and then he dumped me. He had lunched with a woman he liked better and felt it was the right time to explain my shortcomings. I was too petite for him (he was over six feet tall), and I was not emotional enough (he had failed to turn me into a basket case, despite intense effort). Plus, I had Kayla, and he was suddenly unsure whether he wanted to settle down with a woman who had a child. But settling down was not an option from my perspective anyway. He was not marriage material unless I wanted to spend my remaining years being blown here, there, and yonder like a Kleenex in a wind tunnel. And since my objective was to be married, I suddenly wondered why I had been wasting time with a crazy man. Pat had been a foolish interruption and detour from my goals.

Although I was partly sad about the relationship ending, I was partly relieved. Pat was a dud and more of a downer than a dead guy.

⁂

He was drop-dead gorgeous. Spinoza was a hunk. Unfortunately, he was "temporally unavailable" in the same way that some men are "geographically undesirable." This is because he had been dead for over three hundred years.

It was 1992. I was thirty-two and unfortunately still single. As usual, I was taking classes. Specifically, I was at CSUN prepping for a doctoral program at USC.

It was the first day of a CSUN class. I flipped through the course text, *The Great Philosophers*, perusing pictures of the dead blokes I would be studying that semester. René Descartes looked like a snarky know-it-all. "Got fried" perfectly described Gottfried Leibniz's waist-length, overly curly wig. It appeared to have been blitzed by high tension wires. But Baruch Spinoza was the handsomest man I'd ever seen (in this particular portrait on page 103). In fact, he looked a little like Tom, except for the shoulder-length curls.

I knew nothing about these so-called seventeenth-century "rationalists," who believed that knowledge was independent of sense experience. Plus, I was not versed on the other great thinkers pictured in the book, such as St. Augustine, Nietzsche, and Wittgenstein. But I knew the professor would be taking us on an enlightening cruise through the waters of Western philosophy.

Two months later, we had not yet studied the hunk on page 103. In fact, I no longer remembered his name when suddenly the teacher outlined a theory on the blackboard, and I became as excited as the "class" that had finally located its "struggle." I had found my ideological soul mate, and his name was Baruch Spinoza. Like me, this Dutch philosopher argued that the universe was determined and amoral and that humans were arrogant in placing themselves above nonhumans on the Great Chain of Being. It was only a matter of minutes before I reexamined the course book to discover that the hunk and soul mate were one and the same.

"Are you dating anyone?" Lynn asked that night during our usual "girl talk" phone session.

"No, but I have a crush on a philosopher born in 1632," I joked.

"Oh, that's really funny," she replied. "You have a crush on a guy who died in 1677."

It felt like I'd been zapped by Leibniz's electrical wire. I was in shock because Spinoza *did*, in fact, die in 1677.

"Why did you say that?" I asked.

"I don't know," she said.

Lynn had never studied philosophy or heard of Spinoza. I designated this as the first spooky experience of my life. To my surprise, others would follow, and all would end up being linked to Spinoza.[17]

Before this, I'd considered paranormal experiences to be fraudulent, often the result of an overactive imagination. I'd placed great value on logic and evidence. But Lynn's comment had changed my perspective. Suddenly I was unsure about it all.

I vacationed in Europe a year later. I had never really fancied travel, but when I did go out of town, it was to visit someone special, such as a boyfriend or my birth parents or a particular VIP whom I didn't yet know but hoped to befriend. I had never been one for tourist attractions or group tours. They felt like conformity traps. The error with this vacation was that I had designed it without a person in mind. It was an aimless wander from one foreign city to another. And for me, this was a recipe for boredom and restlessness.

The good news was that when I hit Holland, I realized that I was visiting someone after all: Spinoza. He was the VIP whom I hoped to befriend. His aura infused every cobblestone street, delightful Dutch structure, and winding waterway. I suddenly believed I knew secrets about him. Somehow I'd inhaled his spirit. I was in sync. I seemed to understand the synapses in his brain. It was as if his essence was my essence. I had additional unexplainable experiences, and every clue suggested I was in the right place, at the right time, visiting the right person.

It also felt as if I were being led from place to place not by my head, heart, or feet but rather by a mysterious ally called "intuition." I came to believe that there is a secret drawer that goes ignored and untapped by most people, yet it holds powerful tools and insights. I came to believe that cause and effect operate on a more unobservable, immeasurable, and far-reaching level than I'd ever imagined. I was certain the tossing universe had secrets to which humans and science would never be privy.

After my Spinoza trip, I came to rely upon intuition. As a Realtor, I avoided two vacant houses that simply did not feel right. As a hiker, I abandoned a woodsy trail that felt dangerous. Maybe intuition saved my life. Maybe it didn't. I will never know. My odd happenings and link to Spinoza also put me on a certain path within academia and led me to devise the unique animal rights philosophy I hold today.

Spinoza has cloaked me with a spiritual veil, forever changing the way I view things. He has shown me that while the forces toss and turn, there may be sneaky little dwarfs who whistle while they work. And he has taught me that I should have no fear, because in the end, the universe is just like Snow White: It always lives happily ever after.

"Spin"—the man I jokingly call "my husband in a future life"—has made a huge impact on *this* life. He will forever remain a part of my heart.

∽

My real estate business was booming. I'd become well versed on the ins and outs of buying and selling, from values and loans to negotiating and inspections. I could sniff out a money-making deal from fifty miles away with a bag over my head. My clients almost always won multiple-offer situations, even when we were competing against fifteen other buyers. I'd received a flurry of accolades, such as President's Club awards, a trophy for being one of the top real estate agents in the country, and a certificate from the *Los Angeles Business Journal* for my contribution to the community. I had expanded my clientele. I was not only helping ordinary folks get rich but also representing business leaders and celebrities.

In addition, I'd been growing my own investment portfolio. I was thirty-two years old and had income-producing properties in addition to my main residence—not too shabby for a girl who had come to California with $500, a borrowed Volkswagen, and an assortment of naysayers babbling in my ear.

My adoptive father was unaware of my accomplishments because he'd refused to take my calls for three years. It's not like I hadn't tried. I'd phoned. I'd left messages. I'd attempted to catch him at odd hours of the night. I'd even called one of his friends to make sure he was still breathing. She'd expressed sympathy with my predicament. "I don't understand your father. I don't know why he acts this way."

I felt a duty to keep in touch as his child and only living relative, but I also believed it would cheer him up to know that I'd realized some success. Since he viewed money as the measure of a person, I wanted to tell him that when it came to career, I was no longer five feet tall. I was more like Magic Johnson.

I tried to call Dad once again. Surprisingly, he answered.

"Wow. I haven't talked to you in a really long time," I said.

"You've been living in Europe," he replied.

"What? No, I haven't."

"Don't lie to me."

"I'm not lying. Where'd you get that idea? From Ike?"

"I fired Ike years ago."

"I'm doing pretty well as a Realtor."

"Are you married yet?"

"No."

"Men don't want a woman with a kid. You missed that boat years ago. Better get used to spending your life alone."

Dad had always worshipped the dollar, but now he seemed

to be saying that marriage was the measure of success. Was this because I had no husband? Did he need to say "I told you so" about something? Did it make *him* feel good to make *me* feel bad?

"Gotta go." He hung up.

Chapter Thirteen

MY DATE WITH AN UNINDICTED CO-CONSPIRATOR

Michael Meisner and Gerald Wolfe were breaking the law. Their caper was part of a brazen scheme called Operation Snow White. It had been ordered by higher-ups for a so-called higher cause. It was May 28, 1976, and just after nightfall. I was sixteen and living in Atlanta at the time.

The two men didn't have to jimmy open the lock, because weeks earlier they had created fake ID cards (which allowed them to roam government buildings), and they had surreptitiously copied the key to the office of the Assistant U.S. Attorney located in the U.S. Courthouse for the District of Columbia.

This was not the first escapade launched by Michael, Gerald, and dozens of their cohorts. For years, they had been infiltrating, wiretapping, and/or burglarizing the Internal Revenue Service, the U.S. Department of Justice, the Federal Trade Commission, the Drug Enforcement Administration, the U.S. Coast Guard, the U.S. Treasury, the Labor Department, the American Medical Association, and private law firms, just to name a few. The thieves did not steal money or expensive office equipment. It was all about the quest for worthless paper. Of course, at the time, they did not think it was worthless.

The government offices had filing cabinets crammed mostly with nonsense: old newspaper articles and boring memos photocopied from other departments. Bureaucrats shuffled documents from one division to another like desktop paper sorters. But Michael, Gerald, and the other members of their organization believed that these items were pivotal to their mission, so they spent four years sneaking into buildings and making illegal copies.

On this particular night, Michael and Gerald ducked into a third-floor hallway, where they used their duplicate key to enter the dark office. They located the Assistant U.S. Attorney's filing cabinet with their flashlights and then spent hours secretly Xeroxing the papers on government copiers. Afterward, they placed the twelve-inch stack of documents in their briefcase, bolted from the building, and proudly sent their loot to their higher-ups.

Charles was a higher-up.

But Charles had not ordered the illegal break-in, nor did he have knowledge about it. When handed copies of government papers—which happened frequently—he always assumed they'd originated from lawful Freedom of Information requests. Charles's associates knew that he would not want to know about mischief and criminal capers, because he was a barrister and the head of the organization's worldwide legal department.

While Michael and Gerald were in Washington, DC, congratulating themselves on a mission accomplished, it was eight hours later in England, and Charles was entering his office at Saint Hill Manor in West Sussex. This was the worldwide headquarters for the "higher cause." Saint Hill Manor is a tourist attraction today with a fifty-nine-acre estate, golf-course-like grounds, lakes, and compelling views. The mansion on the property was built in 1792. The legal office inside the mansion comprised fifteen desks in a section called the "ballroom." It had a splashy stone fireplace and a wall of windows.

Charles fetched his morning coffee and checked his in-box, which contained dispatches from all over the world.

"Would you say today's coffee is warm and fuzzy?" A colleague toyed with Charles's always-dependable sense of humor.

"Is this an attempt to put adjectives in my mouth?" Charles settled at his desk. "I tell you, the human being can't be trusted with adjectives."

The colleague laughed. "I wonder what we should do about the Department of Health."

"When in doubt, sue the bastards," Charles quipped.

The colleague chuckled again and headed to his workspace.

Charles's fourteen-hour day was exhausting, but it fit nicely with his calling. He and the lawyers under him handled four hundred lawsuits at a time although the pay was a laughable forty dollars per week. It was essentially volunteer work. Many of the cases involved suing someone to get documents because, of course, the organization's leaders had a fatal attraction to paper. Accumulating information was their vocation, avocation, obsession, and life blood. There were already dozens of overloaded filing cabinets on the premises, as well as hundreds at satellite offices around the world, and the fact that no one had ever found a "smoking gun" in these stolen pages was irrelevant.

Back in Washington, higher-ups phoned Michael and Gerald and ordered them to remove additional documents from the Assistant U.S. Attorney's office, so the men slipped into their spy identities once again and prepared to replay their scheme. However, this time when they arrived on the third floor, they encountered a snag called the FBI. Agents interrogated them about their presence. This led to an unraveling of the entire four-year operation, as well as to Gerald's arrest and the issuing of an arrest warrant for Michael, who turned state's evidence and was given immunity from prosecution.

Michael's confession about the underground activities provided ammunition for the FBI to raid the Washington, DC and Los Angeles offices of the "higher cause"—the Church of Scientology—and to find 90,000 incriminating documents, including internal memos. The 156 FBI agents (the most ever used in a single raid) confiscated enough paper to fill a sixteen-ton truck. The seized information led to the indictments of eleven eminent members of the church. All served time in federal prison.

Operation Snow White was conceived with the naive goal of correcting inaccuracies in government paperwork and equipping the church with data that could help them beat their adversaries in court and in the newspapers. L. Ron Hubbard, the founder of the religion, believed there were untruths amassed in bureaucratic offices, and he wanted these files purged of all falsifications. He thought the edits would change the negative perception that many people had of the religion. The image of Scientology is, of course, still unfavorable today despite famous followers, such as Tom Cruise, John Travolta, Kirstie Alley, and Greta Van Susteren.

Although Ron Hubbard was not indicted in the Snow White caper, he was listed by prosecutors as an "unindicted co-conspirator," which meant the government felt he was involved but lacked evidence to pursue him. This term is, of course, nonsensical for obvious reasons. Charles, who was a part of Scientology's inner circle, was not officially named as an unindicted co-conspirator,[18] but he has somehow been saddled with the label for the past forty years. Fifty-nine websites list him this way today.[19]

Despite Scientology's fall from grace in the late 1970s, Charles still felt it had grace for him. He continued to seek spiritual improvement and personal fulfillment through membership in the religion for several more years, even though he was exploited and overworked. He was an Oxford graduate and skillful lawyer making a trifling forty dollars per week, while senior barristers today make around $1.2 million per year, with some earning as much as $3.2 million annually. It was admirable that he was willing to sacrifice possessions and luxury for a "higher cause." Charles remained at the helm of Scientology's legal department for sixteen years, from 1965 until 1981. To survive, he was forced to live off of a modest inheritance and run a cookie shop on weekends.

When Charles extricated himself from the religion in 1981, he became the victim of what some call a "disconnection policy."[20] In Scientology, members are encouraged to sever all ties with those who are declared antagonists toward the religion, even when these "enemies" are relatives, close friends, or colleagues. Charles was considered such a person, since he had been an elite leader in the organization with access to its inner workings and was now on the outs. To this day, Charles is shunned by Scientologist family members, including his son and brother. It is an agonizing situation.

Charles instigated his own "disconnection policy" from

England. He moved to Los Angeles in 1981, passed the California bar, and started a law practice. He was forty years old, was unmarried, and had never earned more than forty dollars a week. He was starting from scratch, just as I had done when moving to LA with $500. And like me, Charles was perceived by many as a heretic. His iconoclasm could not be tolerated by good, little conformity-minded soldiers in step with church policy.

I would meet this "unindicted co-conspirator" thirteen years later on the eve of the Northridge earthquake, and I would fall in love with him before the aftershocks could swallow their first Xanax. There would be a whole lot of shaking going on in both the streets and my heart. While Mother Nature was making a chopped salad out of the city, she seemed to be playing matchmaker with us.

Some might call her an unindicted co-conspirator as well.

⚜

I was number 32439. I had rejected 37630, 37596, and 39731, among others. I was losing hope.

I had joined the dating organization, Great Expectations (GE), in June 1992 after my failed relationship with Pat. I still wanted to find a man to love and marry. This was prior to Internet matchmaking websites. GE in West Los Angeles was the go-to spot for romance. Although it normally cost $1,000 for a six-month membership and thousands more for the long term, my cap was tens and tens of dollars. I was not interested in shelling out big bucks, plus I was a fan of the "frugal" rule. If I could finagle something for free or cheap, I felt compelled to go for it.

GE had made a grave error. When the business first opened, it offered lifetime memberships with transfer rights. In other words, a person could use the service and later sell her membership. Her buyer would automatically become part of the organization forever at no extra cost. GE had unwittingly created a market against itself, and thus quickly terminated this benefit. But a lot of people had already stepped through the loophole, usually locating the already-used memberships via newspaper ads and paying $800 to $1,200 each. I scored my lifetime affiliation for a mere $200.

After joining, each member provided a bio and photos, which were displayed inside thick books on a massive bookshelf. There were probably fifty feet of males and another fifty feet of females. It was a virtual avalanche of eligible mates, and I felt I had a decent chance of appeasing the demons of pickiness and staying within the lines of my itty-bitty box. In addition to bios and photos, there was a VHS library. GE staff made a ten-minute video of each member and placed the footage near televisions and VCRs so other members could watch. Guys could choose gals, and vice versa, but both parties had to agree for there to be an exchange of contact data.

I got saddled with more dates than the Maya calendar. I went out with men, weekend after weekend, for a year and a half without becoming even slightly bewitched. Most of the men were perfectly nice and attractive but simply not my type for one reason or another. I fine-tuned the "let's be friends" line and even turned some of my rejects into real estate clients.

In desperation, I approached two blonde women who worked at the GE front desk.

"I know exactly what I want: twenty years older than me, highly educated, hysterically funny, good looking, and down-to-earth. He needs to love kids and animals. Do you have anyone who fits that description?"

The blondes led me into the library and pointed out Dick, a cocky-looking dude in a toupee, wearing gold chains and a polyester pantsuit. He was leaning against a red Corvette. Disco Dick was a mess and he was barely visible, because his 3,500-pound gas-guzzler took up most of the room in the shot.

"I don't usually date Corvettes," I said. "Do you have any less sporty options? Maybe a nice station wagon?"

The blondes had blank stares, so I thanked them for their help. Rather than strangle myself with Dick's gold chains, I decided to ask for assistance once more. So on the following day, I approached the manager of GE named Keith and repeated what I'd told the blondes.

He said, "We only have one man who fits that description."

"Only one? Out of thousands of guys?" I felt defeated. "Could you show him to me?"

Keith escorted me to the books and flipped to member number 38459. It was Charles. He was blue-eyed, bald, and well-dressed. His bio revealed he was a lawyer and Oxford graduate. This worked for me, but his photos were questionable. In vehicle lingo, he was a bright yellow double-decker bus because he was hamming it up for the camera. His facial expressions were not all that flattering. However, there was one shot that looked natural; he was hiking in the desert unaware of being photographed. Because of this picture, I checked out his video and immediately became ecstatic. Charles spoke with a British accent and was clearly refined, brilliant, handsome, and as witty as a late-night comic. He was itty-bitty box material.

For the first time, I noticed the powerful role that body rhythms play in attraction. I liked the way Charles spoke and moved. It was slow and soothing—nothing like my lickety-split type A demeanor. I reflected on past boyfriends and realized that I did not want a man like myself because it would be draining to have two bulldozers sharing the same space. I wanted a man who could calm me. In return, I hoped to infuse energy and excitement into my partner's life.

"I would like to select number 38459," I told Keith, and two days later, Charles responded to my invitation with "yes."

Dating Charles would be like spending time with the *Encyclopedia Britannica, The Complete Works of William Shakespeare,* and *The Big Book of Jokes* rolled into one. It was a heck of a lot better than romancing it up with a Corvette or even a fully equipped station wagon.

～

We were being watched.

Just because they were kings didn't mean they had the right to scrutinize every bite of my salad and every nibble of pita bread. And their court jesters were even more annoying with their squawking and thrashing about; they were singing, dancing, clapping, and banging on a bunch of instruments. It brought back childhood memories of twice dining in noisy joints. Both times I'd thrown up my meal. Although I kept the food down this time, I wanted to stuff grape leaves in my ears.

It was nine hours before the January 17, 1994, earthquake, and I was on my first date with Charles. Conversation was a struggle due to the racket at the Great Greek restaurant in Sherman Oaks. It was supposed to be folk music. I can't speak for other patrons, but as a "folk" myself, I was considerably more interested in silence. I was told that some of the instruments were the oud, bouzouki, and baglama. I didn't know any of these words. I only knew that I was a soup spoon away from throwing tabouli at a tambourine player. And I was a salad fork away from hurling hummus at a waiter. He was humming in my ear like an in-heat bumblebee.

"Some people call me Bandy Legs or Toad-gone-wrong," Charles joked, pulling the idea from a poem called "The Frog."

I laughed at his remark, but it was one of the few I could hear among the bedlam.

The portraits of kings—George, Constantine, and Alexander who had ruled Greece from 1863 until 1917—were hanging on the wall next to our table. The kings wore regal garb and a stiff look. They peered at me as if I were a Spartan sourpuss who needed to be hauled off to the tower and fitted with an iron mask. I meant no disrespect to their majesties, but I had never been one for noise and pandemonium. I was more of a classical music and candlelight gal.

At 4:31 a.m., there was even more pandemonium. The evening with Charles had ended at ten p.m., and I was asleep at home when the Northridge earthquake hit. It was a magnitude 6.7 and lasted for a full twenty seconds. It technically originated in the slightly less prestigious community of Reseda. Perhaps quake-naming authorities figured if one's house was going to fall apart, it would be comforting to think the home-wrecker sprang from upper middle-class roots.

Bookshelves tumbled. China and other breakables crashed to the floor. A backyard brick wall collapsed. I leapt from my bed and scurried to Kayla's room, only to remember that she had been sleeping with me all along. The three dogs that I had at the time were fine. Paws was on the couch and had narrowly escaped heavy debris and falling furniture. My Dandie Dinmont Terrier had darted into the pantry and was sitting in the corner covered in pancake syrup. My Maltese had ducked under the covers next to Kayla. I immediately telephoned Charles to see if he was okay. He was. All power had gone out, so we sat in the dark talking for half an hour.

Nine highways fractured that day. Power lines fell, 250 gas lines ruptured, and there were more than 1,000 aftershocks—many of them quite substantial. The earthquake was one of the costliest natural disasters in U.S. history at an estimated $69 billion. President Bill Clinton pledged a $680 million contribution toward repairs and low-interest loans. Thirty-three people died and 8,700 were injured. I did not hear how many nonhuman animals perished or suffered.

Sixteen inhabitants of the Northridge Meadows Apartments were killed, but a woman I call Lucky was not. Her happy ending would roll off Realtors' tongues for years to come. The first floor of the 163-unit structure was crushed by the weight of two upper levels during the earthquake. It was flattened so thoroughly that it looked as if it had never existed. Rescue teams scrawled "DB" for "dead body" outside many of the units. It was a grisly scene, and personal effects, such as shoes and clothing, were scattered throughout the courtyard and into the street.

This is where Lucky had lived. But two weeks prior to the disaster, she had purchased her first home from a sales agent in my real estate office and moved from the ill-fated complex. Her vacant apartment was destroyed so substantially that if she had remained a tenant, her chance of survival was estimated at zero. Lucky was not only lucky. According to local Realtors, she had wisely chosen to become a homeowner.

I was fortunate myself. The earthquake caused no real damage to my primary residence or investment properties, except for a rental house in Northridge that I owned jointly with my friend Gary. The pool had cracked, and miraculously this was the only property on which I carried earthquake insurance. State Farm quickly and efficiently repaired the damage.

Although my job as a Realtor had been relatively uneventful, the two months prior to the quake were a tad odd. First, I acquired a suicide listing in Glendale. A depressed young man had perched on the edge his bed, five feet from his caged pet parrot, and blasted out the side of his head with a Smith & Wesson. I was required to preview the place prior to the removal of blood and cerebellum stains from the walls. The walk-through was challenging, to say the least, as was finding a buyer after disclosing details about the death. I am happy to report that the parrot was fine and living elsewhere.

Then I sold Mae West's former property to my friend Lola via a no-qualifying loan. It was a half-acre country French estate with six bedrooms, a pool, and a tennis court. Having a private tennis court in the backyard had always been my dream, so I lived vicariously through the purchase. Days before the close of escrow, Lola announced that the place was haunted. Rather than cancel the sale, she paid a priest to perform incantations and to slop around some holy water. Afterward, she said the evil spirits were gone.

"Thank goodness for that. I hear Beelzebub has a mean backhand." I laughed. Lola didn't appreciate the comment.

❧

It seemed the road *less* traveled might be our road *last* traveled. We were trapped in the desert, and it looked like we were going to die.

Charles was reciting a John Donne poem. "Death be not proud, though some have called thee mighty and dreadful."

"I don't think you're taking this seriously," I said.

Charles and I had been dating for some time, and on that particular day, we'd been viewing desert land he owned north of Los Angeles, near Palmdale and Lancaster. He had a 160-acre parcel, as well as 35-acre and 12-acre lots, in a panoramic and underdeveloped community called Juniper Hills. He also owned two 5-acre pieces in Llano. They stood alone on a beak-sized street called Turkey Ranch Road, which I renamed Tofu Ranch Road. I had even investigated the official—and onerous—process for getting a new street sign.

In addition to practicing law, Charles had profited from land investments during the 1980s. Property values had increased substantially in the area due to whispers about the expansion of the Palmdale Airport (which has never occurred, by the way). Charles's 160-acre quarter section—roughly the same as 145 football fields—was as important to him as Trump Tower was to "The Donald." It had been a money bag. Charles had carried paper when selling the property to Philippine investors in 1989, but after paying off 80 percent of the loan, they'd defaulted. The title reverted back to Charles, and he could resell the asset at his leisure.

I enjoyed visiting Charles's land. Even as a child, I'd loved the desert, partly because I was a heat freak. I reveled in dry 100-plus-degree temperatures and the miles of sandy landscape. The horizon seemed to be tinted with a silvery paint. It was not that I hated green grass, but it evoked fear, unless it was situated on a golf course or in a sprinkler-filled front yard. If the surroundings were too verdant, I figured long pants and a sweater were necessary. Long pants and a sweater meant freezing, and freezing was very, very bad. Of course, in my world, freezing was anything lower than eighty degrees. Snow was, of course, a nonstarter. It was in my "frowny-face" column. I hated snow as much as people hate snow jobs.

Now it looked like I would kick the bucket in my favorite place: the desert. But I didn't want to perish *anywhere* at age thirty-five. "Death" was in my frowny-face column, too.

"I knew we shouldn't have taken that detour into the middle of nowhere," I quipped as I climbed out of the car. I was light and playful. I was certainly not going to let a little thing like facing the grim reaper hamper my relationship with Charles.

"Watch out for scorpions and snakes," he cautioned.

"What?" I panicked.

"They won't bother you if you don't bother them," he added.

"Let's carefully analyze what 'bother' means. I get *bothered* when I see a scorpion or snake, so it stands to reason that they may get *bothered* when they see me."

Charles was relaxed about having his Ford Thunderbird stuck in the sand in the middle of nowhere and quite organized in his effort to extricate us from the ordeal. I was glad, because it meant he was marriage material. I didn't want to someday go to the altar with a guy who became frazzled when under duress. Of course, there was no reason to think I would ever say "I do" to Charles, because he was leery of commitment after two failed marriages. He called himself a "cockroach," which was predicated on his favorite joke.

"How do you get rid of a cockroach?" he would say at get-togethers. "Ask him to make a commitment." The crowd would laugh.

Charles's car was less equipped than the Titanic. Of course we had no rafts, but we also had no water, food, blankets, warm clothing, or means to contact help. This was before cell phones. Plus, there was not a patch of shade in sight. In every direction, there was an eternity of sand and sunshine. Charles partially deflated the tires, which is supposed to keep them from spinning. Then he collected floor mats and a reflective windshield sunshade and lodged them under the wheels.

"Maybe I should watch the flight patterns of birds and look for animal tracks," I said, sounding like an out-of-touch academic. "They could take us to water."

"I don't think the situation's that desperate yet," he replied. "Why don't you get in the driver's seat and slowly accelerate while I push."

The strategy failed, but moments later, luck came rambling up from behind. It was an elderly man in a pickup truck. He informed us that his home was the only one in the area. We were fortunate that he'd been in town. He tied a rope to our vehicle and pronto, he hoisted us from the sand.

During our drive back to Los Angeles, Charles elaborated on his adventuresome life. He'd been kidnapped in Africa at age twenty-two and had once slept all night inside an Egyptian pyramid. After story time, I switched the FM dial from a soft rock station to easy listening. But I got the feeling Charles was not on board with my "improvement."

"Did you have fun today?" I asked.

"I'm the second happiest man in the Northern Hemisphere."

"Who's first?"

"Some guy in Peoria, Illinois. His girlfriend once turned to a *decent* channel on the radio." I laughed.

When we arrived at my home, Charles ducked inside to say hello to Kayla and the babysitter but forgot his reading glasses. I noticed them after he'd left and figured it was the perfect opportunity to devise a kidnapping plot. I sent him the following fax.

I have your glasses. Go to the bank. Withdraw $10,000 and place it in a Whole Foods grocery bag. Then take the bag to LensCrafters and place it in the bushes. Do not contact anyone or your spectacles will be crushed, shot, or otherwise mutilated.

He faxed back.

I need evidence that they are okay and being treated right. Otherwise you will never see your $10,000. Also, I only have a Wild Oats bag.

Our weekly faxing sessions began like this, and months later we were still at it. One night he sent me a widely circulated Internet letter from a man who resented upgrading from Girlfriend 3.0 to Wife 1.0. He had found "Wife 1.0 to be a resource hog, leaving him little free space for other applications."

I faxed back.

I've heard Wife 1.0 is an excellent program. That is, as long as it is run concurrently with Husband 1.0. Unfortunately, Wife 1.0 has bugs when run simultaneously with Jerk 6.2 and Asshole 3.8.

I had fallen in love with Toad-gone-wrong by date three. Now, it was a year and a half later, and he would break up with me shortly thereafter.

Chapter Fourteen

WHIPS, CHAINS, AND THE UCLA PROFESSOR

The mistress's hair was the shade of dried blood.

She strutted around the dungeon in a latex jumpsuit and shiny black boots. Her slave was on all fours chained inside a cage, wearing a blindfold, a posture collar, spandex shorts, a halter top, and fishnet stockings.

"Bark," Mistress ordered.

"Arf. Arf." Slave obeyed.

"And tomorrow you will mow my lawn dressed in Saran wrap." Mistress strummed the cage as if it were a cello. "Then you will worship my feet for an hour."

"Yes, goddess," Slave said.

Mistress yanked Slave from the enclosure, tied her to a medieval rack, and whipped her. Slave screamed.

Charles, who was standing next to me in the dungeon, backed against the wall.

"I hope she doesn't make us clean the floor with our tongues." I flashed a worried look. "I hear she likes to do that."

"This is a joke, right?" he asked.

I was deadpan. Toad-gone-wrong and I were dating again.

The breakup—and my ensuing tears—had been short-lived. The words "I can't see you anymore" on Monday had turned into "Do you want to get together again?" by Tuesday. In other words, Charles had called it quits for a full twenty-four hours. Now we were standing in the oddest of places: an eerie dark chamber on the seedy side of town. We were surrounded by numerous sadistic devices: a bondage table, a spanking bench, a full suspension-type mechanism, wall shackles, a St. Andrew's Cross, and what looked like a bed of nails.

The Chateau Club on Fulton Avenue in North Hollywood was the only licensed BDSM or "bondage and discipline" facility in the country, according to the business's front desk clerk. Customers could pay seventy dollars to rent out a room for an hour, and they could pay extra for one or two girls. Customers who had a thirst for a sadomasochistic fantasy experience came there to play games with either a dominant or a submissive theme. There was no sex or erotic touching allowed. It was against company policy.

Neither Charles nor I had ever been exposed to this subculture. As a real estate agent, I had clients ranging from FHA buyers to wealthy celebrities, but I had never represented an obvious sadist or masochist. Of course, there is the industry-wide joke that "sellers are yellers," indicating that property owners inflict pain and humiliation on their agents. But I don't believe it ever included spanking or whips and chains. No homeowner, to my knowledge, has ever hauled her Realtor into the front yard and put her in the stockades. Pillory-lined streets would hurt resale value.

"Buyers are liars" is another frequently uttered catchphrase. It is true that many purchasers are wishy-washy and seem tortured by the buying process, but I have never met one who wanted to be shackled to the walls and whipped with a riding crop.

I had told Charles, "My real estate client calls herself 'Mistress,' and she's super weird. I need to get her to sign escrow papers, and I'm afraid to meet with her alone."

Charles had agreed to accompany me to the windowless warehouse of the Chateau Club, which Mistress called her "office." The receptionist had led us to a back area called the "dungeon," where we'd found "my client."

"I'll be with you shortly," Mistress hollered at us while continuing to abuse her slave.

We waited patiently near the door. I held a folder of papers against my chest as if it were a bulletproof vest.

"I won't make you lick the floor this time." Mistress eventually pranced over to us. She was clearly bored with her human toy. "I will sign the papers on one condition." She zeroed in on me. "You have to let me tie up your guy and beat him for a while."

"Come on, this is not real." Charles chuckled.

Mistress, Slave, and I could no longer keep a straight face. The whole thing *had* been a practical joke. There were no escrow papers, and we erupted in laughter. The women left the room, and Charles and I spent the remainder of the reserved hour taking goofy photos on the medieval-style contraptions. Many of the shots were not in keeping with the image of a lawyer and judge pro tem (a role Charles assumed from time to time). The picture of Charles sprawled out on the "nail bed" in handcuffs with a pained expression on his face was priceless.

"I'll have to hang this in your courtroom to remind everyone what a guilty verdict means," I said.

⁂

"E" was a relationship wrecker.

He had no business meddling in our affairs. I wanted to attack that measly vowel. Specifically, I yearned to turn "E" into an "F," Lorena Bobbitt–style.

Charles had returned from a three-hour spiritual seminar and announced that his higher power named "E" wanted him to break up with me. This was not a sufficient reason, because "E" was not a sufficient person. In fact, "E" did not exist at all. He was just some pretend entity that a pretend spiritual teacher wanted his students to accept.

Charles liked visiting gurus. I admired the fact that his heart was open to alternative views of reality, but when this creepy little vowel started butting into our love life, it was time to show my true colors as a skeptic.

"There is no E," I told Charles. "It's a lie. There is no invisible entity that wants you to end our relationship."

"No, we are supposed to break up," he insisted. "I can't ever commit to you. That's the plain truth."

I did not want to believe these depressing words. I had no faith in pessimistic predictions. My faith was fully contained in my stamina, perseverance, and feelings for Charles. I hoped to hang on by my fingernails until Toad-gone-wrong had a change of heart.

"E" was not the only spacecraft to lower itself into our relationship. I don't mean to discredit metaphysical adventures or so-called sages (especially in light of my Spinoza experiences).

I actually found these sorts of things interesting, like a new shade of gray that I had never before witnessed. But Charles and I had different goals in the spirituality department. He was seeking "enlightenment," while I was seeking "experience." Charles was a cirrus cloud. He was high in the air, wispy, and diaphanous. He was floating in the ascetic realm chasing perfection. I was of the cumulus persuasion. I was closer to the ground, practical, and more defined. I relied on this-worldliness and discounted the notion of transcendence.

I didn't believe in personal enlightenment, objectively speaking. I viewed people as clouds, drifting here and there, up and down, back and forth. Each person could define her own essence and what personal "progress" or "virtue" meant, but it was a wholly experiential and subjective enterprise. There was no judge from on high who designated Person A as enlightened and Person B as defective. No mere mortal could escape her flesh-and-blood circumstance to become a mini-God, perfect being, or "E" equivalent.

Charles and I had sailed into many spiritual escapades together. He'd taken me to visit a Tibetan monk, who blessed our relationship and dubbed me "All Good Goddess." He gave Charles the name "Fearless, Powerful Life." We wore white; lit candles; and participated in solemn, sacred space behavior.

Charles and I also spent a number of evenings at a warehouse in Santa Monica called the Hard Light meditation center. Charles would do the normal meditation thing: He would sit in the lotus position, try to clear his mind, and think about nothing. I would do the normal type A thing. I would create lists, go over goals, review projects, and jot down philosophical ideas. Attempting to do nothing made me anxious. It felt like a waste of time. And wasting time was almost as bad as being thrashed by Mistress in the dungeon with a belt.

Over time, Charles's line "I'm seeking enlightenment"

evolved into the statement "I am enlightened." Although he said it in a tongue-in-cheek way, I often wondered if he'd been sneaking into "E's" fridge for unsanctioned sips of Kool-Aid. One day, when Charles returned from visiting the Croatian spiritual healer Braco, I confronted him with some "Socratic method" and sarcasm.

"Oh, my goodness." I looked him up and down when he walked through the door. "You are enlightened!"

"That's good. You're making a joke." He smiled.

"Oh, I forgot," I said. "You were already enlightened."

"Yes," he replied.

"So what exactly were you doing there? Enlightening Braco?"

Charles smirked. He had no answer.

"Maybe this was just a topping off. Your enlightenment tank was full, but you were just topping it off?"

"Do you want to know the truth?" he asked.

"Yes."

"I was doing it for you." He chuckled and left the room.

Charles liked to kid about my lack of enlightenment and his overabundance of it. In addition, he got pleasure from mentioning how he and Spinoza shared the same birthday: November 24—a fact I had not realized until two years into our relationship. He regularly teased me about how he had been Spin in a former life.

"I've changed my views. I was wrong about everything back then," he'd jest.

Our E-induced breakup lasted only three days, but there would be more heartbreaking times ahead. I worried that Toad-gone-wrong might never turn into a permanent Prince Charming. And I feared that a lifelong love relationship was for me as unattainable as the cirrus clouds in the sky.

"E" was not the only dark cloud that threatened to flood my parade. There were the satanic shrinks and Rosalyn.

Rosalyn was not a figment of Charles's imagination, a character in a paranormal novel, or an invention by a misguided soothsayer. She was a UCLA professor who let Charles rent a room in her Brentwood home for one hundred dollars per month. She kept the cost low because her attraction was high. She hoped to make Charles her boyfriend and crush pesky competitors like me. She convinced Charles to be the voice on her answering machine, to attend periodic lectures as her escort, and to pick her up from the airport when returning from academic conferences. She even paid for him to accompany her to exotic lands, although she maintained a separate room and never made a pass. Charles professed innocence about Rosalyn's intentions, which I chalked up to the "males are clueless about females" theory.

"She's never expressed any overt interest in me," he explained. But deep down, he knew she saw me as her rival.

Rosalyn was thin and affluent like Cruella de Vil but had no Dalmatians. Her primary bone to pick with me had to do with age. I was a puppy at thirty-five, while Charles was fifty-four and she was seventy. Rosalyn was ten in dog years. She hoped to pry me away from my boyfriend and strangle me with the short leash she'd reserved for Charles.

One day, she fetched my holiday card, examined my signature, and launched a penmanship attack. It was based on her "expertise" in handwriting analysis. Like Robert De Niro in *Meet the Parents*, she thought she'd uncovered lies with her little test.

"Charlotte is a demanding 'princess' type who's not really

interested in you," Rosalyn said to Charles after examining my bold *E* and other cursive.

Just because my *E* was demanding didn't mean I was. In fact, Charles had already labeled me a 3 on the high-maintenance scale, and he had graded me a full 10 for the "being in love" category. As for the link with royalty, I was generally too conflict-averse to be bossy or take the stage as Miss High-and-Mighty. In my mind, I was my childhood nickname: "Missy Mouse," a tiny person with big aspirations.

In addition to Rosalyn, I had to contend with satanic shrinks. They lived in Morro Bay, California, and were probably not real devil worshippers. They just gave that impression. Charles knew Mr. and Mrs. Shrink casually. They agreed to give us couples counseling because we had been having such a bumpy time of our relationship. The speed bumps, of course, were constructed by Charles, who kept calling it quits and claiming there was no future. Although I was emotional and tearful much of the time, I'd always put great effort into veering back onto the road and putting soft rock on the radio for Charles's listening pleasure.

Mr. and Mrs. Shrink took us into their home and showed us the basement, where they had set up lights, chairs, and video cameras for therapy sessions. I quickly learned that these couch doctors had only one plan: to dump the entire couch on me and jump on it. The playbook seemed as if it had been orchestrated in advance. I was their voodoo doll. They needled me with sharp words, sprayed bright lights in my face, and harassed me for hours, exorcism-style.

"Our relationship is on-again, off-again," I confessed.

"He's not interested in you. Don't you understand?" Mrs. Shrink said.

"I think he is," I replied timidly. "He's just afraid of commitment."

"No, he's not," Mr. Shrink said. "He doesn't want you. How can we help you get on with your life?"

"You must strive to be unaffected by anyone or anything," Mrs. Shrink added. "Compromise is a dirty word."

"You have a problem and need to change," Mr. Shrink said. "And couple's therapy doesn't work."

"Then why are we here? And why are you pocketing our money?" I asked. There was no response.

Eventually, I was able to escape from the Grand Inquisitors. I darted upstairs to learn that while I was being ambushed in the basement, Charles had been drinking wine and watching television. I was outraged and glared at the psychologists, who were now standing next to me.

"You defended yourself quite well." Mrs. Shrink tried to smooth things over.

"This was about defending myself?" I asked. There was no answer.

I pulled Charles into another room and exploded. "These people are the devil!" It was uncharacteristic for me to be so angry, but I'd had enough of the terrible twosome's sick games. "I want to leave. Now!"

Secretly, I was contriving a scheme in case Charles refused. I would sneak from the Shrinks' house and take public transportation to Los Angeles, where I would telephone Laura, Lynn, or Gary and ask to be picked up from the train station or bus stop.

"I guess we'll be going," Charles said to the shrinks. "What do I owe you?"

"Three hundred thirty-three dollars," Mr. Shrink replied.

"That figures," I said sarcastically, and stormed out of the house.

Couples therapy cost half the sign of the beast, despite the fact that the beast was fully present. Charles and I left Morro Bay. We faced no further speed bumps on our way back to L.A.

I wanted the relationship with Charles to be a nonstop flight from Single City to blissful togetherness. Charles, however, had a never-ending supply of excuses for why he needed to deboard periodically. He lacked freedom and space. He wanted to stretch his feet. He needed to expand his horizons by meeting new people—maybe even someone who would share a drink with him—because as he put it, "There's only one thing better than drinking before noon. It's drinking before eleven a.m." In actuality, Charles drank little but joked a lot.

When Charles was on the plane, the flight was seamless. We attended the Magic Castle, a casino night fundraiser, a weekly writing group, Oxford-Cambridge Club cocktail parties, California State University philosophy club meetings, classical musical concerts, and even Shakespearean Reading Group dinners for which Charles needed no script. He could recite entire plays from memory. I was dating the man with the big brain, and when I had a question on virtually any topic, I could refer to the human almanac on my arm.

We held makeshift mock trials in which I would play lawyer, presenting one side of a real case. Charles would argue the other position, and our friends would be jurors, deliberating and awarding pretend money judgments. I don't know if it was my last name "Laws," my fake lawyer status at mock trials, or something altogether different, but I regularly received calls from friends asking for legal advice. Lola was one of my best "clients."

"You are the finest attorney in town," she insisted.

The Strong Interest Test agreed with Lola. I'd taken this exam back in high school, and my results came back a tad odd. First, I was apparently equipped to be a lawyer or politician, which seemed wholly reasonable and in keeping with my interests. But Strong got a little wacky when it came to numbers two and three. My second most suitable profession was military officer, and my third was housewife. I told my career counselor that I had narrowed it down to either bombing Iraq or making beds.

Dancing in the aisles was another pastime. Charles and I hoofed it up at the Victorian Ball, where I wore a beaded dress that I'd made for the occasion. And once we stopped by Pleasure's Gentlemen's Club, a Pasadena strip joint. It brought back memories of fleeing from Green Hat and dancing for dollars. I popped onto the stage without permission and boogied for Charles in my bustier and velvet floor-length skirt. Customers thought I was an employee and threw crumpled cash at my feet. The proceeds paid for my favorite supper—steamed broccoli and bottled Evian—as well as for Charles's typical five-course food extravaganza.

Charles liked to eat as much as Scientologists liked paper. He said he could never die before breakfast, lunch, or dinner. He called himself "Pork" and joked that the only meal I could cook was brown rice pizza. Come to think of it, it wasn't a joke. He hated that I had hundreds of small, plastic deli containers scattered around the house, and he recoiled in horror over Kayla's talent for destroying kitchenware.

"How does it make you feel to have brought a ruthless pan wrecker into the world?" he asked.

Kayla regularly shouted "Lover Boy" when Charles came through the front door, and she buried him in balloons, wrapping paper, or newspapers when he fell asleep on the couch. In addition to Pork, Cockroach, and Toad-gone-wrong, Charles named himself Lord Pig and Sniggley Bockett. He affectionately called me Elsie Dumpling, Charlittle, and Babe.

He also created names for my dogs[21] and dubbed them members of the Homeland Defense Force. Cyd, the English sheepdog, was a Bombardier because she could empty a room. Never was rank so rank. George Swossage, a terrier, was a Lance-Corporal and the backbone of the army, but not a thinker. The other terrier, Shaggy, was a lover and not a fighter. He had assumed the title of Grenadier. Last, Spotless the Maltese was very small; you could hardly make her out at all. She was a Fusilier, even though she was really too midgety to hold a fusil. Charles was proud of the fact that my house—as well as the entire neighborhood—had remained free from terrorist incident since the dogs assumed their posts.

Charles and I often went on double dates, once setting up Lynn with a guy who fell asleep in his soup. Actually, only his bangs took the plunge. When he woke, he had a split pea on his forehead. That same night, we made an "odds and ends" call to the cops. An *odd* man with a naked rear *end* was ambling down the street in a hospital gown. He had wandered out of a psychiatric ward. We timed the police response at three minutes, which was impressive. But it was unimpressive to find twenty officers still on the scene of the "crime" three hours later with no *end* in sight.

Leaving the aircraft did not always mean our relationship was on hold. During the three years that Charles and I dated, we'd deplaned together to vacation in Santa Barbara, Lake Tahoe, England, and a friend's home on the Colorado River. We also took a nine-day cruise to Mexico and spent a week at Optimum Health Institute in San Diego. On both of those trips, Charles complained, "You just can't stay with the program."

He was right. I was like water escaping from an uncorked sink. The more structured the environment, the more likely the dissident in me would emerge and rush toward nonconformity. "Following the program" was simply not my style. I preferred to make my own arrangements. I had been a cynic at

Insight when meeting Jed, and I could never have belonged to a structured organization like Scientology.

When it came to conformity, Charles had a different perspective. He felt that when a person signed up for a program, she should follow it. He was disturbed by my disregard for rules, for norms, and for the unspoken mandate that hovered over the ship during our nine-day Mexican cruise. The message was: "Do what the masses do. Swim. Go to shows. Stuff your face. Invest in expensive artwork. Act like a typical American consumer. But above all, do not work."

In retaliation, I did not swim, I did not go to shows, I did not stuff my face, and I did not buy fancy artwork or behave like a typical American consumer. The topper was: *all* I planned to do was work. However, I encountered a slight difficulty: The cruise line had not installed a single electrical outlet in the public areas of the vessel for my computer.

"Sorry, we don't have any plugs," an employee said. "You're supposed to relax and have fun. You're on vacation."

I was annoyed. In the end, I had to settle for the measly plug in the bathroom of my room without a view. I had to charge my laptop there and take it on short jaunts to more stimulating locations. It was a real drag but the only option. There was something about being productive that was important to me, even when on vacation. I needed to feel as if I was wooing success. Tiny victories were like notches on my bedpost, names on my dance card, or check marks on my bucket list. I'd always packed books and writing projects when traveling. It was the only way to enjoy myself for long stretches. I adored spending time with Charles, but my goal-oriented self needed to be drowning in goals. Drowning didn't trigger claustrophobia because each objective was an outlet or opening, potentially leading me to increased self-fulfillment.

By the end of the cruise and with only the juice from my

bathroom plug, I completed a fifty-four-page no-kill animal shelter proposal for a local municipality. I handed it to the mayor on the following week.

The instructions at San Diego's Optimum Health Institute were different. "Stuffing your face" was not on the menu. Starvation was the main course, and losing weight was the after-dinner activity. Many people—such as Charles and I—were there to drop pounds. Others hoped to combat health issues or destress with holistic healing. Guests were asked to attend daytime lectures—mostly on the benefits of veganism—and to participate in a morning exercise class, which was as vigorous as lying on a hospital gurney. I liked Optimum but had no intention of following their rules, because, well, I never followed anyone's rules.

I could take high-impact aerobics classes at San Diego's Bally Total Fitness, so hospital-cot calisthenics were moot. And as an animal rights advocate, I was already a proponent of the vegan diet, so the lectures were superfluous. Although the Optimum food was healthy, it comprised weird things, such as green watermelon juice, durian, crosne, kumquats, cherimoya, morels, and green tomatoes. On the first day, I stared at the hodgepodge on my plate as if it was a pottery project. I took teeny-weeny bites until my nausea reached the level of "high alert." It was one day, two days, three days later, and my stomach sickness had not subsided. Fasting was getting old fast.

Charles ate his pottery like a dutiful camper in the main dining hall with the other guests, while I peered through the window in starvation mode. I could not go inside because the smell of the food caused queasiness. But suddenly I caught a glimpse of a breathtaking sight. It was a red tomato, and it appeared to be as normal as those found at Ralphs, Safeway, or Whole Foods. It was resting innocently in a small bowl near some condiments and trays.

I held my breath so as not to inhale pottery fumes and darted into the room. I nabbed the tomato and caressed it as if it were a ruby. Then I took a huge bite. It was ecstasy. It was perfection.

"That's a decoration," a kitchen worker in a hairnet said. "Please don't eat the decorations."

"I just want normal food," I begged. "Please. Don't you have anything normal?"

"There's raw chayote on the table."

Obviously the hairnet had severed the neurons in her brain. I didn't know what raw chayote was. I didn't care what raw chayote was. Raw chayote was simply not going to work for me. So, with my treasured tomato in hand, I marched to the parking lot and drove to a local health food restaurant, where I ordered a glass of fresh apple juice. The juice came from normal apples on normal trees in the normal ground. This became my go-to spot for the remainder of the week.

Despite my refusal to eat Optimum food, the Charlotte Laws Apple Juice Diet was a success. I lost more weight than any other guest. On the final night of our stay, Charles and I performed in the resort's weekly talent show. He recited poetry, and I danced in a delightfully gaudy red-and-gold belly dancing costume that I'd made. We called our act "Agony and Ecstasy."

Despite the good times and my efforts to lock the hatch and hide the parachutes, Charles would not stay in his assigned seat. There was no natural turbulence in the relationship—only that which he induced. He'd been married twice. One union had lost too much altitude but had landed safely. The other had resulted in a midair collision. The first wife had exited Scientology and was on good terms with Charles, but the second had stayed in the religion and "disconnected." I believed the failed marriages had prompted the commitment-phobic cockroach to emerge.

On the other hand, maybe Mr. Shrink's "he's just not that into you" speech had been on target.

Despite my doubts, I asked Charles to take a baby step. I created a two-month commitment contract. I figured if Charles would not sign, his fear of flying was worse than I'd anticipated. I handed him the document and waited. The cabin pressure mounted. He hemmed and hawed. I wondered if I might need an oxygen mask. Like a typical lawyer, he crossed out sentences and injected his own wording. I held my breath and made sure I could use my seat cushion as a floating device. In the end, he signed. It bonded us for only two months, but it was an improvement over the constant anxiety of wondering when he would step off the plane.

On January 20, 1997, he ended our relationship. My heart ached as if it had a fatal bullet wound, and my tears could have washed an entire fleet of 747s. I knew I had only two choices: give up or not. Quitting was not my style, especially considering the happiness I'd felt with Charles and the difficulty in finding another "perfect" guy to fit inside my itty-bitty box.

Throughout my life, I'd harbored a persistent and painful fear: that I might become asexual or non-romantic. I was always one man away from an attraction to no one. It was scary because it seemed abnormal, unfulfilling, and hollow. I'd look at movie stars and entertainers and find no one appealing. I'd attend man-filled events or flip through magazines of male models. I'd be disinterested, yet my girlfriends would gush over tons of guys. Was there something wrong with me? It seemed like more than pickiness. I harbored a compulsive all-or-nothing mentality, and I felt *nothing* 99.9999 percent of the time.

I was more afraid of finding no one attractive than being rejected by that one man who peaked my interest. I was enormously grateful when a sexy guy came into my life. It assuaged my ever-present fear of "a possible attraction to no one"—an anxiety that stalks me to this day.

This is why I was unable to let Charles go. I also knew that dragging him back onto the plane, despite protests, would do nothing but lead to animosity and possibly a restraining order. So I created a third option and called it the Three-Step Persistence Plan. This process could be written as one of those self-help books that rambles on for 250 pages when the core idea is capable of being explained succinctly in four paragraphs. I will take the succinct route.

Step 1 is to set a date on the calendar at least six months in the future. This is the day that you plan to "coincidentally"—translated as "not so coincidentally"—run into your ex-boyfriend again. You might pop into his favorite hangout; drop by his office under the auspices that you are visiting someone in his building; or get a mutual friend to invite him to a restaurant where you, by chance, happen to be eating. Then you feign surprise and hopefully renew his interest. It is my belief that if a person was once attracted to you, he can be attracted again.

The genius of this maneuver is that you do not need to spend six months weeping like a willow. You can maintain a positive attitude with hope that reunion is possible. Either one of two things will happen: You will follow through with the future meeting, or you will forget about the cockroach and move on with your life. Maybe you will meet a new cockroach. But either outcome is fine because you have avoided the avalanche of agony that traditionally accompanies a breakup. If he rejects you a second time, you can either plan a new date down the road or not. But the disappointment is less likely to sting because time has elapsed.

Step 2 involves bettering yourself. You have an important goal—to reunite with the man you love—so you want to be the best you can be. Improvement may include losing weight, sharpening your mind, obtaining a better job, saving money, fostering a new talent, or something altogether different. Perhaps it is a combination thereof.

The third and last step of the Three-Step Persistence Plan is to show up for the "coincidental" meeting. Woody Allen said, "Eighty percent of success is just showing up." I disagree. It's 90 percent. If you prefer to be more straightforward, you might want to simply contact your ex with hope that he has become more interested over time. I would, however, add that a visual connection tends to be crucial for instigating a reunion. Obviously if you have met someone new or lost interest in the cockroach, the third step is pointless.

I circled August 19, 1997, on my calendar. This was seven months following our taxi into that final gate, where Charles collected his bags and bolted. Until August, the plane would remain grounded, inoperable, and under repair. I would strive to upgrade the engine and reupholster the interior. I would repaint the body and buffer the wings. I would do everything possible to make alluring improvements. And thankfully during that period, I would not feel the usual whips and chains of torment that normally followed a romantic split.

Although I was an experienced party-crasher, I knew there was no assurance I would ever break through the barrier to Charles's highly guarded heart.

Chapter Fifteen

RETURN OF THE MENACING PARTICLE?

Menacing particles walk among us. They nab our parking spots. They pile their dirty dishes in our sinks. They put their work boots on our white couches. Charles had gotten this clever term from Scientology, and he'd periodically volleyed it my direction. I'd used it against him as well. It had been our inside joke.

There had been no inside jokes for seven months. Charles had walked out of my life in January 1997, and now it was seven months later. I had not dated any other men, and I deeply missed Charles. I was still in love with him. The Three-Step Persistence Plan was entering its final stage. I had to concoct a sneaky plot to put myself in Charles's face with hopes of instigating reconciliation. I was unsure how he'd react. Would he roll his eyes? Would he run away? Maybe he had a new honey pie in his cupboard. I figured my chance of success was small. After all, Charles had not contacted me. He was obviously content with leaving our relationship at "good-bye, dragonfly."

The anonymous letter that I sent to him read, "Finally responding to your request from a long time ago." This was nonsense, meant to confuse Charles about my identity.

Then I wrote, "Fine food, imported beer, and gourmet chocolate" in an effort to get his stomach to meet me, even if he refused.

I added, "Drop by for dinner if you're free on Tuesday." Then I mentioned an address on Ocean Front Walk in Venice, California. Lola had sold her tennis court estate at a huge profit and moved to this beachside apartment. I was house-sitting.

My correspondence ended with "Hope you can make it" and no signature. I mailed the correspondence from far away for postmark-deception purposes.

On the appointed evening, I set out to create a delightful dichotomy. Venice Beach was the center of eccentricity, where tourists came to be shocked out of their middle-American values. It was the capital of body piercing, fortune-tellers, muscle men, tattoos, roller skating, homelessness, break dancing, and Hare Krishnas.

My plan was to transform Lola's apartment into a sanctuary of old-world charm. It would resemble the other Venice: the less cheesy one located in Italy—which was, of course, more cheesy when it came to parmesan. When Charles stepped through the door from the quirky beach town, he'd find himself in a Venetian villa with a romantic ambiance and a femme fatale in Renaissance-inspired corset gown.

I smeared vanilla lotion all over my body. I painted my toenails soft pink and styled my long hair. I lit the fireplace as well as three-dozen chocolate-scented candles, which were scattered throughout the apartment. The aroma was that of a decadent dessert truffle. The dinner menu consisted of olives, a crusty baguette, Pinot Grigio wine, imported beer, tofu stroganoff, a salad with grapes and sautéed walnuts, and gourmet chocolate for after-dinner calories. Classical music filled the air, and I set the table for two with a splash of Martha Stewart living. As a final touch, I slipped on high heels and dabbed myself with Realm perfume, which contained human pheromones. It was designed to attract even the most cantankerous cockroach.

I glanced at the clock. It was seven p.m. I was nervous but ready to find out whether the Three-Step Persistence Plan was an epic fail or an epic success. I looked at my supporters in the room. The fireplace flickered like a bouncy cheerleader. The candle flames pranced like majorettes. The stroganoff on the stove sizzled like a marching band, and the ceiling fan roared like an adoring crowd. They all encouraged me to win one for the Gipper.

At 7:05 p.m., Charles had not arrived, and I was filled with worry. I fidgeted with the curtains while peering out the window. At 7:08 p.m., I collapsed on the couch. By 7:11 p.m., I was still having no luck. I thought about dismantling the "romantic evening" and heading home. I figured I'd been a loony raccoon to think Charles would go to a strange place to meet a possibly even stranger person. Only a super spontaneous and brave soul would take a chance on dinner with anonymous.

At 7:13 p.m., my supporters looked dejected, too. The fire no longer cheered. The candles had lost their stride. The tofu was getting overcooked, and the ceiling fan whined as if it needed WD-40. Even the pimento-stuffed olives on the table looked like droopy eyeballs. I wasn't sure who would start crying first: me or them.

But at 7:14 p.m., hope barreled back into the room with a loud knock. I fluffed up my hair, made sure all looked perfect, and opened the door to find Charles. He looked as handsome as ever, and he did not seem disappointed to learn that I was the foreman behind the ploy.

"Oh, it's you," he said. "I was wondering who sent that invitation."

"Come inside. It's been a long time."

"Are you wearing pheromones?" he immediately said. I thought I would fall off the Sistine Chapel ceiling!

"Pheromones?" I dodged the question. "I have a lovely dinner prepared. I hope you're hungry."

"They don't call me Porky Pie Crust for nothing," he replied, showing me that he was the same ole lovable guy.

During dinner, he playfully criticized the United States, although he was equally renowned for attacking his beloved Britain. He insisted that America is overly complicated, offering thirty-four kinds of mustard at the grocery store. He said that the one and only brand in England is perfectly sufficient.

Then he undertook a philosophical analysis of American football, arguing that due to its byzantine complexity, it finds deep resonance in the American soul. He explained how the players are deliberately fashioned as anonymous cartoon superheroes with huge shoulder pads and helmets that hide their faces. They are differentiated only by the numbers on their backs. He contrasted this with the much simpler and less incognito game of soccer in England.

"I'll get you some dessert." I headed to the kitchen.

He followed. "I'll help you. I'm a fountain of goodness."

I strained to reach plates, located in a cabinet.

"You've had the same opportunity to grow as everyone else," he joked as he retrieved the china.

Charles was a riot, and I was still his biggest fan. Our conversation was smooth, playful, and meaningful. It was as if he had never stepped off that plane seven months prior. Dessert led to a romantic walk on the beach. The waves clashed, and I felt like Deborah Kerr in *From Here to Eternity*. Charles reached down and kissed me, and my heart leapt with joy.

The menacing particle was back in my life.

⁓

On the following day, I got a surprise phone call from a woman named Amy. She said that she was my adoptive brother's biological mother. She had put Buddy up for adoption in 1962. Society was brutal on single moms back then. This is the story she told me.

Buddy's natural father, John, was an alcoholic and a schizophrenic. He was an irresponsible womanizer. He was anti-Semitic and wanted to be sure everyone knew he wasn't a Jew. John was charming and smart but troubled.

John was distressed when he placed the gun to his head. He was standing on his father's driveway in Cleveland, Ohio, next to his car. John knew he had a little boy out there somewhere, who had been adopted by an Atlanta family, but he didn't care.

John killed himself that day.

John had impregnated Amy during a fling at a house in Virginia Beach. He was sharing the place with some buddies. He was thirty years old, was a navy man, and had attended Purdue University. He was in town for only a few days and liked getting girls into bed whenever possible. He had no thoughts about consequences or what would happen if the casual relationship led to a baby alone in a bassinette at Emory Hospital waiting for parents to be assigned to him.

Amy had not wanted Buddy to be alone. After giving birth, she'd tiptoed from her bed down to the maternity ward. She had to be sneaky because mothers in her situation were prohibited from seeing their newborns. The adoption agency was afraid she'd reconsider. She had relinquished all rights. She had signed a contract. Her baby boy belonged to "The Agency."

Amy had never wanted to put Buddy up for adoption, but she'd succumbed to social pressure. In 1962, it was considered shameful to be a single mom. John had callously directed her to get an abortion, despite it being illegal at the time. Amy had told him that she was unwilling to skirt the law and risk injury or death with a bootleg physician.

When news of Amy's pregnancy first reached her parents' home, she was quietly shipped off to live with her broad-minded aunt Nancy in Atlanta. Aunt Nancy had a log cabin with vertical timbers on Moores Mill Road. It was set back from the street, and it was as cold as John's heart. The undersized heater was virtually inoperable. Aunt Nancy took Amy to her routine doctor appointments in her Volkswagen bug until the day she gave birth.

Amy saw John four years later in New York, where he was working for a chemical company. He was unconcerned with Buddy's whereabouts. He was unconcerned with Buddy. He was only concerned with getting Amy into bed again. But his charm had lost its razzle-dazzle.

Amy told me that she was now an adoption activist and that she had been searching for Buddy for many years. For some odd reason, Dad noticed her tiny classified ad in the *Atlanta Journal-Constitution*. He'd never looked at the classifieds before, and he has never looked at them since. Frankly, I was surprised that he'd reached out to her. It seemed out of character. Dad told her Buddy was dead. Although Amy could not find her son, she found closure.

Amy and I got together a couple of times, and it was delightful. She also hoped to meet Dad, who agreed to dine with her if she came to Atlanta. She wanted to give the man who had raised Buddy a hug. Amy and Dad confirmed the details on the phone. Then Amy bought a plane ticket, flew to Georgia, checked into a hotel, and called Dad.

"I'm in Atlanta, Mr. Laws," she said with enthusiasm.

"Sorry. I'm too busy," he replied callously.

"What?" Amy was incredulous.

"I don't have any free time. Take care." Dad hung up the phone.

Amy was confused and disappointed, and she broke into tears. She didn't deserve this. She'd already experienced loss with news of Buddy's death, and now she was suffering again.

Buddy was abusing alcohol at a young age just like his natural dad. Had my brother not died in a car accident at sixteen but lived a normal life span, it is possible that self-destructive behavior would have stalked him as well. Genes are powerful. It may not have been Mom's suicide and anger toward Dad that hooked my brother into the bottle. It may have been the tainted blood of John.

⁖

Charles was at a desk with a pen and a pad, trying to push through writer's block while I towered over him.

"Your novel is like your life," I said. "There's no story. Only beautiful words."

"What do you mean 'only'? Words are pretty freakin' important," Charles said.

"A brilliant artist. Maybe a genius. But without a story." I yawned.

"I have a story," Charles said.

"True. Philosophically speaking, no story is a story."

"You're always giving me that analytical crap," Charles replied.

"It's like your life," I said. "No structure. No glue. It doesn't flow. A novel needs structure. So does a life."

"A novel is not a life," he said.

"You jump from character to character, from person to person, from woman to woman… without continuity."

"Are you talking about my book or our relationship?"

"It must be terribly unsatisfying."

"I don't see things the way you do. Freedom's important to me."

"Creativity and freedom are necessities for a writer. Structure doesn't destroy them."

"You know something that really irks me," Charles said. "Besides the fact that you like to confuse the hell out of me. You're nothing but story, honey, and it's a real drag."

"But perhaps my stability is the structure you need. And perhaps I need the beauty and eloquence you offer. Maybe this is why we've been together so long."

"So what are you saying? That I can't finish my novel without you?"

"No," I replied. "I'm saying you may not be able to finish your life without me."

"I knew this was about commitment," Charles grumbled.

Charles and I bowed to applause. We'd been reading a piece that I'd written for our weekly writing group in Hollywood. It was based upon the continual struggles in our relationship. It had been almost a year since the Venice Beach reconciliation. Although there had been no speed bumps or departures from the plane, there was a low hum in our relationship. It was like freeway noise or a dentist's drill. It was the sound of friction. It was the irritating vibration that looms when two people disagree on whether to plunge into lifelong commitment.

We'd been dating for four and a half years, and Charles still viewed marriage as bondage. I saw it as a stabilizing force in one's life. I knew it would permit me to devote more time to volunteerism, to making the world better. If married, I would no longer have to spend hundreds of hours on date preparation or worry whether my boyfriend was going to phone. There would be freedom from anxiety and time-wasting activities.

Thus far, my use of transportation imagery had failed. Charles had not snapped out of cockroach mode when I equated our relationship to a car or aircraft. It was time to rely upon the third member of the "planes, trains, and automobiles" team: the steady locomotive. It was a fitting example for the "little Atlanta girl who could," whose motto was, "I think I can, I think I can."

I explained how our relationship could be a smooth and gratifying train trip rather than an unpredictable roller coaster ride. I told Charles that I'd always hated amusement parks. They're crowded, and the masses flock to them. Many are searching for a quick fix. They are not satisfied with what they have. They assume the grass is always greener. They think the roller coaster will spruce up a mundane existence, but they are wrong.

Roller coasters never lead anywhere. They travel in loops and could be called a waste of time. A person hangs in the air and will fall to her death if not strapped to a seat. Trains have a destination. They are safe and secure. Roller coasters consist of cold, uninviting metal and offer no protection from wind, rain, sleet, or hail. Emotions are continually battered by the elements. On a train, there is comfort, shelter, bonding, and lifelong devotion.

It is difficult to make the world better when clinging to a roller coaster. A person becomes preoccupied with the ups and downs, the potential toppling over. On a train, there is a reliable schedule filled with hobbies, friends, dreams, and goals. There is time to help "the other" or those less fortunate.

Commitment-phobes don't understand the importance of the train. They spin endlessly in circles. When they tire of one ride, they search for another. But the lines are long. It takes energy to keep switching roller coasters. It is draining to keep changing one's mind, going from woman to woman, time after time.

After my metaphor, Charles was silent. It appeared that my arguments had once again failed. Perhaps it was time for the train to pull out of the station without the man I loved.

Shutters Hotel in Santa Monica was our destination on the following evening: June 5, 1998. I contemplated whether this would be the right time to tell Charles that I could no longer tolerate the roller coaster. We were joining Charles's brother, John, for dinner and drinks. This was a special occasion because we had not seen John for many years due to the Scientology disconnection policy. He was still in good standing with the church, while Charles was an outcast.

The Shutters ad campaign read, "Where nothing stands between you and the sand." Maybe I was on good terms with the sand, but something very definite stood between me and my man: commitment. Charles and I walked into the lobby, which had a Craftsman flavor and an inviting seating area. I thought about the name of the hotel and how shutters allow a little light but not enough for a full-on committed relationship. Charles liked to adjust brightness on a whim, based on his mood that day or his desire for freedom during a particular week. I wanted an unobstructed view. I wanted total sunshine. I needed our hearts to be completely open to each other.

Charles and I said hello to John, and hugs were enjoyed by all. Then Charles did the unexpected. He was still that spontaneous soul who had come to Venice Beach to meet anonymous. In the middle of the lobby and in full view of two dozen hotel guests, Charles got onto one knee.

"Will you marry me?"

Charles had finally boarded the train. The cockroach was gone, and I was about to become the proud wife of a menacing particle.

Chapter Sixteen

SURPRISE! MARRIED BY A WITCH

I was marrying a man who liked to say, "I'm ready to do nothing on a moment's notice." But I had no complaints, because I was ready to do everything. I would become the florist, baker, and wedding planner. I would finagle deals. I planned to out-shark the wedding sharks. Many vendors in the "marriage biz" are hustlers. They raise prices 1,000 percent for only one reason: because they can. Since brides and grooms are so *taken* with each other, they often get *taken* by others. They are easy marks.

I began by shopping for a gown. As a collector of clothes, I was not about to carelessly plop down thousands of dollars on the first pretty rag in the first pretty shop. I couldn't be fooled by designer labels or elaborate sales pitches, and I quickly learned to ignore price tags. They were merely foreplay for hard-core negotiations.

"I could give you that dress half-price," a clerk hollered as I was leaving a bridal shop in Studio City.

That was the cue I needed. I was privy to a closely guarded industry secret. Prices were much like Romanian gymnasts: They were highly flexible. Armed with this advantage, I vaulted into every bridal salon in Los Angeles, searching for that perfect "10." I eventually said yes to the dress at Wedding Dreams in Woodland Hills, which was frankly the most exquisite boutique of all. There were enough gowns to bedeck every star in the sky. It was the happiest place on earth, full of hope, tingles, and fairy dust. For clerks, it was good news all day. Beaming brides would try on sumptuous gowns, which jacked up everyone's smiles a little bit more.

A romantic, lacy, high-collar Marie Antoinette frock with a corset bodice would escort me down the aisle. With it, I would live the fairy tale. With it, I would feel confident at my garden wedding. And with it, I would marry the man I adored. But this angelic dress had a devil of a price tag: $4,200. I shook my head and started to leave, but the clerk informed me that the gown was on sale.

"It's in the wrong spot. It should be on the sale rack for $1,250."

I shook my head again. "How about $475 cash."

"Okay," she replied. "It's last season anyway."

Since I had clothing collection disorder and had hit the jackpot with dress number one, I decided to splurge on dress number two. Most brides pay bundles for just one gown, I rationalized. Plus, I liked being eccentric. Buying two gowns was more my style.

The runner-up was an off-the-shoulder medieval-style dress from a different boutique. I nabbed it for a paltry $300.

However, the list price was only $795. I planned to show it off at a family dinner at Villa Pia Cere restaurant on the evening prior to the wedding.

Wedding photographers can be expensive. The average cost to cover a ceremony and reception is $2,500. I decided to go a different route. I headed to CSUN, where I stood outside an advanced photography class until the bell rang. Then I recruited two camera-savvy students for a mere fifty dollars each, not including the cost of the film. They eagerly accepted the marriage gig. It presented an opportunity to beef up their portfolios. They agreed to provide me with the negatives afterward so I could make prints. This plan would lead to success. Their wedding shots would be breathtaking.

Gary agreed to be the videographer; it would be his wedding gift. Plus, he and his band offered to entertain at the reception at no charge. The caricaturist and bachelorette party would be presents from Lynn. In the "fifty dollars or less" category, I obtained each of the following: a triple-decker wedding cake (which I made), the veil (which I created mostly from my adoptive mom's old veil), white shoes, and my bouquet. From the "fifty to one hundred dollars" category, I got designer invitations (obtained at "cost"), flowers (wholesale from downtown Los Angeles), centerpieces (also wholesale), a harpist for the ceremony, Kayla's maid-of-honor dress, and throw-away cameras for each table at the reception. Charles's tux was also inexpensive.

I rejected the tradition of putting bridesmaids in poofy prom gowns. Instead my seven bridesmaids were instructed to wear any black dress they already owned.

I was unable to negotiate a discount on venue. After previewing every appropriate outdoor facility in the Los Angeles basin, I was confident with my final choice: Descanso Gardens, which had majestic views and 160 acres of flowers and woodlands. It was a renowned tourist attraction with stunning botanical gardens, and it had been accredited by the American Association of Museums. Descanso cost a whopping $2,500 plus catering, which added another $3,000. This obviously composed the bulk of my $8,500 total out-of-pocket expenses, but I knew the event would be as impressive as any royal wedding.

"The meal will have to be vegan," I said to Charles.

Charles felt it was important to offer meat, as well as unhampered access to hard liquor and other alcoholic beverages. To do otherwise was what he called "impolite." Charles's peccadillo in this area stemmed from his English upbringing. Although I hated the idea of wasting money as an enabler for the drunk and disorderly, at least booze didn't clash with my value system.

"I'm not going to budge on the food issue," I said.

"You should have looked for a husband on tofu.com or lettuce.com," Charles joked.

In the end, we compromised. I consented to an open bar, while he accepted a flesh-free menu.

It was my wedding day: July 11, 1999. For better or worse, it would be one of the most memorable days of my life. I say worse because I began the day in worrywart mode. I didn't have wedding jitters, but I most definitely had weather jitters. My outdoor ceremony was at the mercy of the storm gods. Thunder, lightning, and heavy rain were expected to gatecrash. And if they showed, they'd steal my thunder. They'd be the drunk and disorderly. I imagined being a soggy bride. I imagined reciting my vows while vowing revenge on the heavens. I imagined tying the knot while wringing out my new gown. It never rains in Southern California, so why the heck was it threatening to rain on me?

On top of that, I was the busy butterfly, flitting here, there, and yonder. I had three hours to do everything. I was mildly panic-stricken because I had no wedding planner, florist, or other prearranged helpers. I constructed the dinner centerpieces. I decorated the lattice tunnel that led guests into the garden. I readied the photo album, which guests could peruse to see relationship snapshots of me and Charles. I prepped the funny quizzes that I'd written. Invitees would later try to guess the correct answers for prizes. I affixed tulle ribbons and supplemental flowers to the wedding gazebo. Gorgeous vines were already wrapped around the structure. It resembled a three-dimensional canvas of Van Gogh and Monet.

"It's fantastic. I've never seen anything like this, and I've been in this business a long time," the Descanso representative said to me as I stood on a chair in my shorts and tank top tying the final ribbon to the wedding arch. Guests were beginning to trickle into the garden.

"What do you mean?" I asked.

"You are doing all this work yourself, and you're *enjoying* it." She grinned.

She was right. Hiring a wedding planner would have been a major gaff. An outsider with outsider opinions, creating outsider details, would have spoiled the insider charm. Charles and I had designed everything from scratch, including our unusual vows. And I'd relished every moment of the wheeling and dealing, of whipping the multifarious puzzle called our wedding into shape.

But I had two secrets. First, I had not told the Descanso representative that Charles and I would be married by a witch. I was afraid she'd give us the old heave-ho. Second, I had told no one, including Charles, about my sneaky surprise. It had cost me an extra $500, and it was designed to burst forth only minutes prior to taking our vows. It would shock my family and friends.

"Where's the rabbi?" the Descanso representative asked a

group of people standing in the gazebo. I was far off in the Rose Pavilion setting the tables for dinner.

Barbara, the witch, overheard the question. She was sad and confused. She had driven six and a half hours to officiate the wedding, and this was the first she'd heard about a rabbi. I knew Barbara from USC. We were friends and had graduated from the doctoral program together. She was not a "double, double, toil and trouble" witch. She was a Wiccan minister and worked as a distinguished university professor in northern California.

The Wiccan religion honors gods and *goddesses*. Practitioners enjoy candlelit ceremonies and celebrating life. Although neither Charles nor I was a witch, our vows contained elements of Judaism and Jainism (for me), Old England Christianity (for Charles), pantheism (à la Spinoza), and references to the Wiccan term "god/goddess" (to dodge bias). I had always viewed the word *God* as sexist. Charles and I had designed our ceremony to be a delicious hodgepodge, unique only to us.

"Am I officiating your wedding?" Barbara approached me, plagued with worry.

"Of course you are."

"Who's the rabbi?"

"You're the rabbi," I said. "I listed you that way on the paperwork." Barbara laughed.

The stream of arriving guests was becoming a great flood. Embarrassed to be caught in beach attire, I scampered toward the dressing room to prepare myself for the ceremony. Thunder roared as if the gods and goddesses were squabbling. The sunless sky was the color of a caramel Frappuccino, and the bulging clouds looked surreal, imposing, and actually quite beautiful. There was no precipitation yet, but I feared everything, including my sneaky surprise (which was dependent upon clear skies), would turn into a muddy mess.

∽

I was in the dressing room, and I was given the cue that I had a brief fifteen minutes to put on my wedding dress, affix my veil, touch up my makeup, and style my hair. The hairstyle alone was a hairy enterprise. At home, I'd rehearsed without success. I'd faced frightful follicle explosions and multiple failures to launch. I knew a space capsule could orbit the earth in less time than it took me to manage my split ends.

I had no wedding helpers. My bridesmaids had been hustled from the dressing room by the Descanso representative. They had been instructed to take their positions and await the signal for the promenade toward the gazebo. Of course, without a halfway put-together bride, there would be no promenade. I dressed at rocket speed but felt combustible. I frantically pinned my headpiece, touched up my mascara, and crossed my fingers that my hair would not nail me to the cross. I grabbed unruly strands on the right and thrust them upward, bobby-pinning them behind the veil. Then I clipped the other side. I stared in the mirror and was dumbfounded. I looked perfect. How could this be? At home, my hair had been a collapsed quiche and a Phyllis Diller horror show. It seemed my fairy godmother had arrived just in time for my Cinderella wedding.

Once ready, I moved outside. Thunder boomed. I hoped the noise would not frighten the horse, who waited for me in the distance with Jack. I grabbed my veil with one hand, hiked up my skirt with the other, and hurried toward the carriage.

∽

I smiled at the horse. This was not just any horse. Troy, as he was called, was my friend for the afternoon. He was the only paid assistant at the wedding. He would pull a burgundy-and-white carriage, which would transport me to the gazebo for the ceremony. This was my wedding surprise. I would burst forth from the woods like a Greek goddess from the Bronze Age.

Troy was a beloved member of my wedding party. I'd initially been hesitant about commissioning his services due to concerns about his standard of living. I'd interrogated the couple who tended him. They'd rescued him from a slaughterhouse. He was a retired racehorse who had once been pumped with drugs and forced to perform. He'd endured painful injuries and had been whipped as many as thirty times per race. When gentle creatures like Troy are no longer profitable at the track, they are often shot or churned into meat for the European and Japanese food markets. Troy was luckier. He had been adopted. The couple sold wedding carriage rides to pay for Troy's food and care and to help cover their household expenses. They assured me that he was loved.

I gave Troy a loving pat on the neck and boarded the carriage with Jack, a professor from USC who had been my dissertation advisor. That day, he was the all-important "papa substitute" or "Y-chromosome stand-in." He would escort me down the aisle. I'd already asked my two dads—one and then the other—to assume the traditional role of giving me away. Both had declined. It was also made clear that neither would attend the momentous affair. My birth father couldn't come because he'd never told his family about me, although he'd promised to do so on many occasions. We'd been in secret contact since the mid-1980s. I hoped eventually to meet his kids—my half brother and half sister—who did not yet know of my existence.

My adoptive dad simply said, "I'm too busy." He added that he would not foot the $8,500 marriage bill, despite the fact that he'd said time and again, starting in childhood, that he would someday do so. On paper, I had two dads. But in reality, I had no dad.

Thankfully, Sharon was my mother on paper and in reality. She and Grandginger had flown into town for the festivities. (In addition, Sharon had been in close contact with me throughout the years, despite the fact that her husband was still in the dark about our relationship.)

I climbed into the carriage. The wind whipped past me as if it were late for a date with the willows, and the bloated clouds looked as if they'd soon lose their lunch. I was counting on Mr. Rain to be a proper gentleman.

∽

Guests were amazed as my horse and carriage trotted into view. Many stood, applauded, and sprang into a chorus of oohs and aahs. The impending storm was almost forgotten. From 300 yards away, Jack and I could see the bridesmaids, the witch, and Charles waiting patiently under the gazebo. They, too, were delighted by my surprise.

I felt like Troy's Helen, immortal and confident. And I felt like my face—and my well-behaved hairdo—could launch a thousand ships. The real Helen from Homer's *Iliad* and *Odyssey* had also been transported to her wedding by a majestic chariot back in 1200 BCE. Because I wanted to make a larger-than-life entrance, I'd asked the carriage driver to circle the area once before dropping us off.

"Here she comes," Charles announced to the crowd.

"And there she goes," he said, as I continued past him and out of sight.

Everyone laughed. I looked like the runaway bride.

Troy took us in a wide loop and then brought us back in view, stopping in front of a pebbled walkway. Jack and I disembarked and moved toward the guests and gazebo while the photographers snapped shots of us. A dozen children, who had been provided with bottled bubbles, blew floating droplets in our direction. I could see my birth mother, Sharon, in the front row of the crowd. She was wearing a rose-colored dress that I'd beaded for her. Around my neck was a Star of David that she'd once worn at her wedding. She'd gifted it to me that morning.

The ceremony included an American Indian prayer, a ketubah (a document listing promises to each other) that Charles and I had created, a poem that Kayla had written, words from the Anglican Book of Common Prayer, and a Hebrew passage that I'd memorized. During our vows, the wind kicked rose petals into the air above our heads. They swirled like halos. Then a double rainbow miraculously appeared on the horizon, punctuated by another melody of oohs and aahs from the crowd. It was as if Mother Nature longed to be a bridesmaid, too. I accepted her into the fold, despite the fact that she was inappropriately dressed in a multicolor gown rather than the sanctioned black. The unusual weather conditions seemed to carry the message that god-goddess was pleased and that the marriage was blessed.

An eleven-year-old Celtic harpist named Gelsey played my favorite song, "I've Never Been to Me." She had learned it for the affair. Gelsey was a musical phenomenon. She had been performing since the age of eight and had just published her first book of harp compositions. She lived down the street from Descanso Gardens.

"I've Never Been to Me" always made me emotional. It illustrated a conflict much like that in *The Turning Point*—a film starring Anne Bancroft and Shirley MacLaine—in which the heroines face an either–or scenario: career or family. But there is a slightly different twist in "I've Never Been to Me." Charlene (the teller of the tale) sings about how she opted for a lifestyle of glamour—hobnobbing with kings, sipping champagne on fancy yachts, and enjoying the bright lights of Monte

Carlo—while rejecting the steady love of a husband and child. She calls her predicament bittersweet.

I was not Charlene, because I had miraculously accomplished both. I had lived the lavish lifestyle: strutting down red carpets, riding in limos, meeting heads of state, and even dating Tom. On the other hand, I also had a beautiful child and was now marrying the man I adored. Life is not a coin with which there are only two options: heads or tails. Life can be magical, like swirling rose petals at a garden wedding or a vivid double rainbow.

I realized that there are two sides to my soul, and without celebrating both, life would be lopsided. Without balance, I would be incomplete. I would be day without night or night without day.

Had I listened to naysayers who wanted me to have an abortion, it is likely I'd have no child. Had I deferred to Mr. and Mrs. Shrink who said to walk away from the cockroach because "he's just not that into you," I'd surely have no husband. I'd trusted my heart, rather than others' prohibitory words. And I'd been lucky. I could not take credit for my good fortune, because perseverance and inner strength stem from nature and nurture, which originate within the mysterious, swirling forces of the universe.

There were tears in my eyes as Charles said, "I do." It transported me back to the refrain of my favorite tune when Charlene sings that although she'd led an extravagant life, she regrets more that she had never been "to herself." I was content because I had enjoyed extravagance, yet *also* been to me.

Following the ceremony, Charles, Kayla, and I boarded the carriage. Troy whisked us out of sight. There was a five-minute sprinkle, but it was more like a refreshing spritz of perfume, unleashing fragrant garden scents. Mr. Rain had remained a perfect gentleman after all.

Ten years later, Jack would attend another couple's nuptials in the very same garden. A group of guests would ask the Descanso representative to describe the best wedding she'd ever seen, and amazingly it would be mine.

※

It was many years after the wedding. I received a cryptic e-mail from my birth father in which he alluded to the fact that his sister had died. I'd never met her. In fact, she'd never been told about me, and I suddenly worried that something could happen to my half brother and half sister, who were in their forties and still did not know of my existence. I decided that I needed to meet them. Plus, I was tired of being excluded from my two dads' lives.

My birth father, the professor, had promised again and again to tell his family about me. First he needed a month, and then he needed a year. Then his kids had to graduate from high school, and finally they needed to complete college. Although he never explained the reason for procrastination, I figured it had something to do with personal image. He did not see himself as a man who would get a woman pregnant, quickly marry her, place a baby up for adoption, and divorce. The professor had rigid ideas about what was acceptable and unacceptable, and he felt he had colored outside the lines. Now the picture was one big mortifying mess, and he could only think of hiding it.

The professor and I had spoken on the phone for twenty-six years and communicated through letters and e-mail. He was careful to cross every *T* and dot every *I*. No one was to know about me. He wrote in a furtive way using fake names, writing obscure sentences, and not including a return address. I chalked it up to paranoia and figured his daily stress must be unbearable. We maintained a secret relationship until the day I asked him once and for all to admit to my brother and sister that they had a sibling. He must have been scared of my left hook, because he countered with a formidable punch to my heart. He suddenly claimed that he was not my father after all and that he'd been pretending all of these years because he'd "felt sorry for me." It was a blow I didn't expect. I retreated to my corner. I felt dizzy and emotional. Was he lying? And if he was not my father, then who was?

My adoptive dad was also ashamed of me. He had stashed me downstairs next to unwanted gifts and department store purchases that he couldn't be bothered to return. I was the dragon china in the basement. He willed himself to forget about me. He had no clear excuse. There was no embarrassment about getting a damsel pregnant, and there was no quickie divorce that he hoped to hide. He was not worried that the neighbors would learn he had a child. After all, it had been an above-board adoption. He simply cut all ties when I became pregnant. Maybe he saw me as irredeemably blemished. Maybe I had punched a hole in some sacred moral standard. But most likely I was part of a disquieting past that he hoped to forget. He had turned his back on Mom after the (attempted) suicide, and he had put a cancel stamp on Tween's file. The three of us were "team loser." We were the morally depraved, the unsightly, the disfigured, and the unworthy. We were Dad's outcasts.

But dragon china has one advantage. It has fire in its belly and flames in its throat. It is not docile or obedient, and it is most ill-suited for basements. So mama dragon and daughter dragon decided to fly to the East Coast for a showdown with my two dads.

Chapter Seventeen

THE TRIP TO NOWHERE

Crashing Dad's condominium complex was a little like sneaking into the Oscars.

Kayla and I arrived in Highlands, North Carolina, while Charles babysat the dogs and chickens[22] in L.A. This was the first leg of our "trip to nowhere," in which I would pop in on my sister, brother, and two fathers. Kayla and I hoped the trip would lead somewhere, but our confidence was wobbly. When it came to "dads," I'd learned that expectation is like root rot. It usually leads to disappointment and loss. Despite many attempts, my adoptive father had agreed to see us only once in the previous twenty-four years. It had been for an hour brunch in Atlanta. That was the only time he'd even spoken with Kayla, who was now twenty-five. We hoped to have our second meeting that day.

Months earlier, Dad had agreed to meet with us on this trip. I'd bought nonrefundable plane tickets, but he'd called later to cancel our rendezvous using a cockamamy excuse about being out of town. His wife, Virginia, later confirmed this was a lie.

"I'm going to lose over a thousand dollars if I cancel this trip," I said to him on the phone.

"Oh well," he replied. "That's what happens sometimes."

For the first time in my life I realized that Dad's word could not be trusted, that he would not be there for me if I needed something. I'd always thought that in an emergency situation, I could count on him as a safety net. But I'd been deluding myself. If he was going to cause me to lose all this cash, he was not dependable.

Kayla and I gathered together our chutzpah and decided to pop in unannounced. This was where "crashing his security condominium complex" came into play.

"I'm a real estate agent and need the gate code," I said to a lady leaving the condo community in her SUV.

This was actually true. I *was* a Realtor in Los Angeles, and I *needed* to get inside the complex. The driver of the SUV happily provided the secret numbers. Kayla and I drove our rental car through the big black gates into uncertainty.

We figured nothing could be worse than the previous day. We'd landed at the Atlanta airport only to realize that my driver's license had expired. No one would lease me a vehicle. Suffice to say that the three-hour ordeal at the rental car counters was unmitigated suffering and our schedule got thrown askew. Our entire trip hinged on driving hundreds of miles north, the California DMV could not send me an extension without an in-person appointment, Kayla's credit card did not have a high-enough limit for her to be listed as the "driver," and the bank that controlled her credit card refused to raise her limit. Then, to top it off, I learned from news reports that a

NASA satellite the size of a school bus was plummeting toward the earth in a fiery death drive.

I dragged my luggage up to the hotel's front desk that first night and spoke to the clerk. We were exhausted and still had no car. "So far this trip has been a disaster. And you know the satellite that's plunging toward the earth? It's going to fall on me."

As was the case during childhood, it seemed as if the malevolent forces did not want me to leave Georgia. I felt trapped and immobile, like a shrub trying to flee a swarm of locusts. I was thankfully rescued on the following afternoon by Bank of America. The institution provided Kayla with credit to cover the car rental. Although behind schedule, we finally hit the road.

Now we were in Highlands outside Dad's hilltop condominium. The attraction of the complex was its view. It looked like a scene from *The Sound of Music*, except it had a few hundred thousand more trees. Was Dad in town? And if he was, would he be civil? Would he be responsive? We nervously knocked on his front door. He answered.

"I didn't recognize you at first." He chuckled in an uncomfortable way.

His wife, Virginia, appeared with a welcoming smile and a cane. She'd just had knee surgery. Dad also had a bad knee, but his problem was significantly more serious and he stubbornly refused to see a doctor. His left leg bowed out, and he hobbled as if he were a bicycle missing a wheel. Virginia invited us into the living room and then scurried out of sight. Later, Kayla and I would wonder if she'd spent this time setting up a sneaky trick.

We sat on the white furniture. I wondered how Dad felt about having the flawed daughter on the flawless couch. He proceeded to play his usual role of jovial host while avoiding any questions about our lives. As usual, he did not discuss deep, philosophical, or intellectual topics, but he was a crackerjack with chitchat. He explained his strategy for convincing the phone company to give him a number with the last four digits "5297," which corresponds to the name "Laws."

"I just tell them I'm old, and I can't remember anything except my last name." He laughed. "It always works."

Then he segued into another short bit. "I tell people that I have been a resident of Highlands for eighty-five years. They say, 'How could this be? You're only eighty-four.' I tell them my mother got pregnant here."

Virginia appeared with a plate of melba toast, and the conversation turned to *Judge Judy* (Dad's favorite afternoon ritual), Obama (whom Dad kept calling "the anointed one"), and his condo (which was listed for sale). Dad and Virginia were making a permanent move to Florida.

Virginia was a peacemaker. She was delighted to see Dad interacting with his only daughter and only granddaughter in spite of his marked level of discomfort, and she wanted to draw out the visitation time. She suggested lunch. Dad rebuffed the idea. She mentioned coffee and dessert. Dad shook his head no. Finally, she insisted on dinner, and he caved. As we were leaving the condo, the reveal or possible "sneaky trick" came into play.

"I want to show you something." Virginia escorted us into Dad's bedroom and pointed at a four-foot-long chest of drawers. "*This* is here all the time."

There was only one item on the bureau: a framed photograph of me and Kayla together on the red carpet at the Malibu Music Awards. There were no other pictures in the room. I was baffled. Kayla was baffled. Did Virginia sneak it onto the desk when she fetched the melba toast? And where did it come from? I had not sent it. It had to have been copied off the

Internet, made into a glossy print, and then framed. Obviously, Virginia could not have done all that while pretending to prepare the food. Maybe she'd had it created months earlier for Dad's birthday, and maybe he'd dumped it in the basement with other rejects until melba toast time, when Virginia miraculously made it reappear. Or maybe not. And if he didn't hate us, why did he act like he did? The puzzle of the curious photograph has not been solved to this day.

Dinner was at the exclusive and pricey Cyprus restaurant. Each entrée on the menu was an artistically displayed concoction from a different land. However, there was nothing vegan, so Kayla special ordered her meal in great detail, sending the waiter on a vegetable-related obstacle course.

"They're from California," Dad apologized to the server.

"I'll have what Kayla's having." I figured cooking two complicated dishes would be just as easy as making one.

"Someone told me you are the number one real estate agent at Prudential," Dad said. This was the only time he deviated from small talk or funny tales to ask about me.

I explained that Prudential is a large international firm and that I am most definitely not number one. I explained that in addition to real estate, I was a councilmember, article writer, a regular on an NBC TV show, speechmaker, and the head of a couple of animal nonprofits. Plus, I had a husband, daughter, dogs, and a bunch of chickens. Dad did not ask me about any of these avocations or vocations, I assume because they did not contribute to the bottom line. *The* bottom line had always been *his* bottom line.

"To be the top agent, you cannot have a life outside of real estate," I said. "It's a sixteen-hour-a-day job. I would not want to be the number one agent. For me, life is not all about making money."

"It *should* be all about making money," Dad countered. "You *should* want to be number one."

As usual, Dad's allegiance to the cash register had reared its head and snarled at me. I could hear the clash of our value systems. His went *cha-ching*, while mine whirred like nature. Dad and I clearly had different priorities.

"I didn't have a life for twenty years," Dad said. "I was only home two hours each day—from six to eight p.m.—then I'd go back to work until midnight. That's why you always asked your mother who the stranger was." He chuckled at this line as usual. "Plus, I had sideline investments. I owned cattle, for example."

"What? You never told me about this!" I was horrified.

"The cattle business was pretty profitable." He smiled, confirming that he had no regrets about making big bucks off the backs of little Ferdinands.

It was then that Kayla handed Dad a gift wrapped in tissue paper. After leaving his condo earlier in the day, she'd bought him a cup from a tourist shop that read "You are loved." He opened it to great discomfort. It was clear that he felt awkward with these words, because he proceeded to ignore Kayla for the remainder of the meal. He hurriedly finished his food, requested the check, and left the cup at the table as he hobbled into the parking lot. Kayla went back inside the restaurant and retrieved it for him.

Although his forgetfulness was surely a by-product of old age, leaving the cup behind was symbolic of how Dad had always left love on the table. He was adept at distancing himself from feelings. Although he knew Kayla and I would be in Highlands for two more days, he did not mention getting together again. We left North Carolina unsure whether we would ever see him again.

The dragon china was still in the basement. But there was a photograph on his dresser. Maybe.

◈

After leaving Highlands on the trip to nowhere, it was time to meet my forty-year-old half sister, who didn't even know about me. I was afraid to pop in on her at work, thinking the shock might be too much. I felt it would be better to let her warm up to the idea through her husband. He would be the buffer.

I phoned her husband at the company where he worked. I'd learned about his place of employment through the couple's wedding announcement on the Internet. I informed him that I was a relative without explaining details, and he reluctantly agreed to meet me in front of his office building.

"I'm your wife's sister." I swallowed hard. Then he swallowed hard.

A brief chat in the lobby of his workplace led to a phone call to his wife, which led to a lunch on the following day at the Olive Garden. Kayla and I arrived at the restaurant early and from my vantage point at the table, I could see people approaching the entrance.

"There she is." I predicted, among a dozen women in the vicinity. It turned out I was right.

"Sis" was astounded to learn she had a half sister. She was a pretty brunette and a cross between Lois Lane and Superwoman. She was reserved and feminine but also smart, scientific, and adept at balancing her important job as an engineer with raising three small children. Like other members of the professor's family tree, she was infatuated with diplomas. She'd earned a master's, B.A., and B.S. She was not surprised that our father had a secret life.

"He's always been sneaky," she said.

With these words, the floor lamp turned "on" in my head. I was floored because I now knew the origin of my smart talent. But the professor's sneakiness differed from mine. While I liked slipping into exclusive events and developing unusual philosophical ideas, he was furtive about his life and actions.

"I'll have the shrimp primavera without the shrimp. Please give me chicken instead." Sis proceeded with a detailed account of how she wanted her meal prepared.

"We can't do that," the waitress replied.

"Yes, you can," Sis countered. "I eat here all the time."

The manager and chef came to the table, and Sis tussled with them over her special request. Kayla and I laughed, figuring food fussiness was a family trait.

Despite "meal-ordering" similarities, I had little in common with Sis. I was a hot pink lily. She was a lovely vase of baby's breath. I was flashy and talkative. She was more taciturn and traditional. I teetered on the edge philosophically. She stood solidly on the balance beam of ideas. She had largely accepted her *Father Knows Best* upbringing, while I had rebelled against conservative Atlanta like a Frederick's of Hollywood corset.

"I'm a Jewish Jain," I revealed at the end of the meal.

"Can you just *be* that?" Sis asked.

"Of course. That's the beauty of religion. One day you're a Jewish Jain. The next day you're not."

Sis let out a soft laugh.

Despite our differences, I realized lilies and baby's breath can come together to make a rich bouquet. I could learn from Sis, and I hoped she felt the same. Our lives could be enriched by difference, by exposure to each other's beliefs, thoughts, and lifestyles. Our hearts could be sisters just as we were.

The next stop on the trip to nowhere was my birth father's hometown.

"Yep, you can reserve a room under a fake name," a Days Inn clerk told me on the phone.

"Ok, I'm the King of Prussia." I envisioned paparazzi and history buffs awaiting my arrival.

The fake name on my room reservation was necessary because of my birth dad's sneaky genes. I figured he would check to see if I was coming into town, and when the reservation clerk said "Yes," he would leave the state in an effort to circumvent me. Months earlier, I'd told him that I'd be vacationing in his area. I suggested our second get-together ever. I was especially anxious to introduce him to Kayla for the first time. Like my adoptive father, the professor initially agreed but later changed his mind. He cancelled after I asked him to tell my siblings, once and for all, about my existence.

"I care deeply about you and feel honored to have you as my dad," my letter started. "But I also feel the time has come for you to tell your family about me. I have waited a quarter of a century. I think it is time. The reunion can be heartwarming and life-enhancing for everyone concerned."

It ended with the following words: "If you cannot tell my half brother and half sister, I really feel that I will have to move toward telling them myself. I don't want to keep waiting and waiting. Life is short. People die and chances are lost."

His response was, "I will not be available to see you after all. I will be deeply involved in travel and sorting out personal and professional issues."

He signed it "Your friend" in his usual cloaked way, as if trying to mask our father-daughter connection. Like my other dad, he did not care whether I lost $1,000 on nonrefundable travel costs. So, like my other dad, I decided to make him the target of an unannounced visit.

Popping in on pop number two would occur following the Olive Garden lunch with Sis and prior to meeting my half brother. Sis had phoned "Bro" about me. He wanted to dine with me and Kayla on the following evening. To my surprise, both of my siblings had agreed to say nothing to our dad, the professor, until after I spilled the beans about our cryptic meet and greets.

I arrived at the university that afternoon and envisioned angry words as I peered inside the professor's history class. I could see the phrase "Fort Sumter" scribbled on the chalkboard and knew I was trespassing on my father's fort away from home. Students were taking a test on the civil war. I quickly bobbed back into the hall before he could spot my prying eyes.

Thirty minutes later, tests were collected, class was dismissed, and the professor stood at his desk in the empty room rearranging materials in his briefcase. Kayla and I crept up to him. When he recognized me, he morphed into the nutty professor, bungling his words.

"Do we… did we… uh… have plans to meet?"

"No, we were just in town and thought we'd drop by and say hello. I'd like to introduce you to your granddaughter, Kayla." I had no expectations. I'd been ejected from my two dads' lives more than once.

"Maybe we could meet for breakfast in the morning?" I made this suggestion because Sis had already informed me that our dad had dinner plans that night with a former congressman.

"Uh… uh… okay… eight a.m.," he agreed, probably thinking it was the only way to lasso loose lips.

Kayla and I docked ourselves in the university cafeteria on the following morning with the professor, and frankly we had a delightful time. He was no longer jittery or uptight, and he counseled Kayla like a caring grandpa on possible career paths. Although she had just broken into show biz and had accumulated an impressive number of acting credits on her Internet Movie Database page, she thought it would be wise to select a backup profession should her first choice fail to bring a regular paycheck.

"Library science is an interesting field," the professor said.

"I'm *not* going to be a librarian," Kayla replied.

"By the way, I brought you a copy of my last book." The professor handed me the four-hundred-page work.

"I'm very impressed," I said. "You did so much research. And you're making such a significant impact on the world."

"Well, I don't know about that." He blushed, clearly pleased with the compliment.

Unlike my adoptive dad, the professor's value system did not go *cha-ching* or revolve around the gold bullion. It reverberated like the Gettysburg Address. It was erudite and inquisitive. Although my birth dad did not obsess over the plight of non-humans as I did, at least he was a writer and intellectual with a philosophical bent. This was almost as good as it gets when it came to gaining my respect.

After almost four hours of conversation—as well as breakfast and lunch at the same cafeteria table—I felt it was time to tell the professor that I had contacted my siblings. Kayla realized I was about to confess and kicked me under the table. It was jarring. This was her first meeting with "Grandpa," and she did not want the admission to muck up a perfect morning.

The kick sent a mild reverberation through the table, and the professor furrowed his brow as if he knew something had happened. But he said nothing. I said nothing. And Kayla said nothing.

Saying nothing turned into a stroll around campus. My birth dad loved playing tour guide and discussing historical happenings in town, as well as improvements at the university. I periodically inserted the words "We need to get on the road" into the conversation, but he ignored them. Finally at 12:30 p.m., I put my foot down.

"We have to go. We have a long drive," I said.

"Are you sure you don't want to have lunch?" he asked.

"We already had breakfast and one lunch." I gave him a hug. "We can't. But we had a great time."

The professor wanted to join us for three meals. My adoptive dad had to be persuaded to have one. The professor inquired about our lives. My adoptive dad played "entertainer." The professor gave Kayla grandfatherly advice. My adoptive dad ignored her when his cup runneth over with heartfelt words. But both men refused to see us until cornered. I suppose crashing is not just about meeting stars. It can come in handy with dads.

One ringy-dingy, two ringy-dingy. I anticipated anger and aggression. My voice would whip through hundreds of miles of pencil-thin phone cables to bring the professor bad tidings. I would ruin his day, his week, and probably his year. I knew he was alone. Sis had given me his itinerary, hour by hour. I figured he'd reprimand me for phoning him at home. I'd only done this once in twenty-six years: moments after Kayla's birth in 1986.

"Don't call me at home," he had scolded me, and I'd abided by his wishes ever since.

This was the next stop of the trip to nowhere. Kayla and I were in Washington, DC, staying at my friend Sarah's place.

On the previous evening, Kayla and I had met my half brother for the first time. He had enthusiastically suggested

Indian food, but we weren't into spices. So he proposed a "chain."

"Red Lobster, Chipotle Mexican Grill, Outback Steakhouse, or Quiznos?" Bro asked.

"Any other suggestions?" Kayla asked.

That's when the "home sweet home" option surfaced.

"California Pizza Kitchen?"

This was a high five.

After we arrived at the restaurant, Kayla went into her usual rendition of no oil, no salt, no meat, no dairy, no bread, no soy, and so forth. The waitress wrote ferociously with her itsy-bitsy pen.

When Kayla seemed to be finished, the waitress smiled. "You're not the most difficult customer I've had."

This, of course, was the cue for Kayla to try harder. She revised her order extensively in an apparent attempt to be the most annoying patron of all time. As the poor waitress scribbled at breakneck speed, Bro chuckled at the sight of his most charming and unusual niece from California.

Bro was handsome and a younger-looking version of the professor. Academically speaking, he was well degreed. Like me, he made an effort to think outside of the box. He was not sneaky like our dad when it came to clandestine actions, yet he had some smart talent of his own. He could peer around the corner of ideas to see a different perspective or come up with an interesting insight.

He was reserved like Sis, but not as peaceful as baby's breath. There was a whisper of rebel in his soul. Just as I had escaped the stranglehold of Atlanta, he'd fled his hometown. But since he'd faced less adversity in childhood, he'd remained closer to home as an adult. He landed a few hundred miles from his roots, while I landed a few thousand.

Three ringy-dingy. Four ringy-dingy. It was time for the

latest showdown. I hated confrontation 6.9 times more than Indian food and 5.2 times more than most chain restaurants. I was standing in the center of Sarah's living room in Washington, DC, when the professor answered.

"Hi." I tried to act cheerful. "This is Charlotte."

"Oh, how are you?" The professor sounded genuinely happy to hear my voice, which surprised me since I was phoning him at home. "Did you make it to DC all right?"

"Yes," I replied. "I had a really nice time with you yesterday."

"So did I," he said.

"I just wanted to let you know." I took a deep breath and then confessed that I'd introduced myself to his kids: my half brother and half sister.

It was then that the pencil-thin phone cables shook from the rancor of my birth dad. I imagined them threadbare and close to the grave. I felt near death as well.

"That is a violation of our original agreement," he screamed. "We originally agreed that would never happen."

He slammed down the phone. I had no idea what he was talking about. There was no "original agreement." In fact, when I'd sent the ultimatum letter (saying I would tell my siblings if he didn't), he had not even asked me to refrain. If he had, of course, it would have made my dilemma all the more challenging.

Sis and Bro got in on the act with a call to their mom. Oddly, she was more concerned with whether her husband was screwing up the crab cakes that he was making for dinner that night.

"She's a liar," the professor told his family. "Don't ever talk to her again."

Then he delivered shocking news to Sis and Bro. He said he was *not* my father after all and that he had been pretending all these years because he felt sorry for me. He said the timing was not right and that my birth mom, Sharon, must have been seeing another man. Although he did not deny marrying Sharon or placing me for adoption, he claimed that I was not his flesh and blood.

Was he inventing this tale to save face? Was this an effort to pacify his family, who may have felt betrayed by his secret life? It permitted him to use the excuse "I did not *think* she was my child, so that is why I never told you." Or was he being forthright? Had I been duped for the past twenty-six years? I felt confused, rejected, and heartbroken. Was this man a stranger or my dad?

Bro and Sis told me they believed that he *believed* what he was saying. But they were unclear about the underlying truth. They were also baffled by their mother's nonchalant response. I simply dubbed her a practical and calming force. Maybe to her it was irrelevant because there would be no consequences either way. After all, they would not have to pay for my college tuition. I was too old to move into the house, and I could easily be excluded from family gatherings.

The professor shot me a scathing and final e-mail: "Your bomb has shattered the family. Don't ever contact us again."

⁓

Some students cheat on tests, but would the professor?

A paternity test would reveal the truth. Bro, Sis, and I had pushed for a DNA analysis and to our surprise, my (alleged) birth dad had agreed to participate. But we all knew the professor wanted to distance himself from fatherhood, so it was decided that Sis would escort him to the testing facility to make sure there was no funny business or sneaky switcheroo with samples.

The Washington, DC, leg of my trip to nowhere was supposed to be spent interviewing members of Congress for an article and having coffee with Supreme Court Justice Stephen Breyer, who had publicly announced on *Larry King Live* that he would "meet any elected official for lunch." I was an elected official at the time as a member of the Greater Valley Glen Council. But instead of conducting interviews or meeting for coffee, I became consumed with the "birth father ordeal." I spent a huge amount of time on the phone with my brother, my sister, and DNA testing facilities. I had been getting unpleasant and sarcastic e-mails from my (alleged) birth dad. And Sarah, Kayla, and I were like war room tacticians, strategizing on how to handle the correspondence. After a nationally based DNA facility was approved by all and the fee was paid, Kayla and I traipsed miles across town so that medical personnel could extract the all-important swab from my cheek. The professor agreed to do the same in his hometown several days later with Sis as chaperone. The results would not be available for two weeks.

That was a long wait. I had gone through twenty-six years believing I had a dad, and now for two painful weeks I would have to wonder. Intuitively, I felt as if I knew the truth. For example, the professor and I had common interests and identical blue eyes. And following the Spinoza experiences, I had become an advocate for interior knowledge. On the other hand, I was also scientific and fully prepared to subordinate gut feelings to the black-and-white findings of the lab report. If the results came back negative, I would be crushed. It would mean Baby Lady had given me the wrong data, or my birth mom, Sharon, was not telling the truth. Sharon had spent two delightful days with me on this particular trip, and she had reconfirmed that the professor was my father. I believed her. I had never known her to lie.

If it turned out Baby Lady's file had been wrong, it would mean I had no known father *or mother*. This would be a disaster.

Plus, I would feel horrible about throwing these strangers' lives into turmoil. During the two-week fact-finding period, I felt helpless and did not know how I'd react to bad news. Would I start my hunt over? Would I declare defeat? I was not one to disappoint my best friend, Perseverance. But there is a first time for everyone, even for "the little Atlanta girl who could."

⁂

Drum roll. The answer was 99.9998 percent.

This was the probability of paternity that appeared on the printout from the testing facility. In other words, my alleged birth dad was no longer "alleged." He was actually my father. My brother and sister told me that any further DNA denials would be DOA. I was relieved, but the professor was distraught and stared at the paternity results for an hour in silence as if he was a weepy sad sack. Was it so bad being my dad? Or was his "upset" merely an act, designed to make his family think he was shocked?

"I don't know which of your fathers is worse for concentrated and sustained villainy," Charles told me on the phone after I reported the professor's unfavorable reaction.

A day later, the jack-in-the-box started popping in and out, as if it was jammed in repeat mode. I got pleasant e-mails from the professor, followed by hostile ones, saying, "Don't ever contact us again." All of the messages were dripping wet with heaviness. Why couldn't he wring them out before hitting the send button? I was being dunked into one emotional pool after another, and frankly it was getting wearing. I felt like packing up my tent, putting out the smoldering fire I'd created, and abandoning the campsite for good.

At one point, the professor said he wanted to orchestrate a "reunion" in Washington, DC, and that he wanted my adoptive family to attend. He described them as the people who had cared for me within minutes of my birth. He was obviously living at an alternate campsite. I figured he hoped to locate hunky-dory adoptive clan, who would say what a sterling childhood I had in order to alleviate guilt or to silence the masochistic instincts that hacked away in his head. The professor's emphasis was on meeting these people, and he stressed that he would be "highly disappointed" if I did not produce them. I had no adoptive relatives other than Dad, who would never attend such an event. Plus, no one had tended me within minutes of my birth. I was officially adopted at two months of age, and my father had always insisted that I was returned twice because I was such a bad baby.

The reunion idea sounded like a comedy roast. The professor suggested speeches, a photo album of my life, and a full-on celebration. I envisioned people at the podium, making jokes such as, "Charlotte is so short you can see her feet on her driver's license." Although the event sounded joyous, it was not achievable. And when I finally convinced my birth dad that there was no one to invite, he sent me another weighty "Don't ever contact us again" e-mail.

Notwithstanding the erratic behavior, I love the professor and am proud to be his daughter. I admire his intellectual and philosophical pursuits. Like my adoptive dad, he is a shade of gray. Despite his allegiance to moral absolutism, my value system is closer to his than to those who raised me. At the writing of this book, we have met a couple of times without jack-in-the-box drama or upset. Our get-togethers were casual and cordial, and he seemed to have amnesia about the former outbursts. Although he did not treat me like an enemy, he also did not treat me like a daughter. I was betwixt and between. I was a semicolon or deep sigh in his life.

My adoptive father (now 92) has also softened with time.

Virginia died, so he is alone. Although he has had no further contact with Kayla, I've met with him three times. Like before, he played "entertainer," called *Judge Judy* his favorite show, and emphasized the importance of money. But he refrained from the verbal abuse that was so common in earlier years.

Both of my dads have anchor problems. After the (attempted) suicide and Buddy's death, my adoptive father unhitched the "mom anchor" and has been floating directionless ever since. He is determined to forget his disquieting past. I am part of that past.

The professor, on the other hand, clings to a "moral anchor" despite being battered and bruised. He embraces masochism and lives with feelings of guilt, embarrassment, and pain.

I am the anchor reminder. I am the dreaded messenger. To remember me is to remember bad news. To see me is to see flaws within themselves. To spend time with me is… well, unbearable.

Despite the ups and downs with kin and the unknowns ahead, I am grateful for everyone in my life. I am even grateful for my two dads. I care about them both and realize life is not about looking back or being distressed over little things. It is not about exploding over tiny mishaps or unkind words. It is not about hiding dragon china in the basement. It is about looking outward, away from oneself. It is about helping those who *truly* suffer. It is about the other.

With that, I smile at the future and brainstorm on how I can best give my heart to the world.

Bonus Stories 1: Additional Autobiographical Experiences

"When Charlotte gets something in mind, nothing can stop her."

Stylist Magazine

"Dr. Laws must have lived several lives in order to have fitted in the huge amount that she has."

Daily Mail

"Charlotte Laws is a really cool lady. A kick-ass lady."

The Jim Christina Show

How to Fake Your Way into a Celebrity Party: Frank Sinatra and George Clooney

By Charlotte Laws
(Published in the Washington Post, 2015)

There are shockingly easy ways to infiltrate VIP events and schmooze with the rich and famous. I am an expert on this hobby. Here are two of my favorite methods.

The first ploy is called "Fake Out to Get In." Much like a magician's sleight of hand, this technique requires distraction. You must invent a believable excuse for the chap or chapette guarding the door, and then sashay up to this person with confidence and deliver an Oscar-worthy performance. In other words, you have to be Meryl Streep in order to meet Meryl Streep. You do not want the guard to think you care one iota about the event or the bucketful of celebrities in attendance. You must convey that you have more important matters to attend to, saying something like "I'm here to apply for a job" or "I am with Building and Safety and need to check the concrete footings."

I embarked upon the "Fake Out to Get In" ploy in 2012 when I wanted to attend a fundraiser for President Obama at George Clooney's Los Angeles estate. The entry fee was $40,000 per person, and as Billy Crystal once said, "Some of my friends don't make that much in a day." Gate-crashing was the only ticket I could afford.

Law enforcement had closed the streets surrounding Clooney's estate, but they blundered when they temporarily removed a blockade. I shot up the road in my Nissan and was subsequently flagged down.

A security guard spoke to me through my car window. "Ma'am, you must turn around and go back down the hill."

Assorted of excuses raced through my head, but then I noticed a Rite Aid bag on my passenger seat filled with recently purchased ponytail holders. "I have an emergency pharmaceutical delivery for..." —here I pretended to read a small piece of paper— "Mr. G. Clooney." I exuded confidence, yet also deep concern, as if to say, "Do you really want poor George to die?"

The guard seemed confused and scanned the area for advice, but there was no one to consult. He looked at me. He scanned the area again. I hoped he would not search my bag to find the Ouchless No Crease Hair Ties; I knew my death-by-hairdo story wouldn't fly. The guard finally relented. "Okay. I guess you can go up."

The area around Clooney's house was packed with catering trucks and service vehicles, so I parked in the only spot available: the actor's driveway. I entered the event to find Robert Downey Jr., Barbra Streisand, Jack Black, and others. The evening was a success.

The "Celebrity Snuggle Up" is another favorite gate-crashing ploy. This maneuver requires you to become chummy with a star just before he or she enters an event, thereby making it seem like you are part of the famous person's entourage. Your demeanor must communicate the sassiness of "I'm this celebrity's BFF," combined with the aloofness of being a "tag-along." As you and your chosen celebrity approach security, you should stare into the distance, count the tiles on the ceiling, or study the scuff marks on your shoes. In other words, under no circumstances should you make eye contact with the guard. You must pretend he or she is as invisible as your invitation to the affair.

You might sweat or convulse slightly as you stand there, wondering if you will be tossed out of the building or sent to jail, but try to be brave. Hide your crushing terror. When the guard gives the signal that clearance has been granted—and this is what usually happens, by the way—you must waltz into the event alongside your star with a business-as-usual attitude. Once safely inside, you should duck into the restroom to regroup or throw up, as you see fit.

What happens if you are game for the "Snuggle Up" but can't think of a darn thing to say to your designated star in the first place? This happened to me in 1981, when I wanted to attend an exclusive party hosted by Frank Sinatra at the Madison hotel in Washington, DC.

I noticed singer Charley Pride ascending a staircase toward the all-important festivities. There was a fortress of security guards in the distance, and I figured this was my opportunity to finagle into the event as Charley's sidekick. I jumped next to him but quickly realized I had nothing to say. Panic set in because the guards were studying our interaction.

Charley looked at me, and I looked at him. It was awkward. Since the guards were so far away, I decided to pretend to speak. No sound came out. I moved my hands in an overly dramatic way and let out exaggerated belly laughs as if I was on good terms with the star.

Charley stared at me like I was a nutcase, but the security guards seemed convinced of our deep and important connection.

When we got to the top of the stairway, Charley gave his name to a woman at a desk while I stared straight ahead, hoping no one would question my presence. Thankfully, we were permitted to enter, and I was able to mingle with Johnny Carson, Henry Kissinger, and Sinatra, among others.

Gate-crashing is a form of life-crashing. It is about living in the bold zone, taking calculated chances, and pursuing your dreams.

And if you see me sashaying down the red carpet or schmoozing on the other side of the velvet rope, don't forget the rules of party-crashing. First rule: You don't talk about party-crashing. Second rule: Maybe you crashed, but I was invited. I am *always* invited. Last rule: If you get caught, I'm not your one phone call, and you've never heard of me.

My Adventure Presenting Animal Rights Philosophy to the FBI

By Charlotte Laws
(Published in the Los Angeles Daily News, 2006)

I got a phone call from Special Agent Andy, an instructor at the FBI Academy. He wanted to pay me to fly to Quantico, Virginia, where I would lecture law enforcement executives and managers from around the world about animal philosophy, keeping in mind "the mindset and methodologies of terrorists and the government's response."

I was hesitant and did what anyone would do. I contacted my family, friends, and criminal attorney. Actually, I didn't have a criminal attorney, but I had a buddy who regularly handled high-profile cases.

He furrowed his brow and cautioned, "Don't do anything. Let me check this out first. The FBI railroad innocent people all the time."

My anxiety multiplied when an animal person said, "Only traitors talk to the government" and a nonanimal friend advised me to take a lawyer with me and to refuse to "name names" when "testifying before the House Un-American Activities Committee."

"I don't have any names," I protested.

A Los Angeles Police Department friend offered the only encouragement. "It is an honor to be invited. Don't worry. I'll tell them you're not a subversive and not to arrest you until after our tennis match next week." She laughed.

Decision day arrived, and my criminal attorney gave me the flickering yellow light, warning me that a visit to the Academy would prompt the FBI to open a file on me.

"Well, I plan to open a file on them, too," I said. "But I won't put any untruths in my file if they don't put any in theirs."

"Go if you want. It's legit, but take my number in case," he replied.

My plan was to serve as an ambassador for the animal rights movement and to convey through my lecture the truth about how animals suffer under human oppression, as well as to present philosophical arguments as to why animals are of equal value to humans and worthy of equal consideration. I wanted my audience to understand that anti-terrorism resources should be used to combat dangerous groups who fly planes into buildings, rather than renegade gerbil lovers.

An ominous feeling tented the empty road and thick woods in Quantico, and the sound of guns slammed through the air. I met Special Agent Andy, a fine host for the FBI, at the first security checkpoint, and he took me on a brief tour of the grounds. He pointed out a pretend town called Hogan's Alley with fake storefronts, including a bank in which actors are hired at twelve dollars per hour to play "robber," "hostage," or "drug dealer" with FBI trainees.

"Do the actors ever win?" I laughed.

Andy gave me a stern look. "We take that very seriously. It is not good to get shot even in playtime."

The presentation room was a small lecture hall with a podium, microphone, and display screen for the speaker, and fixed seats on ascending levels for attendees. I was told that two FBI psychologists would sit in on my lecture. I felt their goal was to scrutinize me (as to whether I might be an underground operative) and to learn how to exterminate the animal rights movement. I felt the others were there to learn.

My presentation began with undercover video footage inside a vivisection lab. It showed a man in a white coat pounding on a beagle puppy and forcing tubes down several dogs' throats. The animals were clearly in distress. I figured cleaning liquids or pesticides would be poured down the tubes since they were routinely tested at this lab. In another clip, monkeys screamed while their penises were electrocuted by scientists.

Andy shouted from the back of the room, "The FBI will prosecute this sort of cruelty if videos like this are brought to our attention."

"Unfortunately, this is mostly, if not completely, legal activity," I replied.

I pointed out that obtaining undercover video is the illegal part, even more so with the passage of the Animal Enterprise Terrorism Act, which states that a person can be prosecuted as a terrorist if he or she causes economic damage to any corporation or business that uses animals. Showing the undercover video could cause investors to sell their stocks, decimating profits.

I said that even if some of the barbarous treatment of

dogs and monkeys in the footage is against the law—such as pounding on the puppies' faces—prosecution tends to result in nothing more than a slap on the wrist. Because animals are property, and because the law generally finds it acceptable to use and kill animals for human gain, imposing prison terms and steep fines on large corporations—who have even larger lawyers—is rare.

During my lecture, I was able to get several law enforcement executives to admit openly that they would break the law, if necessary, to rescue an animal in distress, although they did not specifically agree to break into a research lab or factory farm. This was quite an accomplishment, because prior to the presentation, Andy had privately told me that any FBI agent who did not or could not (for ethical reasons) uphold all U.S. laws would be fired. My audience was mostly non-FBI (i.e., police chiefs from cities around the nation), so they surely kept their jobs.

After the lecture, Andy said, "You were great. Could you come back and speak again?"

"I doubt it. Unfortunately, I don't fare well on long plane rides."

"Well, maybe you could give me the name of someone who could."

"I knew you'd ask me to name names," I said. "I have no choice but to report this in my secret file."

The Nun with the Ruler

BY CHARLOTTE LAWS
(Published in the Chronicle of Higher Education, 2007).

He didn't look like a nun, but my basic computer skills teacher at the community college reprimanded students who touched their computer keyboard before they were told to do so. If he'd owned a ruler, he'd surely be a serial whacker. He was also paranoid about cheating. He thought every student was dying to glance at someone else's paper, so he'd pace the room with an eagle eye.

I convinced my 62-year-old husband, Charles, to take this computer class with me. We sat side by side, and the "nun" got the impression that Charles was cheating. Charles resented being treated like a child, so he was defiant and refused to study. Thus, he got low marks on tests. Whenever he got an answer right, the teacher assumed he'd stolen it from my paper. In addition, Charles kept touching his keyboard during class and getting admonished for it. This made him seem like a troublemaker.

What the instructor didn't know was that Charles had a law degree from Oxford University and was an English barrister, California attorney, and judge pro tem. He had no reason to cheat in an entry-level computer class.

One day, Charles said, "I need to leave class early. I have to be in court."

The teacher shook his head in a condescending manner, assuming Charles to be a criminal in addition to an underperforming bum. "Now, *what* did you do, Charles?"

I revealed that he was sitting as a judge. It was hilarious, but at the same time disturbing to know that a brilliant man who had excelled at Oxford—where showing up for class was never required—could barely survive America's community college system.

Party Crashing for Political Access: Arnold Schwarzenegger and My Pantsuit

BY CHARLOTTE LAWS
(Published in the Huffington Post, 2016)

Party crashing—or gate-crashing, as it is sometimes called—is an art form that I stumbled upon as a teen. I taught myself how to finagle into any event, anywhere, anytime. It required being part private eye, part actress, and part chutzpah machine. I had to think outside the box, throw myself into the role, and whip my brash plan into action. I assumed I would eventually fail, but that never happened. I was lucky in that way.

During my teens and early twenties, gate-crashing was just a hobby, albeit an unusual one. My high school and college friends were drinking at frat parties, smoking cigarettes in the woods, or killing time at the bowling alley, but I had grander plans. I preferred socializing with the rich and famous—movie stars, business moguls, and heads of state—for the same reason people climb mountains: because they were there, and miraculously I could get to them.

Then, I got bored. I was twenty-four and had met just about everyone who was anyone. The celebrity section of my bucket list was "done." My bucket list had kicked the bucket. I'd crashed past the Secret Service more than once and frequented the Emmys, Oscars, and every elite award show in Hollywood. Plus, I had dated the only celebrity who had ever interested me: singer Tom Jones.

As I prepared for gate-crashing retirement, I looked inward and conceded that the main thrill had never been the "party." It was the "crash," the challenge, the feeling of blissful adrenaline. There was something magical about transforming into superwoman and becoming a rebel in high heels. I also realized that this pastime could be much more than glitzy gowns, socializing, and security guards yelling, "Wait! Come back here. I didn't see your ticket." It could aid me with goals.

So, my gate-crashing gears shifted. I attended fewer events, but always with an objective. I might need exclusive interviews for an article or a book. I might hope to snag an acting role, attract real estate clients, or sell my one-of-a-kind clothing designs. On other occasions, I craved famous supporters for nonprofit causes or wanted to push for legislation.

That leads me to "access"—political access. Politics is where the power is, a catchphrase that I realized was true after assuming public office in California, first as the member of a local council and then as a Los Angeles city commissioner. Lawmakers are able to improve society through the initiatives they propose and sign, as well as the bully pulpits they mount. This is why meeting with them—usually at their office or at a fundraiser—is important. If a layperson wants to instigate legislation or lobby for pending bills, he or she may want to grab a little access.

But snagging quality time with big-time politicians can be difficult for those who are not affluent. Obtaining meetings with lawmakers is significantly easier for generous campaign donors as opposed to ordinary constituents.

Fundraisers present a similar roadblock. The cost to attend an event may be $25,000, $45,000, or even $100,000 per person. Gate-crashing, of course, costs zero apart from a little stress and anticipation.

This brings me to Arnold Schwarzenegger and my pantsuit.

It was the mid-2000s when Schwarzenegger was the governor of California. I needed access to him in order to lobby for a pro-animal bill and to suggest a statewide animal commission. The commission was to be tasked with advising public shelters on how to become "no-kill" (ending the euthanasia of dogs, cats, rabbits, et al.).

I put on my lucky pantsuit, got into gate-crashing mode, and headed to Long Beach, California, where I knew the governor and his wife, Maria Shriver, were speaking at the annual Women's Conference. I arrived at the event late, and according to the conference program, Schwarzenegger had concluded his speech in the main hall. Although I assumed he'd left the building, I decided to double-check.

Eunice Shriver was onstage. Behind her were bleachers full of important-looking folks in business suits, and before her was a smiling crowd. I confidently marched backstage but was stopped by a security officer.

"No one is permitted in this area," he trumpeted like a drill sergeant.

I flashed a submissive nod and proceeded to disobey orders. A black curtain separated the makeshift backstage from the full-access areas of the room. Like a mischievous teenager, I waited until the drill sergeant was not looking, ducked under the curtain, and scurried out of sight. Stagehands stared at me, but I pretended to know what I was doing. I was skilled at wandering aimlessly with self-assurance.

Suddenly, Eunice concluded her speech, and the folks from the stage filed into the area around me. I was thankful because I no longer looked like a Cadillac in a bicycle shop. I was now just one of many guys and gals standing backstage in business suits.

"What exactly are we doing?" I summoned the courage to ask the lady next to me.

"We're going to meet the governor," she replied. "I flew all the way from New York just for this moment."

Meeting the governor obviously worked for me, so I proceeded to bury myself in the group. I also purposely avoided eye contact with the drill sergeant and other security guards who led us into a private back room.

"Each of you are on the list. We have your addresses and will mail you a copy of the photograph you will be taking with the governor," a man announced.

Oh no, I thought. I was obviously list-less and became anxious that my ruse would be exposed. Plus, I knew getting a copy of the photo would be difficult at best. While waiting for the governor and Maria, I learned I was standing among executives and board members from major corporations and business firms. These were big-timers with big bucks, the types who could afford those fancy fundraisers. Many had come into town for one purpose: to meet the governor and say "cheese" with him. To fit in with the VIPs, I linked myself with the name of the real estate company where I worked.

"Charlotte Laws of Prudential. Nice to meet you," was my greeting.

Schwarzenegger and Maria arrived with their children, and the dreaded moment arrived. I was wearing the exact same pantsuit as the governor's thirteen-year-old daughter. I was embarrassed. My five-foot-tall stature didn't help matters much. I am pretty sure Schwarzenegger's daughter was taller than me.

The governor glanced over, and VIPs stared at me and cringed. I hid behind an executive from State Farm who was next to me in line. Like a good neighbor, State Farm was there.

"You are wearing the same outfit as my daughter." Arnold smiled as he introduced himself to me.

"Bloomingdales. Teen department. On sale," I said like a member of the too-much-information club. I don't know why I said something so dopey, but I was on the spot and fell on confession as if it were my sword.

"This is my wife, Maria."

"Nice to see you again." I shook the First Lady's hand. We'd met once before. I was not sure whether she remembered. An event photographer asked the three of us to pose for a picture, and *snap, snap, snap*. I would have a collectable photo. That is, if I could figure out how to finagle a copy.

By the end of the two-hour event, my gate-crashing caper had been a success. I got that all-important access. I was able to converse with the governor, who expressed interest in the pro-animal bill and later signed one into law. Plus, I was able to pull the event photographer aside and exchange contact information in order to assure I would receive the picture.

There was more good news. Schwarzenegger arranged for me to meet with his cabinet secretary and senior advisor in Sacramento to discuss my commission idea. The first meeting led to a second and to a dozen phone conversations. Unfortunately, in the end, my commission proposal was rejected. The governor said it was due to budget constraints.

I blame the pantsuit.

Pigeon Man

BY CHARLOTTE LAWS

The "Pigeon Man" adventure was the boldest of my life. And it bordered on what some might call "domestic terrorism."

Slosh. I barreled through a puddle. Dirty water splattered onto my jeans and blouse, but I was oblivious because I was in law-breaking mode. My adrenaline percolated. My body was a vat of caffeine. I was normally a sleepyhead at midnight, but on this particular evening, the dopamine in my brain was the skipper of my ship.

Kayla scurried behind me. She was nineteen and had volunteered to assist her renegade mom. Although our actions were illegal, I was pleased that Kayla was game for the mission. We sprinted through the suburbs of Torrance, California, toward a nondescript house where our partner in crime had stashed the "loot."

Our "partner" had committed "breaking and entering," plus he had damaged property belonging to law enforcement. Kayla and I were technically conspirators because we knew about the unlawful act in advance and had circulated e-mails about it to other conspirators. Because our e-mails traveled over state lines, crimes that would normally fall under local jurisdiction were ratcheted up to a federal level and could have led to involvement by the FBI. Our "co-conspirators" were not the usual suspects. They included a city council member, two people from the L.A. city attorney's office, a deputy from the Los Angeles mayor's office, a city commissioner, two lawyers, a seasoned journalist, and a tenured UCLA professor.

The man who had physically committed the crime was

Red (or "Pigeon Man"), a sixty-one-year-old attorney. He had been a stranger until a week prior, when he showed up at my monthly Directors of Animal Welfare (DAW) meeting.[23] Red shot through the door with a pigeon named Twister on his shoulder. She'd earned her name due to nifty acrobatics. She was the Cathy Rigby of the pigeon world.

"These animals are special," Red said. "Pigeons descended from heroes. They helped people during wartime. We have betrayed them. Now they are routinely killed as pests."

Red wanted the DAWs to help with the pigeon cause. Red had saved Twister from a crow attack, but most of his rescued birds had fallen prey to man-made hazards. Red had 220 feathered friends residing at his Torrance home, including two chickens and four mourning doves. It was unclear whether he was a hoarder (a person with a good heart who was over his head in providing adequate animal care) or merely an innkeeper with a very busy schedule.

Red explained how he always offered freedom to healed patients. But just because they were pigeons didn't mean they were pigeon-brained. They usually chose shelter with Red and dependable meals rather than risk the perils—hawks, falcons, owls, and malicious humans—that awaited them in the open air. Street pigeons live three or four years, while those in captivity can survive for thirty-five. Red was a bit of a hero in his community. Residents knew they could count on him. Sick and injured birds were sent to him by groomers, pet shops, and even veterinarians.

There were two animal control officers from adjacent jurisdictions who called him a godsend. He would care for the most maligned creatures on earth when no one else would.

Angel was a blind baby pigeon who had tumbled from her nest. A lady asked Red to help her, and like 911, he was on the scene in minutes. Angel could not fend for herself in a complicated and vision-mandated world, so Red took her into his home and fed her. They went on errands to Home Depot, they played in his backyard, and Red gave the lady updates on Angel's weekly activities, including the fact that she'd found a mate and given birth.

"I would normally never allow a pigeon to have babies," Red said. "But I didn't have the heart to take her eggs away. Angel needed these two little ones. She was such a proud mama."

Angel and her babies were happy until the day they were murdered.

Torrance Animal Control had a fancy new truck that read "Torrance Police. Excellence through teamwork." They contacted Red about his pigeons. No more than four were allowed per property, according to city law. He had ten days to remove the animals. Red telephoned me about the predicament. The DAWs located two licensed wildlife rescuers, who agreed to take the critters, releasing some and finding homes for the others. I telephoned Torrance Animal Control to inform them that our organization was on the case. I was told that everything would be fine.

But there was no ten-day grace period. The shiny Torrance Animal Control truck and seven police cars pulled up to Red's home on the following day. Officers bolted from the vehicles like military specialists, bent on rescuing hostages in enemy land. But there were no hostages. There was no enemy land. This was not a perilous situation. It was just elderly Red, Angel and her babies, and their feathered friends, many of whom were healing from past wounds.

Red was handcuffed and taken to the psychiatric ward at Harbor-UCLA Medical Center, where an officer laughed. "You will be here for at least seventy-two hours."

Instead, Red was deemed sane and released within three. In

the meantime, two DAWs had driven to Red's home. They confronted Torrance Animal Control, who had taped off the area. They were told to leave. I spoke with an officer on the phone, reminding him that the DAWs would be removing the birds. He was evasive and would not reveal what was happening at the property.

But what was happening at the property was clear to Red's next-door neighbor, who glanced out his window in horror. They were slaughtering the birds, one by one, with lethal injections. The ground was bloody, and syringes were scattered throughout the yard. The neighbor tried to intercede but was informed that all the birds were sick.

"Well, these two sure don't seem sick, do they?" the angry neighbor yelled as two pigeons escaped from the handlers and flew to a wire above Red's residence. They watched the humans slaughtering their friends for a minute and then flew away.

"Get back in your house right now," an animal control officer barked at the neighbor. "And don't come out until we're through."

Distraught members of the community huddled outside of the taped-off area. Some had brought injured pigeons to Red. They pleaded for the return of their loved ones. But animal control was not sympathetic.

"I just want to take my bird home," one guy begged.

"Step away, sir," an officer replied.

Only Twister was saved that day. An officer from the Redondo Beach Police Department, who was also Red's friend, appeared at the scene and was able to finagle Red's favorite bird away from Torrance Animal Control. She said there was a lot of dander in the house, but it was not as filthy and objectionable as the media later portrayed it to be. The home was red-tagged by the County Health Department due to the bacteria, feces, and feathers on the premises. And Red was told that he would go to jail if he set foot on the property. The city also filed charges against him for animal cruelty as a hoarder.

"Oh God, they executed them all. My children have been slaughtered." Red bawled when he learned about the fate of his birds. "They were not diseased. And I was helping them."

Twister was examined by a vet and found to be healthy. How ironic that the one and only saved bird was not sick. But Torrance Animal Control still clung to their story that all the other animals were too diseased and undernourished to be allowed to survive. I would soon have proof to the contrary, and I would learn that Torrance Animal Control had been negligent, in addition to being outright killers.

The shocking phone call came on the following day.

"They may have overlooked some of the birds in the house," Red said. "There were a couple living on top of boxes in the hallway. I bet they're still there."

It was illegal to enter Red's home. It had been padlocked by law enforcement. And we could not ask the city of Torrance to make a further search, because we believed they would kill any remaining birds. They had reason to hide evidence and to cover their tracks. There was an animal cruelty case pending, and officers would be deemed negligent—and cruel themselves—for leaving pigeons behind to starve, suffer, and die. Plus, if birds were found to be in good shape, the evidence could be used against Torrance. No reasonable jury would believe that Twister and a few of her lucky feathered friends (located after the fact) were in good shape, while all the others were irreparably diseased. I called my friends in Los Angeles city government and pleaded with them to search the home.

"It's outside our jurisdiction," a lawyer from the L.A. city attorney's office told me. "We can't meddle in Torrance's affairs. There's an agreement between cities."

I spoke to the mayor's office, a city council member, lawyers, a city commissioner, and a newspaper reporter. All offered the same advice: "Tell Red to break into the house."

The Animal Enterprise Terrorism Act, which turns some infractions into domestic terrorism, was about to be signed into law by Congress and the president. But there was another absurd law already on the books called the Animal Enterprise Protection Act, which also protected "animal enterprises." I was not sure whether Red's house qualified under the definition, but I was certain that I was a conspirator and could go to jail. I also knew the poorly written legislation was subject to the whims of law enforcement. Of course, if I was deemed a terrorist or criminal conspirator, I knew some of the most respected folks in Los Angeles government were as well.

While Red made preparations for the big heist, e-mails between me and the other conspirators whizzed back and forth. A UCLA professor agreed to drive the getaway car. She had never before committed a crime. We discussed the possibility of blaming the illegal break-in on the Animal Liberation Front by scribbling "ALF" on the door. But that idea was dropped because Red believed he could make it look as if no one had entered in the first place.

Red sneaked up to his house with his flashlight that day. He cut the padlock from the front door and replaced it with his own. He'd photographed it earlier, and a locksmith had sold him an identical model. No one would ever know there had been a switcheroo. The break-in would happen just before midnight.

"He's heading into the house. So far, no cops." The university professor gave me a blow-by-blow account of the caper from her cell phone in the getaway car.

Red's house was in shambles. His legal files and computer hard drive had been confiscated by police, and an envelope with $3,000 was missing. He tiptoed from room to room with his flashlight until he saw a beautiful sight. It was a little boy pigeon, who normally nested in the back of a closet. He was perched in the center of the dark bedroom. He seemed to wonder where everyone had gone. Red was inside the house for exactly thirty-eight minutes.

"He's out. Oh, my goodness, he's got a pigeon," the professor hollered into the phone. "Get down here, now."

That is when Kayla and I jumped into our car and drove to Torrance. We sloshed through mud puddles and up the grassy lawn of the house where Red, Twister, and the newly found pigeon were staying.

"Here he is. Isn't he a beauty?" Red said.

A veterinarian checked out the little boy and deemed him fit.

I put Red in touch with a big shot criminal attorney, who was a friend of mine. He was one of the lawyers who had successfully represented Michael Jackson in the well-publicized child molestation case. Shortly after "Big Shot" was hired, all animal cruelty charges against Red were dropped.

On the day following the illegal break-in, I got a second shocking phone call from Red. "I think there may be another pigeon in the house. That little boy's brother likes to hide in the living room corner near the ceiling. I'm going back inside tonight."

"Oh no!" I howled. I seemed to be trapped in an *I Love Lucy* episode.

The following evening was a repeat performance with the UCLA professor in the getaway car and the furtive midnight rescue. Red found the sibling as expected, and we got him checked at a bird clinic.

"He's in perfect shape," the veterinarian announced.

Despite the dozens of poor birds who had been murdered,

three pigeons had been saved. And Red would not be the birdman of the county jail.

Bill Cosby and Drugging: My 34-Year-Old Secret

By Charlotte Laws
(Published in Salon, 2014)

"Did I ever drug you?" Bill Cosby joked when I entered his dressing room at the Paramount Theatre in Oakland, California, in February 2005. He was performing at the venue, and it was "between shows." I was accompanied by my husband and stepdaughter.

His comment was meant to defuse tension because a woman had just come forward, saying she had been drugged and raped by him. It was obvious that Bill was feeling uneasy about negative media attention. I wondered if his decision to hang out with me and my family one-on-one for forty-five minutes was part "damage control." I was not his close friend. I was more of a friendly acquaintance. Perhaps "friendly acquaintances" can expect more attention when thirty-four-year-old secrets are involved.

Bill knew that I knew. I could feel it. I had known the truth since that memorable night in 1981. Bill had drugged my close friend, whom I will call Sandy, and then had sex with her. Bill met Sandy in the casino at the Las Vegas Hilton around 1979 or 1980. She was in her late teens or early twenties, thin and medium height with hazel eyes and straight brown hair that fell just below her shoulders. They immediately began a consensual intimate relationship. At the time, Sandy was sexually adventuresome, dating a number of men around town.

Sandy was not a would-be actress and had no major career aspirations, other than possible enrollment in the U.S. military. She did not date Bill with an eye toward professional advancement, and to my knowledge, he made no promises of this sort. She simply liked his company. She also came to appreciate the few hundred dollars he gave her following each date.

"I don't know why Bill always leaves me money," she told me. "He must think I'm a hooker. But I don't want to tell him the truth, because I like getting the cash."

Sandy had no job and lived in a downscale apartment in a dreggy section of town. Those extra dollars came in handy at rent time.

Sandy introduced me to Bill in 1980. I was twenty years old. The three of us sat alone in his dressing room at the Las Vegas Hilton. He coached me on my college plans. He was the incarnation of the wise and protective patriarch, a role he would play on a national scale when *The Cosby Show* launched in 1984, making Cliff Huxtable a household name. I particularly appreciated his commitment to causes and his down-to-earth nature. He was not only an incredible talent, he was a caring and generous soul.

"If you grow your hair down to your waist, I will give you two thousand dollars," Bill told Sandy.

She did not react with enthusiasm. But then again, she was not a bubbly person. Her temperament was more like a panther: sleek and even-keeled.

Then he looked at me and smiled, "What's your favorite clothing store?"

"Suzy Creamcheese," I said. This was a popular local boutique.

"If you help Sandy grow her hair down to her waist," Bill said to me, "I will buy you a thousand dollars worth of clothes at Suzy Creamcheese."

I figured Bill had a "thing" for long hair in the same way that some men have a "thing" for feet.

Sandy never grew her hair. She was not motivated by money. But she did come to me one morning a year later to tell me that something bad had happened. Bill had drugged her. She was not angry. She was baffled, stunned, even shaken by the experience. Plus, she felt betrayed.

"Bill drugged me last night and then had sex with me," Sandy confided. "I just don't understand it. It's not like I would have said no to *anything*."

He had given her two pills and said, "These will relax you." She trusted him and swallowed them. She figured they were vitamins or herbal medicine. They did not relax her; they flat-out knocked her unconscious.

"He didn't need to do it," she repeated. "I just don't understand why."

Did it turn him on to see a woman "out cold," or was this all a mistake? Maybe Sandy's body had reacted to the pills in a bizarre and unexpected way. I was willing to give Bill the benefit of the doubt, although Sandy felt his actions were intentional.

She did not view the encounter as rape, because she was already in an intimate relationship with him. I likewise did not categorize it as a sex crime, because it was Sandy's experience, and she had a right to define it any way she wished. I was only the bystander, the friend, the shoulder to cry on. Of course, now that I am older, I look back and realize that when a woman is unconscious, she cannot ever consent.

Sandy had no idea what happened to her that night. She knew it involved sex. She could tell by the way her body felt afterward. It never occurred to either of us that Bill might be drugging other women. We both assumed the encounter was a one-off. After all, Bill was charming, intelligent, attractive, and famous. He did not need to sedate women in order to secure dates. He could not possibly have a dark side.

I moved from Las Vegas in 1982 and fell out of touch with Sandy. But I stayed in touch with Bill. One evening we were alone in his dressing room.

"Have you seen Sandy?" I asked.

"No," he replied. "I haven't seen her in years."

It occurred to me that the "drugging date" may have been their last.

In an effort to elevate Sandy a few notches, I disclosed, "She was never a hooker. You probably thought she was."

"Really?" He was expressionless. I could not tell whether he already knew or was surprised.

"She needed the money for rent," I added. "That's why she never told you."

He nodded, indicating he understood and was cool with it.

In 2005, I had arrangements to attend Bill's show in Oakland and to go backstage with my family. But days prior, I got wind of the allegations against Bill. I was shocked and in a quandary. For the first time, I realized that Sandy's ordeal had *not* been a one-off. Plus, I was a witness. I could corroborate this woman's story. But should I? Was it better to leave it to the courts and law enforcement? After all, I was not a victim. Bill had always treated me with respect. He had given me advice and been generous with his time. He had never offered *me* a pill.

I was also unclear how to handle the backstage mingle. Should I cancel? Should I question or confront him? Should I be polite? I chewed on this for hours, finally deciding to keep the arrangements.

After Bill tossed out his opening line, "Did I ever drug you?" I took a seat across from him in his Oakland dressing room. I introduced him to my husband, Charles, and my stepdaughter, Sibylla.

"What style do you think this is?" Bill asked in an upbeat way, alluding to the room's furnishings.

"Art Deco," Charles replied.

"What do you do, Sibylla?" Bill asked.

"I'm an astrologer," she replied.

"Sibylla is going to tell you if you're going to be a success," Charles said. Bill laughed.

"Charles is not only funny," I finally spoke. "He can recite entire Shakespearean plays."

"You like that, don't you?" Bill grinned at me. He loved the idea that poetry had swept me off my feet.

"You can make up anything at this point, and she'll think it's Shakespeare." Bill winked at Charles.

The conversational tone had been set; it was friendly and humorous. There would be no confrontation or interrogation. We calmly discussed politics and national news stories—except, of course, that certain news story about a certain comedian. It was the elephant in the Art Deco room. We also talked about the criminal justice system and Bill's favorite subject: education.

Ironically, Bill was concerned that certain reform schools might be pumping youngsters with drugs.

"Could you check into this for me?" Bill asked, since I wrote a newspaper column.

I said, "Sure."

I did *not* say, "I know someone else who has been pumping youngsters with drugs!"

I was usually a rebel, outspoken and controversial, but on this particular evening, I opted to be pleasant. I gave Bill a friendly good-bye hug, still uncertain whether I should come forward. It was not long before a number of women corroborated the first woman's account about drugging and rape, and I assumed my testimony was not needed.

I assumed wrong.

In the years since, I've tried to reach out to Sandy to get further details of her story. I even hired a private investigator. But I've never been able to track her down. Her full name is common, and some people aren't as easy as a Facebook search. But I've never forgotten the conversations we had, or the ones I had with Bill later.

Last week, media outlets reported that the victims had never been taken seriously. Sexism was apparently the broom that had swept their allegations under the collective American carpet. It took a male—comedian Hannibal Buress—to peel back the wrapper, to put the issue in the spotlight and make the public examine it.

Edmund Burke once intimated that bad things happen when good people do nothing. Since I want to be a good person and I don't want bad things to happen, I have decided to tell my story. I realize I am late. I realize I am not a victim myself. And I realize I did not help my sisters in 2005 when they needed me most. But I also realize that it is better to be late than silent.

Although Bill has refused to comment on the allegations, I'd like to pose some questions, echoing Sandy's sentiment of "Why?" Why drug a willing sexual partner, especially when you are a man with an otherwise good and caring heart? Why risk a successful career and a phenomenal legacy on a couple of stupid little pills? And why turn a country that loves you into one that is no longer sure? Why, Bill?

Please tell us why.

Playing Pranks on the Governor

by Charlotte Laws

I was playing pranks on California's governor Jerry Brown, and my accomplices—Lynn and Lina—were convinced that he was reciprocating with his own sneaky tricks.

It all started when actor Ed Begley Jr. phoned me in a panic. I had recently met with him at his home to explain how the Directors of Animal Welfare program worked. I'd founded this organization, which provided political representation for animals in communities throughout Los Angeles.

"I can't speak at the Bakersfield event," Ed said. "Do you have the phone number for the lady in charge?"

I gave him the information. "I'd be happy to take your spot if she needs a replacement."

"That would be great," he replied.

I knew Governor Jerry Brown—the mayor of Oakland at the time—was also scheduled to speak at this Democratic party function. (I'd gotten to know Jerry and some of his close friends months prior, and I'd spent a great deal of time hanging out with them.) I figured if I was allowed to take the stage, I would make a fool of myself. I always acted like a moron in front of Jerry. Frankly, he intimidated the heck out of me.

When I was not feeling stupid around him, I was in a huff. I was offended by his offhanded remarks. He was offended by mine. We were both provocative with our opinions, and our goal-oriented personalities collided like linebackers on opposing teams. Prior to meeting Jerry, I'd gone through life as a "most valuable player" when it came to ambition and drive. But Jerry made me look like a lazy benchwarmer. He was hugely accomplished and determined to succeed. He was Walter Payton and always fifty yards ahead of me, despite the fact that I was twenty-four years his junior and should have been faster with the ball.

"You know why we clash? Because we're so much alike," I said to Jerry in Los Angeles one evening as he climbed into his car.

"You're right. Have a safe drive home," he replied.

We'd been at a party with others from his entourage when he asked me to fetch him white wine. I assumed it was free until I reached the bar. When I was informed of the ludicrous ten-dollar charge, I became annoyed, convinced that Jerry was trying to con me into paying for his overpriced beverage. I knew he was cheap, personally and professionally. It was good that he was careful with taxpayer dollars, but it was bad that I was facing a loss of face and funds. What Jerry did not know is that (like him) I knew every penny-pinching pass in the playbook.

"Who wants to buy a drink for Governor Brown?" I hollered.

"I'll do it," a man volunteered.

"Thanks," I replied.

"Some guy at the bar bought you this drink." I smacked the wine down in front of the Governor, causing some of the liquid to slosh onto the table. Jerry smirked.

Despite the ceaseless scrimmage between us, I was fond of Jerry. I considered him an out-of-the-box thinker and a brilliant leader. He inspired me to fight harder for my goals, and I thought I could learn about politics by hanging out with him. After all, I was a novice in the field, only recently getting elected to the Greater Valley Glen Council. He had run for president three times. He had been a two-term governor, and he would be elected to his third and fourth terms in 2010 and 2014. I had worked on his political campaigns.

My admiration for Jerry increased when I learned that he had a soft spot for the truly forgotten and oppressed: nonhuman animals. Past skirmishes between us became irrelevant. Suddenly he was elevated in my mind from "brilliant guy and great leader" to "brilliant guy and great leader with a heart."

It was the weekend of the California Democratic Convention in Los Angeles, and I was having breakfast at the Holiday Inn with Jerry and members of his entourage. Jerry was at the far end of the table, out of earshot.

"He wanted me to find him the cheapest hotel in Italy," one of his aides said to me. "I told him I had better things to do and added, 'You have plenty of money. Why do you want the cheapest hotel anyway? What are you going to do with all your money when you die?'"

"'I'm leaving it all to the animal shelter.' That was the governor's response," the aide said. "I thought I would faint."

The second surprising moment happened that evening. Jerry told me about his recent trip to Mexico, during which he had dined with Governor Pete Wilson's wife. With dampened spirit, he explained how his dinner guest had noticed a daddy longlegs on the wall, reached over, and whacked the insect, killing him.

"It was such violence against a living being," Jerry stated in a serious tone.

"Violence against a living being? I can't believe you just said that, Jerry! I'm so impressed!"

Now I was in Bakersfield, a city renowned for petroleum, alfalfa, and cotton—and not for combating late-night boredom. The event organizer had telephoned me after speaking with Ed Begley Jr. She had explained that there was only time for Jerry's keynote speech. My words would go unheard. I was secretly relieved. Since Jerry was going to be there, I probably would have tumbled from the podium or broken my nose with the microphone.

Although the governor was surely accustomed to my never-ending supply of stupidity, I was not keen on a repeat performance. As compensation for cancelling my speech, the coordinator offered me Ed's already-paid-for suite at the DoubleTree hotel and tickets to the affair. I invited gal pals Lynn and Lina to join me in downtown Bakersfield for the adventure.

Our mischief began after the event. Jerry told us he was tired and going to spend the rest of the evening in his room. We knew his room number. He was staying in room 362 directly under us. We didn't know anyone else in town, and we just could not pry ourselves away from him. It was just too tempting, and we were just too bored. We laughed like giddy teenagers and made every effort to spy on Jerry. We jumped on the floor in our suite, peered under his door from the hallway, and watched him through his window. At some point, Lynn and Lina became convinced that he was playing along with our childish stunts and peering at us as well.

"He's hiding behind the curtain, watching us," Lina said. "Don't look. Don't look."

"No, he's not." I stood exposed in the middle of the parking lot like a gawky big rig. "I don't see him."

"He's there," Lynn said, hurrying to her car. "Don't look at his window."

Then we launched a boilerplate prank phone call.

We rang Jerry's room, and when he answered, Lina asked, "Is Mary there?"

Jerry informed her that she had the wrong number, and for some reason we thought this was really funny. But we freaked out when the phone in *our* room rang ten minutes later. No one knew we were staying at the hotel except Jerry and the lady who had orchestrated the event.

"H-h-hello?" I stuttered into the receiver.

"Is Lori there?" a voice on the other end said.

"You have the wrong number."

To this day, Lynn and Lina are convinced that Jerry was pranking us back, but I find it highly doubtful.

Although I chalked up the odd experience to coincidence, I decided to infuse meaning into it. I chose to think that the universe was interacting with me, that it wanted me to work to positively impact the world, to continue to help both nonhumans and humans.

I thank Governor Brown for the inspiration.

FUNDRAISER MANIA

BY CHARLOTTE LAWS
(Published in Simon Magazine, 2004)

Not long after I got elected to the Greater Valley Glen Council, Kayla confronted me. "You never do anything fun anymore, Mom."

"What are you talking about?" I asked.

"You haven't crashed a celebrity event in years. I guess that's what happens when people get *old*."

A week later, I did what any annoyed parent would do: I finagled my way into three star-studded fundraisers. They were designed to raise money for Senator John Kerry, who was the Democratic presidential nominee at the time. It's not that

I was a Kerry devotee, and frankly I was not even a Democrat with my "decline to state" status, but my schedule just happened to coincide with all three events. Why miss forking over thousands of dollars, especially when one can waste them on the financially insatiable political process? Actually, I spent zero. Party crashing was the only ticket I could afford.

Although volunteers and campaign staff surely did their best, the disorganized Kerry breakfast in San Francisco was a 4 on a 1-to-10 scale. When you consider the $1,000 price tag for the event, it was more like a 2. I was able to wiggle into the event with a city attorney friend who had bought a ticket. We waited with hundreds of other people in winding lines like the Delta ticket counter in order to have our metal detected. I was found to be metallic due to the zippers on my boots.

"Zippers on my boots? You've gotta be kidding." I grinned at the somber Secret Service man.

The tables were crammed together like an overstocked furniture store. There could be no waiters, because even the guests had to squeeze into their chairs. The cold breakfast was already on our plates, and for a vegan, such as myself, it was a culinary nightmare. The sausage was touching my other food, thus resulting in severe contamination and, of course, mental anguish. My attorney would be contacting the Kerry campaign. I drank not only my orange juice but the juice belonging to the absent guest to my left before parceling out my food to the carnivores at my table.

It was announced that San Francisco mayor Gavin Newsom had come and gone. Before the event even began? How indicative of what the morning would be like: a less-than-adequate experience for the guests, although rather profitable, I would assume, for the Kerry camp.

The $500-to-$1,000-per-person San Jose event that evening was so poorly planned that I left before it started. I figured maybe Gavin Newsom was onto something. The lines were not like an airline ticket counter. They were more like soup lines under a repressive Communist regime, curving down the street, onto the next block, past the third traffic light.

Luckily, I was escorted into the event early as a VIP by the Kerry people. I was not really a VIP, but because I'd been elected to my council, some people were impressed. This was especially true at events deprived of major league players.

There were meat-filled hors d'oeuvres, severe overcrowding, and nowhere to sit. In fact, there were only ten already-taken chairs in the entire place. What about the grandmothers and their orthopedic shoes? I half expected the fire marshall to burst through the door, but of course, "bursting" would have been difficult. I wondered about the clueless refugees lined up on the sidewalk. Where would they be placed?

The Los Angeles fundraiser at Walt Disney Hall on the following evening consisted of a top-notch concert, with a pre-show dinner for couples who wanted to spend $25,000 to eat with Senator Kerry and his wife. Why buy a car when you can have mashed potatoes and a steak?

The lines into the auditorium were refreshingly short and orderly until the high-paying guests came out of their pricey dinner and crowded around the entrances, refusing to stand in line with the commoners—you know, people who had spent less than $5,000 for a ticket. They seemed to be thinking, "I paid big bucks, and I'm not about to wait in line."

I had been lingering on the sidewalk without a gate-crashing game plan until I realized the big donors presented a big opportunity. I shimmied into their collage of colorful party gowns, and during the excitement of the moment I gained entrance. I went through Secret Service screening. Thankfully no boot zippers or other metal accoutrements set off sirens.

As I ascended a final escalator into the bash, a Secret Service agent yelled at me. "I didn't see your ticket! Come back here."

I pretended to be deaf. Luckily, no one came after me.

People did not immediately take their seats in the concert hall. Studio executives and talent talked "deal-making," while the elected California officials—of which there were many—flashed the expected smiles. As a novice politician, I shook a lot of hands, then grabbed an empty seat in the third row.

The show began. With a theatrical waive upward, Billy Crystal burst onto the stage, "Hello, people in the cheap seats." There was a roar from the $1,000-per-person balcony.

Robert De Niro, Leonardo DiCaprio, Ben Stiller, and other actors introduced performers to the stage. The teleprompters were in full use for everyone except Neil Diamond. Even the words to Barbra Streisand's songs were on three carefully positioned screens. She's quite talented, but doesn't she know the words to her greatest hits by now?

Following the show, a pretty woman strolled toward a side stage portal. Assuming she was VIP bound—and probably a VIP herself—I latched onto her, hoping the security officer would mistake me as her friend.

My plan worked. He thought I was her gal pal. "The party is backstage. You two come with me." (It turned out she was an actress.)

The star-studded gathering was held in a dressing room. I struck up a conversation with Senator Kerry. "My friend Sheila gave you and your wife a massage a couple of weeks ago in Santa Monica, and she told me all the details."

Without missing a beat, Kerry laughed. "Yes. She was great. She knows about all the kinks."

I hobnobbed with Leonardo DiCaprio, Robert De Niro, James Brolin, and Neil Diamond, among others. Jamie Foxx and I reminisced. He had once been my real estate client.

I struck up a conversation with Ben Affleck, who was hanging with Ben Stiller. "My friend said she went out with you."

"No, we just had sex," Affleck joked. The three of us broke into laughter.

The Kerry campaign raised $5 million that night and $9.5 million from all three California events. I can tell you that there is such a thing as being "fundraised out" and that L.A. clearly won the game, mostly because politics *is* show business. And who better to master the art of the show than Hollywood?

SEAT FILLING FOR THE STARS: SITTING PRETTY OR SLAVE LABOR?

BY CHARLOTTE LAWS
(Published in the Huffington Post, 2012)

You've probably heard of filling someone's shoes, but have you heard of filling her seat? Award shows tend to be televised, and producers want a full audience for camera-panning purposes. This is especially true for the first fifteen rows of the theater, where celebrities sit. At some point, a famous attendee may need to perform onstage or accept an award; thus, a substitute is temporarily hustled into her spot. This substitute or seat filler may be required to play musical chairs, or she may remain in one place all evening. It depends on the needs of the producer.

My mission was to go undercover at a televised show called Teachers Rock, which was to be broadcast from the Nokia Theatre in Los Angeles. I applied to be a seat filler with hopes of learning how this highly unusual profession works. Could this be the key to unemployment? Could filling seats fill bank accounts? It turned out the answer was no because the salary is zero.

I received my congratulatory e-mail. I was one of the 827 people chosen to receive no pay for volunteering to be near the rich and famous for four hours. This was almost as good as helping hungry children. I had a warm and fuzzy feeling knowing I'd be assisting an affluent TV producer and Hollywood's biggest stars with their empty seat dilemma.

I hoped my altruism would not go unnoticed, as I read the stringent rules associated with my important new job. The dress code required long pants and a sweater. This made total sense considering the temperature that day was 110 degrees. Furthermore, I was excited to learn that I would be standing in the delightful heat in a long line—something I do regularly as a hobby—for two hours prior to the show.

I was told to wear flat shoes, which meant my embarrassing shortness might end up on national television. Yippee. I was not allowed to dress in red and had to leave my camera at home because photos were not permitted. Plus, talking to stars was a big no-no. Of course, everybody knows that famous people only talk to other famous people. I think it's a law.

The end of the e-mail mentioned the repercussions for not following rules. I could be ousted from the event and prohibited from what I call future slave labor opportunities. Although I am normally a rebel, I didn't want to tangle with the seat filler police and thought the words "fired from indentured servitude" could hurt my résumé.

As I drove to the event in my woolly mammoth pantsuit, I thought about the poor souls in their air-conditioned homes, missing the bumper-to-bumper traffic on the 101 freeway. I envisioned my two-hour wait in the heat and wondered if I could pay a "line stander" to hold my seat filler slot.

Upon arrival at the Nokia, I was astonished to learn that my fellow seat fillers were postmoderns. They'd reinterpreted the instructions, creating their own personal reality. They'd translated "long pants and a sweater" to mean "sleeveless, cotton sundress." They'd decided "flat shoes" meant four-inch-high pumps. They believed crimson, scarlet, and burgundy were not really red at all, and they thought cell phones that took pictures did not qualify as cameras.

I meandered through the line in my Arctic wear, conducting interviews. Everyone was upbeat. A college student named Derrion said he was there because he liked helping the seat-filling company. I asked, "Isn't that like doing charity work for ExxonMobil?"

Felicia, an actress, told me that she once broke the "no conversation" rule with Paris Hilton, who handed her a glass of champagne at the 2009 MTV Music Awards. They sipped together in ringside seats. "So you were drinking on the job?" I asked.

Jason, a burly construction worker, once sat between Cheech and Chong at a show. I asked him what that was like, and he said, "Well, I didn't smell marijuana, if that's what you mean."

Others in line had rubbed shoulders with Katy Perry, Britney Spears, Tina Fey, Amy Poehler, Luke Bryan, LeAnn Rimes, Carrie Underwood, Ashton Kutcher, Jermaine Jackson, and Gwen Stefani. All loved being seat fillers and didn't mind the lack of pay, although they admitted it was really uncompensated extra work.

It was almost showtime. The postmoderns and I were led into the auditorium and told to fill empty seats. Unlike the Grammys or Oscars, the Teachers Rock event was low profile. I figured it wouldn't lead to celebrity encounters, free-flowing champagne, or anything unusual.

So you can imagine my surprise when I met a space alien.

"I'm a retired private investigator," a senior citizen next to me said. "And this is my wife. She's a Grobanite."

I'd never heard of the planet Groban. In fact, I'd never seen a spaceship or been abducted from a field in Nebraska. I tentatively shook the woman's hand, hoping she would not examine my reproductive organs.

"What galaxy is that in?" I asked. She laughed and explained that she was a fan of the entertainer Josh Groban, who would be performing that night. I was relieved because frankly I wasn't in the mood to leave Earth, especially in my woolly mammoth pantsuit.

The show ended after live performances from Groban, Garth Brooks, Dierks Bentley, and the group named "fun." I moved out of my row with other seat fillers when a supervisor said, "Don't even *try* to go backstage." With that, I donned my own postmodern lens and went backstage, where I schmoozed with chef Curtis Stone and the king of his own planet, Mr. Josh. In my defense, I didn't *try* to do anything. It just happened.

Bonus Story 11

THE DEVIL MADE ME DO IT: MY GRANDPA'S LIFE AND MURDER

It was a spooky, sunless day in 1948 when forty-five-year-old Ernie Yost studied the "Hells Half Acre" carving on the front steps of his Fairmont, West Virginia, home. He had chiseled the words years prior, deeding the property to the devil. This seemed perfectly natural, especially now that he'd have no use for the place. He knew he'd rather be dragged behind his neighbor's pickup than let his soon-to-be-ex-wife, Nellie, put her greedy hands on it.

Ernie was a little like Krazy Glue. He was stuck on the idea of murder and destruction. He was a toxic soul who had been victimizing Nellie for years. He was demented by ordinary standards, although he had never been evaluated by a mental health expert. Ernie was mesmerized by the pentagram-bedecked pamphlets in his basement; they spoke about spells, rituals, black magic, and Satan. He had concealed his secret religion so as to avoid public persecution. Life as a devil worshipper was a lonely one indeed.

Then there was the eerie, life-sized satanic doll, sitting upright at the dinette in his breakfast nook. He had been talking to it for days. In his deranged world, it *was* Nellie. After all, it looked just like her. As an ex-upholsterer, Ernie had known how to stuff muslin with packing material so that it resembled a woman's bodice. Then he had molded a plaster neck and head, and with the flair of a master mortician, he had constructed a ghoulish face using acrylic paints and some of Nellie's abandoned cosmetics. The eyes had a particularly nightmarish expression. Fistfuls of dirty straw were used to fabricate Nellie's hair. The figure looked like a mad woman, a fitting match for Ernie.

Ernie was feeling financially pinched since Nellie had extricated herself from six years of beatings and emotional torment. She had moved in with her sister and filed for divorce with my grandpa, the prominent lawyer Tucker Moroose, at her side. Ernie wanted reconciliation because he craved his human punching bag and didn't want his bank account drained. Plus, how dare a pesky woman walk out on him?

The postman dropped off a letter from the court, which ordered Ernie to pay temporary alimony, to refrain from selling his house or personal effects, and not to harm Nellie in any way. Ernie did not sob or sulk when he opened the envelope. He cackled like a demon and descended into the basement to implement his plan.

Ernie had another convenient skill. He knew how to build bombs. He was an expert mechanic and gathered together the necessary supplies: an alarm clock, a six-volt automobile battery, wiring, a wick, scales, and kerosene. Then he piled paper, shavings, and wood near the furnace and cleverly rigged two contraptions to explode that day at four p.m. They would destroy the little home and everything inside. Then the meddlesome court could stuff the burnt remains up its judge's bench for all he cared.

But the dog would not die.

A female, black cocker spaniel mix named Tutu had spent most of her life on the couch and in a special corner of the kitchen. Ernie picked her up, placed her outside on the wooden porch, and locked the door. Tutu leaned her body against the house, as if she feared the trees would swallow her up or the sky would plummet to the ground. She did not realize the porch held promise for a new life, while the interior was likely to become a cauldron of smoke, flames, restless ghosts, and caustic memories.

With his .38-caliber Smith & Wesson revolver and a pouch full of shells, Ernie drove his car downtown and parked it on Quincy Street. His stride was deliberate and upbeat as he entered a three-story beige building with a flat roof where McCrory's dime store was situated on the ground floor. No one, including the lamppost and tree out in front, could have suspected his plan for revenge and his faith in the powers of darkness.

Ten minutes later, my grandfather, Tucker, would be shot in his office, suite 204.

"I have a feeling something horrible's gonna happen." My grandmother Ginger had relayed this to Tucker weeks prior. My birthmother, Sharon, was six years old at the time. Her twin sisters, Sheila and Shirley, were five.

Tucker had film star looks. He was a successful, bespectacled forty-year-old lawyer, who had sprung from penury and hardship. He had energy and determination. Many people in the county had not recovered from the callous jolt of the Great Depression a decade earlier, but Tucker was not among them.

Ernie entered my grandfather's waiting room at nine a.m. on Wednesday, April 7, 1948, to find Nellie and Tucker's secretary, Mrs. Corley. He observed the hardwood floors, oak baseboards, weighty brass fixtures, and pebbled glass windows that slid up and down. The door into Tucker's personal office had a divider with speckled, opaque glass. This meant Mrs. Corley could see shadows and general outlines of images through the glass but no detail.

Nellie had a solo appointment with Tucker and squirmed at the sight of her husband, who slid next to her and asked her to forget about the divorce. When she refused, he insisted she abandon her request for alimony and for half of the property. Ernie did not mention the bombs; he had rigged them to explode seven hours later so as to allow time for disassembly if his wife acquiesced.

"I won't push you around," Ernie said. "Just come on home. I need you, Nellie."

"No! You're a vile and hateful man!"

Mrs. Corley was typing and could not hear the conversation between the couple but knew it was contentious. Tucker arrived and passed through the waiting room into his private office. Nellie followed. Ernie followed Nellie and shut the door.

Ernie blurted out, "I know the two of you are plotting to steal my house and all my money! And I know you're having an affair!"

"That's a damn lie. I will call the police and have you thrown out of my office." Mrs. Corley could hear Tucker's angry words through the wall, and she could see faint images through the opaque glass divider.

Ernie pulled out his gun and blasted Nellie in the throat. Blood stained her blouse, and she fell to the ground.

Mrs. Corley scurried from the outer room and down the hall for help.

Tucker tussled with Ernie and, in so doing, lost the middle finger on his right hand to a bullet. Then he was shot three more times: in the shoulder, chest, and head. When Tucker appeared lifeless, Ernie placed the revolver's barrel against the pale skin of Nellie's forehead, recited a witch's incantation, and ploughed a shell into her brain.

I'd walk a mile for a Camel, Ernie thought as he relaxed in a chair and smiled at the two motionless bodies before him. He pulled a cigarette from his pocket, had a few puffs, and shot himself in the temple. Ernie was slumped over with the Camel dangling from his mouth when the authorities arrived. According to the *Fairmont Times*, "He was leaning in a crazy angle, and the blood was trickling a stream onto the floor." It was a bizarre sight, the kind of thing one might see in a horror flick about demons or voodoo.

Ernie was not dead and was rushed to State Hospital. Nellie had perished, as had Tucker later in an ambulance.

The cocker spaniel, Tutu, thwarted the bomb plot, according to newspaper articles.

Ernie's daughter, who lived in a nearby county, contacted the police that day because she was concerned about the welfare of Tutu, who in her words "was probably trapped in the house." She thought the dog needed food and could die of neglect.

The police arrived at Ernie's property on Chesapeake Hampton Road to check on Tutu, who was huddled against the back door surrounded by smoke. They broke into the burning home to find the satanic doll, literature on black magic, and the remnants of bombs in the basement. The bombs had exploded but had done minimal damage. If the flames had been left to spread, they could have completely destroyed the house as well as other properties in the neighborhood. The volunteer fire department extinguished the fire.

My great-uncle Jal Moroose was working when the shooting occurred. He was Tucker's headstrong younger sibling.

"Did you hear about your brother?" a colleague asked Jal. "He's dead. The killer's still alive at State Hospital."

Jal was enraged, heartbroken, and determined to finish off Ernie. Tucker had been the family's father figure; the younger siblings relied on him. Without his guidance, strength, and financial support, the household would surely crumble.

Jal dashed home, retrieved his gun, and set out for State Hospital. It was as if he had sniffed some Krazy Glue as well. He did not care whether he was incarcerated for life or shot during his attempt to kill Ernie. All that mattered was vengeance. Senselessness seemed to be contagious in Fairmont that day.

Jal barreled into State Hospital with the loaded gun.

"Where's the crazy man? Where's the crazy man?" he shouted, waving his weapon in the air. Nurses and people in the waiting room screamed; many fled. Jal made his way to Ernie's room.

Jal's prison term was avoided, and his impetuousness was forgiven. He was saved by pure luck. It was 12:21 a.m.

At 12:20, Ernie Yost had died.

※

Grandpa Tucker is my hero. I feel great affection for him and get tearful imagining his struggles and final moments. The odd and gruesome tale of his murder was the beginning of my investigation into his life. I interviewed witnesses who had come to his legal office and to the Yost property on that dreadful day. I visited Fairmont and met some of my cousins. They helped me piece together additional details. I perused old letters, photos, and official documents. I met members of Nellie's family, who surprisingly still reside in Ernie's home. They gave me a tour of the property, including the bomb-damaged basement, which has never been repaired. The house looks much like it did in 1948, except the exterior has been painted a charming white. I saw the schools that my grandpa had attended, the businesses he had frequented, the office where he had worked, and the places he had lived, including my great-grandparents' farmhouse on Dewey Street.

✦

A black funeral curtain hung over the front door of the Moroose farmhouse on Dewey Street. Tucker lay lifeless in a casket in my great-grandmother Margaret's living room, while over a hundred bereaved visitors presented plates of food and flowers.

As a youngster, Margaret had worked as a shepherd in the mountains of Campobasso, Italy, which is located southeast of Rome. At fourteen, she married my great-grandpa, Nick. Lack of employment and poverty forced them to immigrate to America in 1914. They arrived at Ellis Island on the ship *Adriatic*, which departed from Naples. According to my relatives, the boat was filthy, and the trip was a disgusting experience. West Virginia was a popular destination for Italians because of its coal-mining opportunities. Margaret and Nick raised nine children, including Tucker. There would have been eleven, but a set of twins died at birth.

With the murder of Tucker, my grandmother, Ginger, fell into a deep pool of grief. She wanted to stay afloat for the sake of her three young daughters. The Moroose family kept Ginger buoyant for those first few days after Tucker's death by administering sedatives and by making sure she was bathed and walked. But Ginger later recalled those days quite differently: as an attempt by the Moroose family to silence her with tranquilizers so Tucker could be given a Catholic funeral. Ginger claims he got one.

A tussle over religion had ensued years earlier when Tucker decided to join Ginger's favorite Baptist church. He had become disillusioned with Catholicism, calling it "cruel" because all members of Catholic families were not permitted to be buried in the church cemetery. There were persnickety rules to be followed, which Tucker found offensive.

But it was money rather than religion that became the supreme conflict between Ginger and the Moroose family, and it crescendoed after Tucker was gone. A bitter fight in the Dewey Street farmhouse over finances led to the end of their relationship.

"You're lucky," Margaret said to Ginger, referring to the bank account and property that Tucker had amassed prior to his death.

Tucker was not yet a mogul but had been rapidly expanding into a highly successful attorney, major landowner, and "big fish" in town. He had also won the widely acclaimed Fairmont State Orator competition, and the Republican party had asked him to run for political office as a U.S. congressman or senator.

"Lucky?" Ginger was incensed. "I just lost my husband and have to raise three small children on my own. I have no skills. No job. You call that luck?"

"You have a lot compared to us," Margaret replied.

"No one has offered to help me, and there's only eight thousand dollars in life insurance," Ginger said. "And you've wasted a thousand dollars on a tombstone. You're as crazy as Ernie Yost. That's money we all could have used."

In his will, Tucker had left his mother $1,000, and she had splurged on a fancy headstone.

"Tucker was my favorite child." Margaret became teary-eyed. "He deserves the best."

The Moroose family had struggled since the Great Depression, and they perceived Tucker as their best hope for a middle-class life. When he died, they felt as if they had been knocked from their horse. They were jolted into despair and remained that way for years. Without Tucker, the oasis in the distance was a mirage. Tucker had been supplementing his siblings' incomes, putting one brother through law school, paying for books and school supplies, and helping his mom to afford food. Many dreams were buried with Tucker in his coffin.

His brother quit law school on the day Tucker died.

Margaret's husband, Nick, had passed from a heart attack, and Tucker had been informally anointed "man of the house," despite the fact that he was not the eldest son. The oldest, Philip, worked in the coal mines like most Fairmont males and never had a nickel to his name.

Tucker could have won an award for energy and perseverance. In his teens and twenties, he loaded up the running board of his 32 Model Ford at six a.m. each day with carrots, beets, lettuce, and other vegetables from the family garden. Then he hauled them into town and sold them before immersing himself in back-to-back high school classes—and later college courses and even later law school courses. At night, he worked in a pool hall until one a.m. racking billiard balls and doing general maintenance. He often slept on top of a pool table until five a.m., when he would head home to repeat his arduous routine.

The Morooses were as poor as a family could be.

"We had a family of nine children, and we lived on only a few dollars each week. Somehow we survived," Great-Uncle Jal explained to me on the phone.

The Moroose farmhouse on Dewey Street was in the poor section of town. It appeared roomy from the outside but was actually cramped. Three to four children had to sleep in each room. There were metal beds and European bureaus. On hot days, Margaret wrapped her arms with stockings to avoid sunburn. She baked bread every morning in an outside oven and grew flowers in addition to the vegetables Tucker sold at market each day. Self-sustenance was a critical component of survival.

Unlike many in Fairmont, Tucker did not drink or smoke, and he had little time to socialize; persevering was a full-time occupation. He wanted to prosper, something that was difficult as a young lad growing up in a small town where most boys could not see past the mine shaft. Mining was the default career path. Ginger often baked Tucker's favorite food, lemon pie. After a few years of courting, they married.

"Jal told me what you said yesterday." Margaret continued the verbal battle with Ginger at the Dewey Street farmhouse. "You wouldn't have married Tucker if he hadn't been a lawyer."

"Yes, that's what I said. I was only being truthful."

"You're a horrible person," Margaret replied. Ginger could barely hold back her tears as she stormed out of the farmhouse. Ginger loved Tucker, but she was pragmatic. She wanted a husband with intelligence and ambition. She wanted to be linked with an eagle rather than a canary from the coal mine, and she was already making a concession by marrying someone of lower status. She had come from aristocratic stock, after all. Also, by connecting herself with a Moroose, Ginger was putting herself at risk. Discrimination against Italians was rampant in Fairmont back then, and Tucker had been in the line of fire many times.

Forty years before I was fighting prejudice in Georgia, my ancestors were fighting it in West Virginia.

*

It was prior to Tucker's death. Tucker had just moved his family—Ginger, Sharon, and the twins—into a home he'd purchased in an upper middle-class community.

"My papa says you have to move. Only whites are allowed," a neighbor boy hollered at Sharon (my mom at six years old), who was playing ball in the front yard. "My papa's talking to the judge and getting you kicked out of your house."

"What?" Little Sharon headed in his direction.

"There are deed restrictions, dummy. You're in violation."

In addition to the covenants, conditions and restrictions (CC & Rs), which prohibited minorities from residency in this well-heeled community, many neighbors were prejudiced against Italians. Several suggested that Tucker keep his family inside or look for a property elsewhere because dagoes destroyed the integrity of the neighborhood. Tucker even received a threatening letter from the Ku Klux Klan with a newspaper clipping titled, "Black Family Killed in Southern California House Fire after Refusing to Move from White Neighborhood." Taking no chances, Tucker quickly sold the home and moved his family back to the poor side of town.

Tucker was lucky in one sense: He had light skin as compared with most of his Italian brethren. This meant he could dine inside Fairmont restaurants. Dark-skinned Italians and blacks were banned. Tucker took pains to camouflage his ancestry. In his twenties, he suggested the entire family change their last name of "Amoruso" to the less Italian-sounding "Moroose." All complied with the exception of a sister.

Italians could not belong to the Elks Club or golf course called the Fairmont Field Club, which was established in 1912. The Elks became embroiled in a civil rights controversy in 1973. A federal court threatened to deprive them of tax-exempt status unless they welcomed everyone. They agreed to comply, although some clubs remained all-white into the twenty-first century due to a lack of black applicants. Today, there are no black members at the Fairmont Field Club even though discriminatory policies were abolished decades ago. African

Americans have bad memories about the facility and refuse to be associated with it. In 1978, there were only two Italian members. One was my cousin.

There were dozens of lynchings of Italian Americans in the United States in the late nineteenth through the early twentieth century. In fact, the largest mass lynching in U.S. history was perpetrated not against African Americans but against eleven Italians in New Orleans in 1891.

Anti-Italian sentiment was also embedded in Ku Klux Klan ideology. The KKK's membership ballooned in the 1920s when a reported three to five million Americans joined. In 1926, a parade of thousands wearing KKK garb and white hoods marched for four hours in Fairmont with hopes of frightening and intimidating spectators. A large photo of the Klansmen appeared on the front page of the local newspaper.

When Tucker finished school and looked to open a law office, he encountered resistance. His newly signed leases were twice cancelled by landlords who had been initially fooled by his light complexion but who later learned of his Italian roots.

"I like you. I just didn't know. I had no idea you were an inky dinky," one landlord said.

"I'm not. I'm Italian," Tucker replied.

"That's what I mean. You're so light-skinned. I'm sorry. I can't lease to an Italian. I'd lose my other tenants. I'm sure you understand. You need to drift on."

Attorney Worley Powell came to the rescue. He was not threatened by the idea of a newcomer edging in on his turf even though Tucker was bilingual and sure to capture the Italian market.

"You're with me," Worley said as he made space in his legal office for Tucker.

Worley practiced law in Fairmont for 46 years and

eventually became a candidate for circuit court judge. He died in 2001 at the age of 97.

My family is thankful to Worley. He was a cushioning presence during hard times.

∽

I feel a connection to Tucker. Like me, he aimed for that rainbow in the sky, despite roadblocks put in his way. Like me, he bucked the trend, refusing to conform to the expectations of society. And like me, he developed his own unique value system.

Tucker swore off alcohol, renounced the religion of his family, and refused to surrender to the default career path of the day: coal mining. But most important, Tucker rejected the defeatist mind-set that was all too common in West Virginia in the 1940s. He remained optimistic in the face of naysayers, a practice that has been integral to my life as well. Tucker will forever be missed.

I will never abandon his memory.

Author Biography

Charlotte Laws has authored best-selling books as well as over a hundred articles in noted publications, such as the *Washington Post*, *Salon*, the *L.A. Daily News*, *Huffington Post*, *Gawker*, *Newsweek*, and the *Los Angeles Times*. She starred on the NBC show *The Filter* and has been a weekly political commentator on BBC television for the past three years. She has appeared on CNN, Nightline, Fox News, MSNBC, *The Oprah Winfrey Show*, *The Late Show*, and *Larry King Live*, and she has been the subject of articles by the Associated Press, the *New York Times*, the *San Francisco Chronicle*, the *New York Post*, the *Guardian*, and the *New Yorker*, to name a few.

Laws was a Los Angeles politician for eight years and worked with the FBI. She has experimented with twenty-eight occupations, some of them quite unusual. She has been an executive director, an actress, a cab driver, a private investigator, a stand-up comic, a backup singer for an Elvis imitator, a city commissioner, and a bodyguard for a prostitute.

Laws penned the award-winning books *Rebel in High Heels* and *Devil in the Basement*, and she was voted one of the "thirty fiercest women in the world" by BuzzFeed. She has a doctorate from the University of Southern California as well as two master's degrees and two bachelor's degrees. She completed postdoctoral work at Oxford University, England.

Laws is an internationally known animal advocate and anti-revenge porn activist (often called "the Erin Brockovich of revenge porn"). She lives in Los Angeles with her husband, her three rescue dogs, and an assortment of rescue hens.

Twitter - @CharlotteLaws
Facebook - https://www.facebook.com/charlottelawsfans/
Websites - www.CharlotteLaws.com and
www.UndercoverDebutante.com

Endnotes

1 The relationship with Tom Jones is detailed in my memoir *Rebel in High Heels*.

2 As a chip chatter, I was given chips by casino high rollers. Some chips were used for gambling, but the rest went into my bank account. Details about chip chatting can be found in my book *Rebel in High Heels*.

3 Animals do not voluntarily do flips, ride bicycles, or jump through hoops. They perform these acts because they fear punishment. In 1989, a showroom dancer videotaped Bobby Berosini slapping his animals and beating them with a rod. She publicized the footage. This prompted a public outcry, and the Stardust canceled his show.

4 In September 2018, I spoke with eighty-one-year-old Freddie Roman, who claimed no memory of the incident. It is possible hotel security did not mention that I'd been sexually assaulted, because it seems unlikely he would have forgotten something so disturbing. On the other hand, perhaps his memory has simply deteriorated with age. I also spoke with the Las Vegas resort where the incident occurred. A receptionist told me that there are

most likely records from the early 1980s but that I would be able to get a copy only if the legal department agreed to release them. My phone messages to the legal department went unanswered. A week later, I telephoned the security office at the resort and was told there are no records from the 1980s.

5 Steve Bunce, "Richie 'the Torch' Giachetti: Boxing Trainer Who Rose up from Cleveland Underworld to Assist Larry Holmes and Mike Tyson," *Independent*, March 24, 2016, https://www.independent.co.uk/news/obituaries/richie-the-torch-giachetti-boxing-trainer-who-rose-up-from-the-cleveland-underworld-to-assist-larry-a6949276.html. Retrieved March 1, 2019.

6 Ibid; also Carlos Acevedo, "Richie Giachetti: 1940–2016," *The Cruelest Sport*, February 4, 2016, https://thecruelestsport.com/2016/02/04/richie-giachetti-1940-2016/. Retrieved April 8, 2018.

7 Michael Katz, "Boxing: Giachetti a Hard-Knocks Man," *New York Times*, November 13, 1978, https://www.nytimes.com/1978/11/13/archives/boxing-giachetti-a-hardknocks-man-marks-of-experience-waiting-for.html. Retrieved March 1, 2019.

8 Thomas Hauser, *There Will Always Be Boxing: Another Year Inside the Sweet Science* (Fayetteville: University of Arkansas Press, 2017), 117.

9 Larry Holmes and Phil Berger, *Against All Odds* (New York: St Martin's, 1998), 183.

10 He allegedly made arrangements to have boxing promoter

Don King killed. Dan Coughlin, *Let's Have Another* (Cleveland, OH: Gray & Company, 2015).

11 Steven Pinker, *The Blank Slate* (New York: Viking, 2002), 375.

12 Tamsin Saxton, "Why We Are Secretly Attracted to People Who Look Like Our Parents," *The Conversation*, February 25, 2016, https://theconversation.com/why-we-are-secretly-attracted-to-people-who-look-like-our-parents-54590. Retrieved March 1, 2019.

13 Speciesism revolves around the flawed assumption that humans are superior to nonhumans. This prejudice leads to the exploitation of nonhuman animals.

14 Richard Sullivan and Ellie Lathrop, "Openness in Adoption: Retrospective Lessons and Prospective Choices," *Children and Youth Services Review* 26, no. 4 (April 2004).

15 Kayla (who is now in her thirties) has clothing that I wore back in high school and college. I hope these items will someday belong to Kayla's kids. It's gratifying when belongings are carried around the corner for future generations to cherish, a feeling that few know in today's convenience-based, throw-away world. High-tech and brand-new are in. Simple joys and pass-downs are out. It is unfortunate. I'm sure my grandmother would agree.

16 Roughly six million animals are dissected annually in high schools across the nation; these animals include cats, fetal pigs, rabbits, frogs, rats, and birds. Dissection is big business and extremely costly. Although a large number of high schools—and even middle schools—engage in

this wasteful, expensive, and absurd practice, 90 percent of U.S. medical schools, including Harvard and Stanford, have "eliminated old-fashioned laboratories in favor of… humane alternatives" (see http://www.pcrm.org). If those who are in the final stages of becoming advanced health professionals do not need to kill animals to learn, why do secondary school students?

17 My paranormal experiences will be detailed in an upcoming book. Suffice to say, there were a number of odd happenings, and many were impossible to dismiss because they were evidence based and/or witnessed by others.

18 Some say Charles was officially named as an "unindicted co-conspirator" in a later case against Scientology, which involved breaking into government offices in Canada.

19 Search conducted in August 2018.

20 The church claims there is no disconnection policy. Perhaps they are using a postmodern lens and saying that there is no written rule to this effect. Perhaps members are simply *encouraged* rather than formally required to cut ties with those who have been "declared."

21 Paws had died of old age by this point.

22 In addition to rescue dogs, I had nine rescue hens.

23 The Directors of Animal Welfare (DAW) is a political nonprofit organization that I started and headed up for many years. It still operates today in some communities.

www.ingramcontent.com/pod-product-compliance
Lightning Source LLC
Chambersburg PA
CBHW020416010526
44118CB00010B/274